"As long as you're havin' a good time."

"As long as you're havin' a good time."

A History of Johnston College 1969-1979

William McDonald & Kevin O'Neill

FORUM BOOKS
REDLANDS / SAN FRANCISCO

Cover photo by Paul Corneil

National Library of Canada Cataloguing in Publication Data

McDonald, Bill
        As long as you're having a good time : a history of
Johnston College,
1969-1979 / by Bill McDonald and Kevin O'Neill.
Includes bibliographical references.
ISBN 1-4120-0946-4
        I. O'Neill, Kevin   II. Title.
LD4701.R66465J64 2003   378.794'95   C2003-904183-2

TRAFFORD

This book was published *on-demand* in cooperation with Trafford Publishing.
On-demand publishing is a unique process and service of making a book available for retail sale to the public taking advantage of on-demand manufacturing and Internet marketing. **On-demand publishing** includes promotions, retail sales, manufacturing, order fulfilment, accounting and collecting royalties on behalf of the author.

Suite 6E, 2333 Government St., Victoria, B.C. V8T 4P4, CANADA
Phone   250-383-6864   Toll-free   1-888-232-4444 (Canada & US)
Fax   250-383-6804   E-mail   sales@trafford.com
Web site   www.trafford.com   TRAFFORD PUBLISHING IS A DIVISION OF TRAFFORD
HOLDINGS LTD.
Trafford Catalogue #03-1315   www.trafford.com/robots/03-1315.html

10   9   8   7   6   5   4

Dedication

This book is dedicated to Edward K. Williams, architect of the Johnston academic program, and a friend whose patience and tenacity made the ten years of the College possible.

Contents

Preface

At first glance there is a formidable list of objections to a book of this sort. Of all the genres of history, that of colleges, especially small private colleges, is arguably the most tedious and self-serving. Inevitably written by a member of the history department with forty years of monotonous experience at the institution, such books affect high seriousness over the founding charter, and deep emotion over the chapel in the sunset. None but the most rabid of alums can get past the first chapter. Further, our institution, Johnston College, is little known; it had only fleeting national notice to attract a reader or to justify a general study. Unlike its distinguished predecessor, Black Mountain, Johnston was not shaped by major American intellectual or artistic personalities, and is unlikely, therefore, to capture the gifts of a well-known "outside" biographer. And perhaps most damning, the authors are both partisans — Johnston faculty members since its beginning — without formal training in historiography.

In the face of these things, we believe the narrative of this small college to be eminently worth the telling. The bare circumstances themselves are arresting; the introduction of a brash, rebellious community into the body of a stiff-necked, conservative institution is inherently dramatic, even melodramatic. And it is a tale which constantly moves beyond its own particulars to wider matters. It cannot be broached without reflection on the late 1960's in America, and on the rise and fall of intentional communities in our national history. At one level a simple outgrowth of the Age of Aquarius, the Johnston Experience also conjures up utopian views of education as venerable as those of Rousseau and Plato. It is representative of a group of schools (Kresge College, Santa Cruz, Hampshire College, Fordham's Bensalem, Berkeley's Strawberry Canyon, and so on) which have, in the 1980's turned more traditional or simply ceased to exist. And since Johnston was such a baffling mix of ideology and drama, perhaps a philosopher and a literary critic are, after all, the right persons to offer an account of its life.

Supported by generous grants from the University of Redlands Faculty Research Committee and by Johnston alumna Kathryn Green, we began the project with some seventy taped interviews of faculty, administrators, and a cross-section of alumni/ae. Then came the written record. Self-consciously an experiment from the beginning, the institution meticulously saved every scrap of paper, both in an official archive and in the files of every administrator and most faculty. We have now sifted through over a hundred file drawers of material. David Riesman advised us at the beginning of the project that written records would be of little help to us, and in general he was right; the bulk of the material was finally tangential to our purpose. But some files of correspondence and some devoted minute-takers at crucial meetings made the months of reading worthwhile. We quote liberally from interviews and correspondence in our text, seeking to capture a flavor of the Johnston experience for strangers to the story.

In addition to our cultural and scholarly purposes, this is a personal history. It is the history of our lives as teachers, and of the lives of colleagues and friends. We know and have worked with every person in the book, argued and allied ourselves with each, taught and learned from all. One of the guiding tenets of the college was that feelings count, and that they enrich rather than detract from understanding. Our feelings run deep. Even so, we have tried to be evenhanded with those persons who

disliked the college, and even with those who openly
sought to close it. We hope that hard work, serious reflection, and the passage of time have transformed those
feelings so that they illumine, rather than obscure, the
history of the Johnston experiment.

For the Second printing

Kevin and I are delighted that Trafford Publishing has
agreed to produce the second printing of our history of
Johnston College. The book has brought the early days
of Johnston alive for several generations of students,
and brought us many comments from alums, colleagues,
and interested educators around the country. The Center
is prospering now in ways unimaginable in 1979, and
we hope that this account of the commitment, blunders
and sheer intensity of those first ten years can serve the
Community well into the new century.

Technical reasons have, for better or worse, compelled
us to reprint the first edition exactly, which means that
the typos and other errors that our friends have teased
us about over the years will remain in perpetuity.
Perhaps that's best: this was emphatically our take on
Johnston's evolution, the considered and passionate
vision of two participants, not distanced outsiders or
professional editors. By now its idiosyncrasies and
prejudices are part of our heritage, and revisions might
water down the immediacy in which we wrote. Reprinting
also preserves the design and selfless work of Keith
Jordan, JC '79, who single-handedly made the first
edition possible. So here's the unretouched original,
dressed up in one of Paul Corneil's classic photographs,
and ready to tell its story to those who will take the Center
into the future.

All proceeds from the sale of the book go directly to
the Johnston Center Director's Discretionary Fund.

Introduction

"I dinna care what you're doin', as long as you're havin' a good time."
— James Graham Johnston

"...coining the thing known into a thing never heard before."
— Nietzsche

The chapel of the University of Redlands is a monument to the school's beginnings. Its imposing presence declares the central place of religion — until fairly recently the Baptist religion — in Redlands' history. The classical revival facade and New England steeple dominate a picturesque, almost cinematic campus: wide lawns bordered by scores of California oaks; old dorms with spacious balconies; prosperous, healthy students.

The chapel's interior is, if anything, even more imposing. It seats over 1500 people, more, in fact, than are enrolled at this small Southern California liberal arts college. Four tall stained glass windows process down the cream-toned east and west walls, declaring in Victorian allegory resurrection and the hope of Christian victory. A wave meander pattern, more cream on a soft blue field, runs along the walls beneath these windows. It draws the eye to the wide stage, to the permanent risers behind it, and finally to the focal point of the entire building — an enormous stained glass triptych of Jesus offering the Sermon on the Mount. It is a dark window; Jesus is in Raphael blue, his hand stretched toward his listeners, his body almost indecipherable in the loose robe. His followers, many in deep reds, fan out below him. Some are enraptured, while others seem disinterested or stare out at the space before them, unwittingly setting an example for inattentive audiences to follow. The window towers behind anyone who approaches the lectern at midstage. Sitting in the center seats, the listener looks up to see beyond the speaker of the day the figure of the Redeemer Himself, blessing, as it were, the words to be uttered.

On the afternoon of March 14, 1979, Douglas Moore, nine months into his tenure as the University's seventh president, announced to an all-university audience a dramatic change in University organization. It was the first such assembly of the decade. The audience, following the window, divided itself into sections: curious but largely unexcited students in the front rows; a number of keenly interested faculty in the further rows, and a small, fanatically interested group of students in the normally deserted balcony. Moore came to the podium in a three-piece suit, its blue slightly duller and darker than that in Jesus' robe. Normally a quiet, informal speaker, his style was assertive, confident. The heart of Moore's new vision of the University of Redlands lay in these words:

> Johnston College...will cease to exist as a separate college but will become a programmatic division within the University.

> ...the University must be brought together as one institution, under one Board of Trustees, one administration, one budget, one certificate of accreditation and one on-campus system of governance.... Specifically, Johnston College will

become the Johnston Center for Individualized Learning. This Center will have one administrative officer responsible to the Academic Vice President. It will be an undergraduate program for resident students. Its external degree program will be reassigned to the Whitehead Center and its Masters' program to the division of graduate studies. The present faculty are under contract for from one to three years. Over the next three years appropriate faculty/student ratios will be established with faculty size then being determined by student enrollments.... Inasmuch as the Johnston College Board of Overseers will cease to function in its present form, all members of that group who are now not Trustees will be invited to belong to and participate in the President's Advisory Council, and selected members of the Overseers be evaluated and considered for vacancies (present and future) on the University Board of Trustees....Where it is not possible to renew Johnston faculty contracts, every effort shall be made to reassign such persons to other areas of the University....

As Moore finished, the students in the balcony threw a hurriedly made dummy over the edge of the railing. Suspended by a hangman's rope and bearing a hard-to-read sign, it swung disjointedly over the exiting crowd. A few cameras flashed. Moore thought the effigy was of himself — his speech had anticipated, even welcomed personal attacks as a test of his mettle — but it was not. It was yet another allegorical figure in the chapel, a slovenly embodiment of Johnston College, looking as defeated as its namesake. It swung for a time, then hung still. From his perch, the blue Jesus continued to bless the poor in spirit and those who mourn.

What ended in this manner had officially begun a decade earlier when "Johnston College of the University of Redlands" opened its brand new buildings to 182 students on September 3, 1969. But the beginnings of the college lie deeper than even that year. They extend into the lives of three central figures, and through them into the paradisal visions of the 1960's in America, and through those into the long traditions of egalitarian, alternative education which have surfaced regularly in our country since its own beginning.

Section One

1968-71:
Beginnings

The trouble with experiments in higher education is that they never fail.

— William Devane

CHAPTER 1

Visions of a College: Armacost, Orton and McCoy

I

Discussion of a cluster college on the University of Redlands campus began as early as 1961. The first conception of the new college was put forth by University President George Armacost and his Board of Trustees. They envisioned an alternative college which would train young people for careers in international business, the foreign service, and related professions.

The time for expansion seemed perfect. The postwar baby boom had produced an unprecedented number of college applicants and higher education was generally regarded as a necessary condition for social and financial success. Small private liberal arts colleges were a preferred, because exclusive, road to such success. Redlands was located in one of the fastest growing and attractive areas of the country. The University was naturally eager to take advantage of these conditions and attitudes.

Internally, the University seemed well prepared for

growth. It had been founded in 1907 by the American Baptists and had enjoyed a steady, if modest, success. It had survived the Depression and profited from the dramatic changes created by the return of veterans to school after World War II. Under the leadership of President Armacost (1945-1970), it had reaffirmed its mission as a conservative college with a strong Christian orientation.

Southern California, a bastion of Christian conservatism, provided a dependable pool of students, who were also attracted by the lovely campus and the New England look of the town of Redlands. Founded by wealthy easterners as a health spa and winter resort, it contained hundreds of turn-of-the-century Victorian homes. These gave the city an air − and a citizenry − of genteel permanence not often found in the Los Angeles area.

Framing the decision to expand was the wish to preserve the small college atmosphere traditionally prized at Redlands. So the University decided to use a version of the cluster college idea successfully employed by the nearby Claremont Colleges. The idea was simple: the University would add units, each with its own academic identity, faculty, student body, governing board and mini-campus. The new colleges would be autonomous in several respects but each would remain under the overarching control of the University President and his Board of Trustees. In this way colleges could be added without diluting the Christian focus of the University.

A college for international business and foreign service would be the first addition. An embryonic form of this plan was approved by the Faculty Council in early 1967, with the implicit understanding that this addition might be followed later by others − a school of fine arts, a center for the study of religion, and perhaps even a law school.[1] But these ambitions could not be undertaken until the University obtained the necessary backing. Though Redlands had a respectable endowment it was not a rich school. Outside support was necessary to finance its new projects. It found such support in the person of James

Graham "Jimmie" Johnston.

Johnston was a Scots mechanic who had emigrated to the United States in the 1920's and joined the fledgling International Business Machines Company. When he retired in the 1960's he was in charge of that corporation's overseas operations, and a millionaire several times over. He wanted to do something worthwhile with his money, and in such a way that his philanthropy would also preserve his name (he was childless). Johnston found a project for his philanthropic impulse through his friend Dr. Dwayne Orton, a Redlands alumnus who also worked for IBM as head of international education programs.

Orton had been a university administrator at Raymond College, the experimental division of University of the Pacific. He had maintained a keen interest in alternative higher education in general and in his alma mater in particular. Orton was aware of the University's expansion plans and saw the Johnston gift as an opportunity to found a college which would make higher education both more efficient and more suited to the demands of advanced industrial civilization. So when Jimmy Johnston sought Orton's advice on possible uses for his money Orton suggested that a naming grant for a new college at the University of Redlands might be ideal.

There was a certain irony to the suggestion. Johnston had emigrated to the United States as a machinist and had very little formal education; he had quit school in the sixth grade. Yet he was sufficiently impressed by his friend's proposal that he decided that founding a college named after him was just what he wanted. So after some dickering — there was a point at which Orton and Johnston almost took their money and expertise to UOP — he offered a naming grant of $1.5 million. $300,000 was made available immediately, with the rest accruing gradually to the University as the seventeen Johnston family legatees died. He added an additional grant of $250,000 in 1970.

The University began an ambitious building program

in 1968. It constructed two dormitories and a classroom/dining hall complex as well as a new library/computer center in the open fields on the east end of the campus. Loans totalling $3.5 million were secured from the Federal Government, in expectation that the Johnston grant and tuition from new students would defray repayment costs.

The building program was a bold, perhaps even a rash move. Johnston's grant was generous but was also certainly inadequate to fund a new college. (Compare the $20 million with which Hampshire College in Massachusetts began its operation.) Both Armacost and his Board understood the gravity of the risk, but they felt confident that the new college would attract just the publicity necessary to raise fresh money.

So the college began to take shape, and Orton was named chairman of its Board of Overseers. He too had a vision of what Johnston College should be, and it was not precisely that of Armacost and his Trustees. His experiences at IBM and at the University of the Pacific had convinced him that much of American higher education was not nearly as productive as it might be. It did not prepare its students to become problem-solvers in a complex and changing world. Colleges were too insular, and too dedicated to teaching the content of traditional disciplines. What was needed was a new approach in which disciplinary courses would give place to interdisciplinary problem analysis. Orton foresaw a school in which faculty and students would group themselves together to understand and solve real-world problems. The gap between traditional liberal arts education and the demands of late twentieth century society could thus be overcome. Founding such a college at the University would have an additional benefit for Orton; he believed his alma mater was atrophying in its stubborn conservatism. The new college would be a "gadfly" to its parent institution, helping it make the transition to a new age.

Orton's large but sketchy vision of higher education

was shaped by IBM, whose business was the efficient production and distribution of useful information. The vision was technocratic and progressive; impatient with learning as an end in itself, Orton believed that learning applied to the world's problems would eventually produce real solutions. His dream college would be a kind of problem-solving laboratory in which students would be trained to master and apply a set of intellectual skills.

Jimmie Johnston's motives — to do good work in the world and to preserve his memory — go some way toward describing Dwayne Orton's as well. Johnston College was a deeply personal mission and came to dominate the last years of his life. He died in 1971 and the student center is appropriately named for him.

George Armacost was the man with whom Orton had to work to bring his dreams to life. They shared a considerable common interest in innovative education. Armacost's doctoral degree was earned at Columbia Teacher's College. From 1929-32 he taught in the progressive elementary and secondary schools run by Columbia in Scarborough and elsewhere. He then worked in the 'experience curriculum' and 'pupil participation' experiments in the state of Virginia in the 1920's.

His exposure to progressive education did not leave him an uncritical admirer. The weakness of such programs, he felt, lay in their "lack of coherence; the teacher who began a class with the question 'what do you want to do?' normally faced chaos."[2]

But he did recognize that more traditional forms "excluded students from classroom decision making" and he hoped to redress that wrong. His notions of innovation for Johnston College extended to problem-solving learning, and to combining knowledge of international business and government with an ecumenical moral vision ("the 'essence' of the Old and New Testaments, not a doctrine").[3] They did not extend to student decision-making beyond the classroom. As early as 1960 Armacost told his Board that "eternal vigilance is necessary to keep our Christian institutions from being corrupted by popular cults.... Our job is to help students recognize significant independence and nonconformity in support of principles as distinguished from beatnik and superficial substitution of oddities of dress and behavior such as the growing of beards as symbols of revolt and nonconformity."

In 1964, despite such protestations by Armacost, the Board felt obliged to warn him against the "freedom of a bohemian community." And it was true that certain of Armacost's ideas were considerably more liberal than those of many of his Board members. He felt that he had achieved concessions from them concerning the potentially "far-out" new college on the strength of his personal word that order and decorum would be maintained. He convinced the Board that a conservative college that adhered to the old values could also be educationally progressive without surrendering its commitment to overseeing the moral and intellectual development of its charges.

It is important to remember how deeply conservative schools of Redlands' type were in the 1960's. A few anecdotes may help. Academic Vice President Marc Jack Smith once went to the home of English professor Jack Mitchell, at Armacost's instigation, and demanded that Mitchell shave his beard. Mitchell refused and — coincidentally? — he was asked to leave the next year. Board or administrative inquiry into the church affiliation of prospective faculty members was routine. For several years admissions director Ken Corwin was instructed to keep a double filing system for applicants. Baptist applicants whose high school records made them risk cases were put in a special category. Armacost would personally review these files to see whether ways might be found to admit as many such students as possible. There were very strict parietal rules in the dormitories; any males found beyond the limits of the living rooms in women's dorms were routinely suspended or expelled. And when the Communist Bettina Aptheker appeared on campus as a speaker in 1968 (invited by a group of conservative seniors, but in defiance of Board policy), the entire group of twenty students was suspended and graduated *in absentia*

Johnston was to be innovative, then, but within the severe limits set by a conservative tradition which, Armacost boasted, kept the University "twenty years behind the times." The college was to be the culmination of his twenty-five year presidency, the embodiment of the dramatic but responsible progress Redlands had made under his leadership. The dream of Dr. Field would be achieved without compromising the religious mission of the school; Redlands would be a true Christian university at last.

Thanks in large part to Dwayne Orton's negotiating skill the Johnston grant came to Redlands in 1966. By the spring of 1967 the search for a founding chancellor had begun, and the fourth actor on the stage was about to be introduced. This was not an easy job to fill because there were not many people willing to take on such a demanding assignment. Success would demand an ability to work well with Armacost and his conservative Board on the one hand, and with the college students of the late 1960's on the other. Since the new college was severely under-capitalized, much more money would have to be raised, and raised quickly. The chancellor, then, needed to be an educational visionary, a first-rate diplomat, a solid administrator, and an aggressive fund-raiser. He should also, ideally, be a practicing Christian, preferably a Baptist.

It is hardly surprising that the individual chosen — Presley C. McCoy — fell short of perfection in meeting this profile. What is surprising is that he accomplished a good deal of what was expected. But McCoy was a remarkable man in many ways. Born in California but raised in the Midwest, he had been brought up in a home where religion and education were literally married; his father was a minister and his mother a teacher. He went from this home to a small Baptist college in Ohio (Denison) and then to an urban graduate school (Northwestern) where he earned a doctorate in political science. He then taught for a few years at Denison before taking a job as an administrator with the Danforth Foundation. He worked for that organization for eight years (1956-64), then for the next five as head of the Central States College Association, a consortium of twelve liberal arts colleges in the Midwest.

Armacost knew McCoy by acquaintance and reputation. They first met briefly in 1962 when McCoy interviewed at Redlands for the position of chair of the speech department. McCoy was offered the job but turned it down.

Armacost called McCoy in January of 1968 and asked if he would be interested in heading an "experimental college with an international emphasis." McCoy was definitely interested, and an exchange of letters led to an interview with Armacost and the Board. He was offered the job late that spring.[4] The University appeared to have found their man. He was bright, articulate, energetic and progressive; he was firmly committed to innovation within the context of a Christian framework of values. He had a national reputation as an educator. He had good administrative experience, and he had sufficient charisma to draw students and raise money from donors.

Just before the offer was extended McCoy met with Dwayne Orton in New York. The two men agreed to meet for lunch at the prestigious, somewhat stuffy University Club in midtown Manhattan. McCoy — bluff, hearty and stocky — dressed as always in oddly matched slacks and jacket that never seemed to hang just right on his muscular frame — walked into the club and looked around, a bit hesitantly, for Orton, whom he had never met. Even in the elegant surroundings Orton stood out. He was an East

Coast aristocrat and looked the part. He was slim, silver-haired and ascetically handsome even in his mid-sixties. He wore a perfectly tailored charcoal suit and eyeglasses that gave him the look of a distinguished senior professor. As they sat down to lunch the two men found that they had much in common despite the obvious differences in appearance. Both were great talkers. Orton was extraordinarily articulate and wholly confident in public settings. He could deliver ex tempore speeches as if they had been carefully written and memorized. But as the afternoon wore on and the lunch dishes were cleared it was McCoy who did most of the talking.

His talk, unlike Orton's, had no orderly surface. McCoy created visions and images in his resonant Midwestern voice. He did not so much present arguments as conjure up vivid and alluring pictures of worlds that might be. If Orton's dreams were couched in careful prose, McCoy's emerged as discontinuous episodes, stories — even myths.

McCoy was determined that Orton understand everything he wanted to do at Redlands. Without Orton's support, McCoy knew, he had no chance. So he went into detail. "Dimensions of learning," "sensitivity training," "living-learning community" — the phrases were unfamiliar to Orton but what they seemed to represent struck deep chords in him. After an hour of exposition McCoy sat back, flushed and eager, to allow for Orton's response.

"Wonderful! Absolutely wonderful!" said Orton. His eyes sparkled behind his patrician glasses. "But you know that what you're spelling out is not what Armacost has in mind."

"Why not?" countered McCoy. "He told me that he wanted an experimental school, like their January 'interim' semester, and that there would be lots of social science and an international emphasis."

"They're interested in a business program," Orton replied.

"Well, that's fine with me" said McCoy. "If the basic

design is right, then business is as viable a field as any other."

"Did you tell Armacost everything you're telling me?" asked Orton.

"Well, no. And he didn't ask me for details. We talked a lot more generally about things."

"Did you ask him for details?"

"No. It was his interview. I assumed he would find out what he wanted to know. He was very interested in my religious background." McCoy hesitated. "And I guess I was a little cautious. It sounds like such a great opportunity. I didn't want to put him off."

"He's very conservative, you know," said Orton.

"And so is Redlands," nodded McCoy, "I know that. And that's why your full support and that of the Johnston Board, is so important to me if I'm going to take this job. Without that the thing isn't going to get off the ground."

"Except for this sensitivity training – I don't know about that yet – you've got it."

"This is unbelievable," McCoy blurted out. "My gosh, you're a businessman who really sees the need for innovation in education. I can't believe my luck."

"That just tells me how much you need to learn about business executives," Orton said with a smile.

From that luncheon on, McCoy and Orton were allies. They shared a vision very different from that of George Armacost. They made an implicit pact: they would not so much openly defy Armacost as pursue their shared understanding of innovation in higher education, despite the conservatism of the parent institution. It was hardly, as some University officials came to think, a conspiracy against traditional education and the "Redlands way," but it was a chance to create an alternative for American higher education, a chance not likely to be offered to either man again.

In order to appreciate the differences between McCoy and Armacost we now need to flesh out McCoy's background and educational ideals. Perhaps his most interesting and radical notion was the incorporation of T-grouping and sensitivity training into higher education. He was not the only educator to use such training but was the first to make it the central focus of a college.[5]

T-grouping ("T" for "training") began almost by accident during a Federally-funded civil rights project carried out in Connecticut in the years following World War II. The Government was interested in finding ways to establish better relations between black and white civic leaders in cities in which blacks and whites competed for the same industrial jobs. The meetings were organized and run by psychiatrist Dr. Kurt Lewin and his staff.

Lewin's staff met each night to analyze what went on in that day's meetings. Before long the civic leaders began to sit in on these meetings and to listen to the meeting tapes along with the professionals. As they listened they began to remark on the process rather than the content of the meetings. It became clear that how people looked and talked made at least as much difference as what they were saying; people's styles helped or hindered decision-making and problem-solving. If an individual's style antagonized others in the group this antagonism would appear as opposition to that person's ideas.

Sessions began to be devoted to raising sensitivity: that is, individuals would begin to say how they felt about other people's styles. The expression of feelings, and personal confrontations, replaced examination of "objective" issues. And it was found that such expressions of feeling, despite being painful, gradually reduced intra-group tension and made decision-making more efficient.

Thus group encounter was born. Two concepts were crucial in these first generation sensitivity groups. First, in group decision-making individual feelings counted and needed to be expressed. The second was that "feedback" — telling other people just how you feel — was the proper means for expressing and validating such feelings.

It was also found, both by Lewin and by many later studies, that such sharing was most effective if it were overseen by a trained group leader. The leader's role was to act as a sort of emotional traffic manager and mediator. When transactions between participants were not going well the trainer would intervene to make sure that the confronting individuals were listening to each other accurately. Leaders were not so much authority figures as "facilitators"; they helped people work out problems but did not legislate solutions.

Two other features of group process deserve mention. First, a group always operated in the "here and now." Any reference to situations outside the group would detract from immediate feelings and occlude the group's purpose, which was to clarify relations among its members, not do therapy for individuals in the group. Second, a group had no pre-established agenda. Even though such groups helped decision-making, they were not themselves decision-making groups. Their purpose was to give vent to feelings and to hear such venting, in whatever order the feelings occurred.

Thus groups had no hierarchy, no outside reference and no internal structure except that determined by the flow of feelings. They were quintessentially anarchic and operated on the notion that from the chaos of feelings would emerge community.

This first generation of sensitivity groups enjoyed great success in government agencies, notably NASA, and high technology companies such as TRW. Their success depended on the T-group's ability to coordinate the work of individuals from many different technical and business backgrounds. In companies and agencies that needed to pool the planning skills of a variety of working groups affective openness meant greater decision-making efficiency.

First generation groups were firmly pragmatic rather than expressive or therapeutic in character. Feelings counted because of their impact on group process; they had little intrinsic value. But the implicit assumption in group work — that the unfettered expression of individual feelings empowered both group and individual salvation — soon emerged as an explicit principle. This led to a second generation of groups which were frankly therapeutic and geared to assist the individual to greater self-expression and freedom. Such groups borrowed both theory and practice from traditional psychoanalysis and from the client-centered, humanistic psychology of such thinkers as Carl Rogers. Roughly stated, their purposes were to help individuals express feelings, to "own" those feelings as valid, and to work through such feelings to achieve greater personal integration. On one level feelings thus expressed might indicate the presence of neurosis; on another, feelings were seen as valuable in and for themselves. In both cases the expression of individual feelings was useful for the individual.

Using a group setting to express feelings was thought to speed up the process of self-disclosure; for many people it was easier to show feelings when others were doing the same thing. Groups provided "targets" for feelings: people learned to free themselves from affective inhibition by practicing with other group members, in confrontations, or in revelations of attraction or affection.

This second generation of groups became part and parcel of the "counter-culture" which began to surface in California in the decade preceding the opening of Johnston College. This inchoate movement placed the individual-as-feeling at the center of its universe of values and supported any method which promised to free that individual from social restraint: sensitivity groups, psychotropic drugs, sexual liberation. The "counter-culture" rejected the goal-oriented pragmatism of mainstream American liberals and celebrated the moment. Insofar as sensitivity groups could celebrate rather than manage feelings they were part of the movement.

Presley McCoy discovered sensitivity training only one year before he was hired as Chancellor of Johnston College — and he discovered a primarily first-generation form. Though McCoy was well read in the works of the leading humanistic psychologists (e.g., Rogers and Rollo May) and more or less believed their optimistic vision of individual development, he had little practical experience in applying their therapeutic suggestions to his own life. He got that experience and became a "convert" to sensitivity training because of personal concerns. While with the Danforth Foundation he and his wife joined a discussion group that met every other Sunday. It was a group of professional people — doctors, lawyers, an engineer, a physicist — who discussed books on human relationships.

McCoy was frustrated by this group because no one opened up about his or her own experience. McCoy knew that he and his wife Doris Lee had serious problems and that this was true of others in the group. But he felt that the group's training, as intellectuals and technocrats, had made the simple expression of feeling too difficult. Group members intellectualized everything; the discussions were clear, cheerful — and false.

McCoy had what amounted to an affective Cartesian revelation: "I began thinking, 'You know, this is just what goes on in classrooms. We discuss things intellectually because it's safe — this school of thought, that school of thought — but as far as any internal commitments are concerned, these are ignored. Feelings have nothing to do with it.'" He wanted to break into the discussions, to admit that he needed help rather than fine words, but he "...didn't dare because there were all our images to sustain and protect...it was a shame; I think of all the lost opportunities...."

McCoy got his chance to reveal himself when a friend told him about the Center for Creative Growth in Athens, Georgia. The friend and his spouse were going to spend some weeks at the semi-rural retreat and he invited Pres and Doris Lee to come along. They agreed. They spent the next several weeks working in separate sensitivity groups exploring their feelings about themselves and about each other. It was what McCoy had been looking for: "The thing I liked about the Center was that it at least dealt with human feelings. It was okay to say how you felt about someone else and yourself in what you hoped was a protected environment that would not do you in...."

He immediately applied what he was experiencing to his nascent vision of a more affectively open academic environment:

> Speaking autobiographically, a big part of the motivation for trying to bring together affective and cognitive dimensions was the difficulty in having and establishing the kind of growth relationship I wanted in my marriage.... Educators and education do not want to deal with the affective dimensions of learning, yet that...is where our motivation lies...of all the things Johnston attempted to do, whether it did them well or not, one of the most important was to give full attention to both dimensions, that is to our true nature.

Thus was the educational "philosophy" of Johnston College conceived.

McCoy's plans coalesced rapidly after the Athens experience. He saw that sensitivity training could be used in education both pragmatically and therapeutically. The incorporation of techniques for expressing feelings into the academic setting would make learning both more efficient and more creative. Students would see how their ideas related to their own feelings and would thus invest the ideas with more passion. Such ideas would then be learned more thoroughly and applied more carefully because they would not only be ideas, they would be ideas rooted in the depths of oneself, in affective interaction with one's fellow learners.

McCoy had little knowledge and less understanding of the second generation, feeling-for-their-own sake groups which identified with the psychotropic and anti-establishment movements. He acknowledged the importance of human feelings and the fact that they should be studied.

But fundamental to his thinking was the use of feeling to achieve the double goals of greater learning efficiency and enhanced personal development.

In this spirit McCoy began to think through how academic classes could also be sensitivity groups. In a class specific content and methods provided the group's raison d'etre; this could not change. But each class could also serve as a forum for eliciting the feelings of class members about the material, and about its mode of presentation. Thus time in a class should be devoted to discussing student reaction to class content, and to talking about the class process by means of which content was learned. In this type of class the teacher, like the sensitivity leader, ceases to be simply a figure of intellectual authority and becomes instead someone who helps the student to express feelings and to find the best individual way to learn.

For McCoy this process of thinking through the relations between sensitivity training and classroom learning was an exciting process because he quickly found connections with the other elements in his vision of reform in higher education. T-grouping was now a means to the larger end of educating individuals for both self-development and community service. The nub of McCoy's vision of good education was that it could help people to solve problems both within themselves and in the world.

McCoy divided education as he divided the world: there were individuals, cultures and nations. Each area had problems specific to itself and education must teach individuals how to recognize and perhaps solve such problems. Thus a reasonable college curriculum should organize itself around each of these dimensions of human existence — the personal/interpersonal, the cultural/intercultural, and the national/international. The ideal college would have "dimensions," just as life itself has dimensions; its offerings would consist of a variety of methodologies which could be applied to each dimension of human experience to throw light on its problems and to suggest solutions.

The first and central concern of education must then be with the problems which affect the individual; McCoy felt that people could not devote themselves fully to the problems of other cultures or nations until they felt at home with themselves. He did not mean that personal problems cannot be a function of larger social and economic upheavals, only that whatever the source of the problem the individual feels it on a personal level and must first deal with it on that level, as a set of affective reactions.

This bias reveals the roots of McCoy's educational philosophy and makes even clearer why he found sensitivity training so appealing. McCoy was a deeply committed liberal Protestant and a thorough-going American. For both traditions the individual stands at the very center of the world. Larger groups are nothing more than congeries of individuals whose sole end is to serve each individual. In that light education must begin, and in a sense end, with the individual, and all its institutional trappings must be constructed with this absolute value in mind.

The pervasive problem that affects individuals in McCoy's vision is that old chestnut, alienation. McCoy's understanding of alienation was not so complex, nor so economically and socially based, as that of, say, Marx. In fact, McCoy's individualism made it impossible for him to think seriously in terms of class consciousness or abstract modes of labor-based alienation. Alienation had to be felt to be real.

Nor was McCoy's alienation that sense of antisocial absurdity embraced by the "beat" generation and post-war French intellectuals. He did not believe that human life was absurd or that free people must always live outside society. He had little in common with the hippies, whose alternate lifestyle was a rejection of the dominant culture. No, McCoy's understanding of alienation was predictably derived from those Protestant theologians and moralists who fed his own tradition. Alienation in this tradition was a felt condition arising from a sense of personal separation between man and his environment – from the earth, from his fellow men, and from his own deepest spiritual yearnings.

The culprit in most such accounts is technocratic civilization, which threatens the autonomy of the individual by reducing her to a cipher or a function. McCoy's specific villain was the multiversity with its technocracy of learning, its rigidly professional academic departments and its emphasis on research. McCoy felt that such institutions dehumanized students by reducing them to non-entities. In his eyes education should exist for the individual; its processes must never reverse the proper relation between man and institution, a relation in which, ideally, institutional structures exist solely to enhance individual development. Thus the overall aim of his educational program at Johnston would be to provide individuals with the knowledge, skills and emotional motivation to overcome feelings of isolation and to equip them for a positive re-entry into a larger world.

Over lunch at the University Club McCoy explained all this to Orton. Alienation would be overcome partly by the establishment of a communal academic setting appropriate to the task. Johnston College would contain conventional academic structures such as classes, administration and record-keeping. But these would go on in a community based on rigorously egalitarian principles and with a minimum of internal hierarchy.

Here we see an inevitable outcome of McCoy's valuing of the individual. In a world where individuals constitute the measure of value it is necessary to reduce social divisions to a minimum since no person is any more a person than any other and acquired skills should only give individuals power in areas circumscribed by such skills. Thus a teacher might have more power in the classroom when discussing his area of expertise but that power must not be generalized to wholesale control of class process. The teacher's status in the learning community would be equal, politically, to the power of a student, an administrator or a staff member.

The next political implication Pres derived from this theory was that his ideal college community should make its decisions by consensus, a method widely used in sensitivity groups. This method was first used by the Society of Friends, or Quakers. Its ground rule is that the group makes decisions only when every group member feels in his/her heart that he/she "can live with" the decision. This means that the decision cannot be one that contravenes any voting member's deepest moral convictions.

Before a decision is taken, then, group members search their consciences to make sure that the decision will not undercut their moral sense or that of any of their fellows. Within this system the lowliest community member has the power to block major decisions, and decisions taken represent more than political compromise or majority victory: they express the shared belief of all, and their best judgment.

The idea of establishing Johnston as a consensual community led McCoy to several allied ideas. Faculty should hold neither rank nor tenure. All community members should be evaluated on an equal basis. All such evaluations, be they of student work or faculty performance, should be done in narrative rather than quantitative form because that comes closest to preserving the unique value of the individual. The consensual idea also led to the very important idea that learning should be organized through the mechanism of negotiated contracts, in which student and faculty would agree to a shared academic plan and proceed according to it. And it has direct political consequences; all decisions at Johnston were subject to community approval. All information-gathering and proposal-writing relevant to decisions had to be shared among all community members. Thus were born the plenary community meeting and the committee structure, in which all committees had equal numbers of faculty and students.

Finally, since personal experience was fundamental to any kind of problem-solving, it would be the subject matter for the first year of study. Alienation must be attacked at its true source. In McCoy's original plan the beginning student would take all work in what McCoy called the "personal/interpersonal dimension," in classes whose focus was personal problem-solving. Only in one's second and third years would one branch out to study the great world in the intercultural and international dimensions.

Dimensions would thus replace academic departments. They would have directors analogous to T-group leaders: guides without being despots. Dimensions would be loose confederations of faculty and students from many disciplines who would pool interests and skills for as long as they needed to study specific personal, cultural and national or international problems. Alienation would be mitigated by creating flexible learning groups whose work would begin and end with a specific, jointly chosen task.

All these things would be done at once. Pres was committed to the idea of an institution that was itself an experiment. He was impressed by educator Paul Dressel's phrase "academic tinkering"; McCoy derided schools that tried a few new things for a few years, then abandoned them for another fad. Nothing about education was learned from such hit-and-miss changes. McCoy's school was going to be an experimental model that would be tested for a three year period.

Thus McCoy's vision. His college would be a learning community ruled by consensus, in which individuals would be helped toward self-development and worldly skills through the incorporation of sensitivity techniques into the learning situation. Those same individuals would overcome dehumanizing alienation via their inclusion in, and maintenance of, an egalitarian community of learning. The community would approach the business of education as that of acquiring skills to understand and solve personal and world problems. They would do this under the aegis of a structure which divided human experience into the three overlapping regions of the personal/interpersonal, cultural /intercultural and the national/international. Faculty without special rank or tenure would pool disciplinary skills in helping students understand themselves and the world, and all community members would oversee the daily business of running the college. This vision was a heady combination of romantic individualism, belief in an egalitarian community and technocratic pragmatism. It combined belief in learning as problem-solving with a certain distrust of technocracy, and a belief in the absolute value of the individual and his feelings with a commitment to life in an intentional/consensual community. It allied traditional disciplinary skills with free-floating problem-solving in *ad hoc* learning groups, and jettisoned traditional academic departments altogether. All in all McCoy's vision was a radical, highly inventive combination of pragmatism, humanistic psychology and utopian Protestant communalism which was a far, far cry from the school for international business envisioned by the University.

II

On the first Monday of August, 1968, Pres McCoy began his tenure as the Chancellor of Johnston College. His office for this planning year was located in the northeastern corner of the University's gymnasium. Pres had a desk and a yellow pad of paper: no faculty, no staff, not even a secretary. Looking north across Colton Avenue he could see the empty field that was about to become Johnston. He was already anxious about how the field would be transformed. Architects' sketches that had called for airy dormitories with wide windows and balconies had already been reduced by budgetary considerations to blueprints of cement block buildings with small windows, no balconies and fully enclosed lobby areas. The windows could not be opened because of the heating/air conditioning system. But this change seemed minor when compared with the sheer excitement of beginning: "Gosh, isn't this fun," McCoy thought to himself. "I'm about to actually start a college, just myself."

On that yellow pad he sketched many of the ideas we have just reviewed, then began adding refinements that would make his more general vision work. Learning would go on in seminars, tutorials and independent studies. Each seminar would have its parallel T-Group to work with any affective problems the class might generate and to promote group dynamics. There would be a full-time staff member engaged in institutional research to monitor the progress of the learning groups, and a coterie of professional psychologists on the faculty to oversee the first year of interpersonal studies. There would also be a class that every student would take and every faculty member teach — the "Quest for Meaning" seminar, which would provide the springboard to self-discovery for the year's academic activity. The original class should have 100 students and 10 faculty. The combination of classes, T-groups, resident experts, a shared seminar and a low student-faculty ratio would continue for three years.

Students would live by an honor code worked out by the community. They would work in each of the dimensions in successive years, do senior theses and have off-campus intercultural and international experiences. They would receive written evaluations for their work and their academic file would consist of such documents. Every member of the community would be evaluated in this way — faculty and administrative staff as well as students — though of course the evaluations of faculty and staff would differ from those of students.

McCoy wrote two key phrases on the yellow pad: "learning how to learn" and "living/learning." The first emphasized that process counted as much as content.

Though subject matters might change with time, methods of learning remained relatively more stable, and therefore more fundamental to education. The second phrase meant that life in the dormitories should be integrated with life in the classroom or in the internship. Just as McCoy wanted to integrate reason and feeling in the classroom, so he wanted to integrate student life with student learning. This translated into the idea that some faculty should live in the dormitories and that faculty offices should also be located there; classes would ideally take place in dormitory lobbies or in the dining hall/student center. Following instructions from President Armacost there would be no duplication of expensive educational equipment. Johnston students would use University science and language labs, the University library and gymnasium, and most art and music facilities. And, in the manner of the Danforth Foundation, spouses and children of faculty and staff would be included in as many college functions as possible.

Finally, McCoy proposed to enlist a group of academic consultants to flesh out these very general plans. But McCoy decided that in keeping with the open spirit of the school, no curriculum would be established before the faculty arrived, just one month before the school opened. A second group of consultants would be hired to design a sensitivity training program specifically designed for the academic situation. And in the prospectus to be published each year there would be a listing of faculty and their current academic interests. That was the sum and substance of what McCoy wrote down in his first days as Chancellor.

We note in this plan no mention of international business or diplomacy, and there is no evidence that Armacost or the University Board were consulted beforehand about any part of the plan. It was Pres' vision alone, and he went ahead singlemindedly to make this the shape of the new college. In fact, he did not learn until a few days after he roughed out his college that there was to have been a major emphasis on international business and diplomacy. McCoy believed that he had carte blanche in designing his college and Orton encouraged him in that belief. Even after he learned of the original plan he more or less ignored it and went his own way. "I would never have taken the job," he told Orton a few weeks later, "if I had known they just wanted a school of business. That isn't...my strength."

Budgeting for the planning year was relatively simple. McCoy was allotted a sum of money drawn from accumulated interest on the Johnston grant and from a Ford Foundation grant which the University had recently received. He was given an operating budget of $100,000, including funds for consultants and for recruiting students and faculty. This was not lavish, but it was adequate to the task.

Once the plan was sketched and a budget provided, McCoy began to assemble the group which would make his college a reality. He first hired an executive secretary, Ms. Marilyn Prihoda. She was everything he needed. McCoy tended to be a typical visionary; he was a dreadful record-keeper and his sense of time was defined more by the enthusiasm of the moment than by more objective calendars. Marilyn, though not a visionary, did know how to get Pres where he needed to be at the right time, and she kept files and correspondence in order and current. Without her steadying, orderly presence the vision could well have remained just that.

Pres also needed a person who could prepare admissions brochures and grant proposals, as well as establish relationships with the University's office of public relations, the development office and with local media. He found that person in Ms. Lee Jones.

Lee was an experienced professional. She has worked in similar positions at Cal Tech and then at Prescott College in Arizona, an alternative college which built its program around the Outward Bound experience. She was unhappy at Prescott and was driving through Redlands to Los

Angeles to interview for a job. On an impulse she decided to stop, in response to a recent form letter describing the Johnston position which she had received in the mail. She knew nothing about Johnston, almost nothing about Redlands.

She telephoned the University's development director, Gil Brown, who immediately invited her on campus. She accepted the invitation and Brown was sufficiently impressed to recommend that McCoy interview her, which he did. Lee recalls the meeting:

> We had lunch. It was very exciting because we didn't talk about the job at all. We talked about education. And by the time we finished Pres was talking about where I was going to sit in that tiny office.

Lee still had to get Armacost's approval.

> We walked into Armacost's office. There were three chairs, one for Pres, one for Gil Brown. I sat in the middle. Gil introduced me and said, 'I believe you have her resume on your desk.'

> Dr. Armacost looked up and said, 'Yes, I have it. But what we really need is somebody who can get this college open on time. Do you know anything about flow charts?' I didn't, particularly, but it didn't sound like a very difficult thing to learn. So I said 'Sure'.

> I realize he was hiring me to get someone who would run around making sure that all the loose ends were tied up and the deadlines met.

Lee was both competent and informed. She knew the world of higher education and the ins and outs of successful grantsmanship; she also, crucially, knew something about how alternative institutions operated. She was an excellent journalist and publicist. During the first year it was her hard work that helped Johnston gain national attention even before it opened its doors. Pres added two more secretaries — Doris Stockman and Sally Hickok. Both were extraordinary people who soon became effective administrators at Johnston and later went on to successful careers in that profession. Their enthusiasm, added to Lee's energy and Marilyn's precision, gave Pres an impressive working group before the first faculty were hired.

But Pres did need a small cadre of faculty to help in the planning process and to take over some of the day-to-day administrative and promotional jobs so he could be free to accomplish his primary objectives: to hire a full faculty and recruit students. During the first weeks he succeeded in hiring three people: John Watt, then a professor of Chinese history at MIT; Roger Baty, a Rhodes Scholar from Montana just completing his doctorate in Anthropology at Stanford; René Françillon, a Swiss economist/administrator who combined academic training with practical business experience.

The choice of these men must have assuaged any fears on the part of the University administration about the direction the new college might take. Two of the three were highly cultivated Europeans, one of whom could teach international business, and the third, Baty, had grown up in Beirut and studied in England. All were accomplished academicians with impeccable credentials and only John Watt could be characterized as liberal. Both Baty and Françillon seemed the soul of decorous conservatism. Baty was a plainspoken Westerner whose long experience overseas did not diminish the impression that he would be more at home on his father's ranch than in a college classroom. Françillon, for his part, looked like precisely what he was: an intelligent, cosmopolitan Genevan economist, polished by his years as an international businessman. Even Watt, whose longish hair and air of genteel dishevelment marked him as something of an exotic in Redlands, came from the best schools and had fought the Communist insurgency in Malaya in 1951. If these people were a bit more worldly than the general run at Redlands, they were also first-rate talents whose backgrounds appeared to be consistent with the mission of the college.

McCoy hired these three in a manner perfectly consistent with his general approach to his task. Watt recounts how it happened to him:

> I got this call from a guy named Pres McCoy. And he talked a blue streak for about twenty minutes. I'd never heard of the University of Redlands. When he finished he said that he'd like to meet me at the Statler Hilton in Boston. I'd hardly said a word...I'd never met a real academic hustler like him before. They don't grow them in New England, you know.

To Watt's astonishment Pres began their lunch with a fervid description of the new college, detailing how it would help students to know themselves before they were compelled to learn about the world. He described the egalitarian structure and sensitivity training, and then immediately offered Watt the position of director of the international dimension.

Watt was both overwhelmed and intrigued. Here was a stranger regaling him with visions of a new college which would create a new educational universe, one that Watt found immensely appealing. Watt decided: he left the security and respectability of MIT for a school that did not yet really exist, located on the campus of a small University he had never heard of and which was far more conservative than any school with which he had ever been associated.

As the Watt and Jones stories indicate, McCoy did not interview — he sold. He would obtain lists of Danforth

Fellows who had recently completed their degrees, and to this list would add the names of other promising young scholars culled from academic friends and from the chairs of graduate programs at leading universities. He would then screen the people mentioned on the lists, and interview those who looked most promising. Since the academic excellence of the candidates was already assured, the emphasis in the interview would be on discovering if McCoy's vision of the new college was consonant with the educational views of the candidates. He also knew that Johnston posed real risks for scholars bent on a traditional academic career, and felt he had to convince them that the challenges and opportunities the program afforded were worth that risk.

Faculty candidates met McCoy anticipating that they would have to present themselves as capably as they could. Instead, most found that they had already been hired, so long as they could live with McCoy's vision. "Generally," said McCoy, "I would decide ahead of time whether I thought this was a person I wanted. I would look only for obvious personality problems."

McCoy did look for excellent young teachers as well as good scholars. Youth was the operative word. He wanted people sufficiently talented to help him flesh out his idea but sufficiently inexperienced to offer those talents for a modest salary. And that is what he got. Of the charter faculty there were six persons under 30; the average age was 34, and only five were over 40. Four faculty were of foreign origin (from Japan, Spain, Switzerland and Britain) and five of the Americans had lived for long periods overseas, primarily in Third World countries where their parents were teachers or missionaries. It was a stellar faculty, recruited by persuasion and enticement to participate in the new enterprise. George Armacost called them "the most respectable group of faculty ever hired at Redlands."

But the hiring of the first Johnston faculty member also provoked the first of many crises between Armacost and McCoy. The Johnston charter was vague at many crucial points. It gave the new college "autonomy" in three areas: admissions, academic policies and graduation requirements. Pres McCoy took this to mean that he could make academic appointments on his own, as long as he cleared them with the Board of Trustees. In late August, Pres received a call from Armacost. It had become clear that Pres was not submitting the dossiers of prospective faculty to the President for review and approval. "Oh, by the way," said Armacost, "as a personal policy, I must approve all your appointments."

"I thought the Johnston Board had that responsibility." replied Pres, "because they are responsible for the academic program."

"No, Pres, they should all be channeled through me," said the President firmly, "I have final authority in all University business."

McCoy immediately sensed that this was a major issue. He was sure that Armacost's criteria for hiring Redlands faculty were so different from his that many qualified people would be rejected. Smoking, drinking and beards were behaviors McCoy considered irrelevant; he did not think Armacost found them so. Pres called Orton, who cut short a Tahiti vacation to meet with Armacost. The meeting took place in the dining room of the President's official residence on the campus. Armacost's wife, Verda, was present as well.

"I will approve these appointments," said Armacost loudly.

"No, you won't!" retorted Orton, nearly shouting.

Emotions rose. Armacost pounded the table; tears welled in Verda's eyes. The meeting finally broke up without either side publicly conceding. But in the event Pres won. As a matter of courtesy he took most candidates to meet the President, and the President would offer an opinion, "But if he (Armacost) said, 'Don't hire that guy' and I wanted him, I went ahead and hired him anyway." Though Armacost never explicitly conceded his power in this matter he surrendered it *de facto* and left faculty appointments in the hands of McCoy and his Board of Overseers.

On other academic issues McCoy and his small staff walked a tightrope between pacifying a President and Trustees eager for specific academic plans and their conviction that they must wait for the assembling of the full college community before such plans were made. The Johnston people also felt that it was politic to leave their intentions as vague as possible to avoid unnecessary friction.

There is one clear instance in which the Johnston group deliberately tried to fool Armacost and the trustees. This took place early in 1969, and is best recounted by John Watt, one of the participants:

> We were having dinner in the presidential dining room and I remember the dinner to this day. We had hamburgers that had been cooked about forty-five minutes and were black on both sides. Almost indigestible. And afterwards Pres got up and made a speech. Then I was invited to present this curriculum. And of course we were agreed that we wouldn't have any curriculum until we had the faculty, and we weren't going to have the faculty until next August. Chadwick (Wallace Chadwick, longtime University Trustee) and George weren't prepared to wait that long. So we had made these flow charts.
>
> I didn't know anything about what a flow chart was. I'd never seen one. But Lee Jones did (!) and she found an elegant printer and we constructed these things. And the printer took them away...and made these beautiful sheets.
>
> So I was playing the role of the evening class lecturer, where you know people are going to be

tired and you just have diagrams and indicate everything. And they were very complicated charts. Terrifying, in fact. But they didn't make any sense.... And I was very serious, very English. At about 11 p.m. I was just beginning the third chart when they said, 'Well, I think your presentation has been adequately...well...we think it's...um...time to go.' And that was it. We weren't asked to make any more presentations on the curriculum. I didn't tell Pres what I was doing, exactly, but I think he knew....

Watt left the trustees, and Armacost, with the misleading notion that Johnston possessed a detailed academic plan; he also extinguished all curiosity about it by overwhelming them with his murky Oxbridge elegance. Comically, a version of the infamous Watt Charts made its way into the first Johnston catalog. There was many a faculty member who arrived for the August 1969 planning sessions filled with terror about working at a place whose design was utterly beyond his or her understanding....

It might appear from all this that Orton, McCoy and their crew spent a good bit of time trying to hoodwink Armacost and the Board into supporting a college far removed from the original plans. This comes very close to former President Armacost's current view, which he defended with considerable vigor fifteen years after the event. He argued that if McCoy and his team had in fact founded a school for training in international business and foreign service the University would have been in better position to recruit the career-minded students of the late 70's and early 80's — and he may have been right. But in Armacost's view neither McCoy nor Orton ever had such an intention. They were both "egomaniacs" who came to the University with other ideas and consciously undid the University's long-term plans.

Thus the school meant to crown Armacost's presidency ended up as his great failure. "It was my baby" he asserts, "but Pres and Dwayne had their own agenda.... Johnston College was the greatest disappointment of my life." Armacost argues that McCoy and Orton got away with imposing their own, divergent plan because he (Armacost) was too willing to be trusting and did not want to seem overly controlling. He did ask for information, he says, but it was just not forthcoming.

Our study of the documents, including the extensive 1968-70 correspondence between Armacost and McCoy, bears out some of this but finds much of it too simple. Armacost did write letters demanding information while at the same time asking, even pleading, for more consultation. The letter of July 3, 1969, is typical:

> I realize that it has been more than a month since we have had any direct contact. I don't like to be issuing letters always asking you to come, or setting a time for you to come, for I feel we should have the kind of relationships in which the development of your plans, when anything comes up which involves budget, or any other items which should be taken up with the president of the University, that you will feel perfectly free to pick up the telephone and call me. You have a standing invitation to discuss with me at any time any topic which should be considered because of the very important relationship which we have...which is an integral part of the University and cannot be separated from it.

Sometimes he would even appear to conspire with McCoy in the education of the Board of Trustees.[6] And McCoy, in his zeal to guard the integrity of an experiment which Armacost and his Board had never explicitly approved, did make a political mistake in not consistently seeking to co-opt the president in his enterprise. He should have faced the contradiction in demanding a four-year pact of virtually absolute trust from a man he was consciously excluding – for whatever reasons – from the college the man himself had helped found. Instead he accepted too easily the word of University faculty and the president of another Southern California college that Armacost could never be made sympathetic. Neither man showed much knowledge of the other in their early, crucial dealings.

This is all the more dismaying in view of the potential similarities between them. McCoy did very much want an international program and was not adverse to enrolling students of international business and diplomacy. In fact, he hired people specifically trained in these areas. He believed, however, that one could not produce a richly educated internationalist without altering the forms of American higher education, while Armacost wanted to confine innovation to the classroom and had no interest in a full-blown academic experiment. Armacost, in turn, was not opposed to many parts of McCoy's educational philosophy. But he mistakenly believed that innovation once begun could be easily controlled. He publicly supported portions of the McCoy program – once he found out what it was. And on several occasions he fended off outraged alumni and townspeople during the first year of the college's operation and cautioned Redlands faculty against premature judgments.

Of course, Armacost had his own stake in the success of the college. But for a man often accused of autocracy he did make heroic efforts not to meddle. He peppered McCoy with letters of advice, relevant publications and pleas to be included – but he made few explicit demands. He remained reticent even though it became clearer and clearer, as time went on, just what McCoy intended. These intentions now regularly appeared in public statements, in the media and in promotional literature, as well as in the pattern of faculty hiring. As the design of the new college emerged Armacost complained frequently about the lack of structure, rejecting as irresponsible Pres' notion that such plans could only be developed when the community had assembled. He also expressed distaste for the T-groups but he was not strident on this matter until years later. And he continued to use the term "innovative" in a different way than McCoy: Armacost meant reform; McCoy meant something closer to revolution.

Still, it is remarkable that Armacost permitted McCoy to proceed with this planning virtually unhindered, despite poor communication and the clear indications that the new school was diverging farther and farther from his original plan. Whatever his motives, it remains a shame that two men with a shared desire to create a new educational opportunity suffered such a lack of mutual understanding.

There were explicit disagreements aside from the skirmish over faculty hiring. The single substantive struggle took place over the issue of student life, an area in which lines of authority were unclear. McCoy believed that co-ed dorms of some sort were an important part of a "living/learning" experiment. Armacost found such arrangements too liberal, not to say immoral; they could certainly not be permitted at Johnston when they were forbidden on the main campus. After much discussion McCoy finally gave up; Armacost had the last word. However, McCoy continued to talk to prospective students as if Johnston people would have complete control over their dormitories, and the realization that this was not true caused an uproar when the students arrived on campus in September of 1969.

McCoy and Orton developed the Johnston Board of Overseers with exceptional care. They were bound by the Johnston charter to have three Redlands Trustees on their Board and they had no control over which three. Beyond this, they tried to recruit a Johnston Board which would be sympathetic to alternative education and tough-minded enough to protect the experiment from undue interference. Board members should also, ideally, be rich, active and preferably young. Here the two men were remarkably successful. They enlisted a distinguished initial group which included a former American ambassador, the president of Alberto Culver, the politically active husband of a member of the J. C. Penney family and the granddaughter of Willilam Danforth. The core Overseers — local physicians, lawyers and industrialists — were less well-known but equally dedicated, and it was these people who maintained Johnston's freedom of action during the planning year and thereafter.

McCoy now had a faculty, a staff, a Board and freedom of action, as well as an embryonic plan. One ingredient remained — students. It is one of the abiding mysteries of Johnston folklore that McCoy was able to persuade 182 students to commit themselves to a college that did not yet exist. Director of Admissions Ken Corwin, who worked with McCoy that year, recounts the "miracle":

> We started in October, 1968, with myself and a staff of three. All we had was the three-dimension structure, a highly qualified faculty (in the process of being hired) and the international program. And of course, we plugged the small school with personal relationships, but everyone in private education does that. We didn't even have seminar-tutorial structure at first. And we found quickly that all this had great appeal and sold easily....

By the early months of 1969 McCoy, with Corwin's help, had already recruited the 100 students he originally sought. But as McCoy found more faculty prospects he began to press Corwin to find more students, and he intensified his own recruiting efforts all over the country.

By stretching admissions standards and ignoring the University's profile for acceptable candidates, Corwin and his staff eventually admitted a total class of 182. Of these (according to Corwin and many of the charter faculty), roughly two-thirds were really qualified to cope with a program as potentially demanding as Johnston's. Still, the altered admissions standards did not produce a bad group of students. Even with risk cases and given the indifferent SAT performances of the more alienated matriculants, it is impressive that the average SAT total score of the entering class was about 1150, considerably above the Redlands average.

The planning year was over. McCoy had done what he set out to do. He had seventeen faculty, 182 students and a trained staff. He had at least a rudimentary idea of what the new college would be about and he had successfully avoided making it into the school that the University wanted. His only real defeat had been on the issue of living autonomy for students — an issue which would soon come back to haunt him.

NOTES:

1. The impulse to expansion was not new. An undated manuscript written by the University's first President, Dr. Jasper Newton Field, called for "...a college of fine arts, a college of medicine and other professional courses to be introduced as the "institution grows and its facilities will permit, thus making it eventually a university in the full sense of the word." President Armacost took this vision seriously. He had already continued or initiated programs such as the Schools of Music and Education and the program in communicative disorders, which bid fair to fulfill Field's plans. Johnston College represented another, admittedly larger step of a long-cherished institutional dream: someday the University would live up to its grandiose name.

2. Address to the Johnston College Community, September 9, 1969.

3. *Ibid.*

4. McCoy was told the following story of his hiring by a former Board member: "You and a man from the Thunderbird School of Business were the two finalists and we were discussing the pros and cons and it was coming up pretty even. It was clear to me that you were the stronger candidate, but what really persuaded everyone was that your wife didn't smoke. That did it; they voted." Armacost confirmed a somewhat more genteel version. This story, and the subsequent quotations from McCoy in this section are, unless noted otherwise, taken from a two-day, twelve-hour interview between McCoy and Bill McDonald on June 16-17, 1981.

5. The more widely known program at Kresge College, Santa Cruz, in fact began a year later than Johnston.

6. "I note in the excellent report on Johnston College objectives a

statement 'that Johnston College will have complete educational autonomy.' I hope it can have this and this is our intention. We have a number of trustees and others who are still open-minded about the relationships which should exist between Johnston College and the remainder of the University. When you say 'complete educational autonomy' there is an implication which may cause questions to develop unnecessarily. I am therefore suggesting that we try to avoid the use of statements which appear to be extreme. In other words, Johnston College will have educational autonomy but when you say 'complete' we may provoke discussion and conflict unnecessarily." (September 9, 1968)

CHAPTER 2

Pilgrim Pines

Oak Glen, some fifteen miles east of Redlands in the San Bernardino Mountains, is principally an apple-growing region. But it is not a one crop town. Every fall Oak Glen exports Red Delicious and Jonathans, and every summer it imports thousands of Southern California children to populate its second leading industry, church camps. There are three major camps in Oak Glen, chief among which is the United Church of Christ's "Pilgrim Pines" — the name declares the sentimental protestantism of its founders — standing just beneath the steep southern slope of Wilshire Mountain. It is a large facility, entertaining some 3500 campers in weekly shifts during the summer season.

Nine modern wood cabins spread irregularly across the narrow declivity. Each one bears the name of a religious leader or a place of religious importance or, in a few cases, a college. Each has a roomy cement porch, twelve bunks and automatic heat; you need not rough it at Pilgrim Pines unless you choose to. There is a pool, a volleyball court, a dining hall complete with lectern and wooden cross. There is, in short, everything necessary to the pleasure of the young and the promulgation of the faith.

By September 2, 1969, the summer camping season was over; all the children had gone home and an autumnal quiet replaced the clamor of kids away from the city for a few blessed days. But early on that warm afternoon one final line of ancient yellow school buses climbed up out of the smog below. These bore an older, but equally evangelical crowd: 182 college students eager to create a new institution.

They had arrived in Redlands during the last twenty-four hours. A stranger to the campus could have seen that they did not fit easily there, either in the two just-finished cement-block dorms meant for them, or on the shaded, peaceful lawns of the main campus. Even the Johnston faculty and staff, let alone the University elite, were not prepared. They had only seen photographs in the hastily prepared "Welcome Book." High school yearbook pictures, most of them, they showed short hair carefully combed in place, neat dresses or modest ties, wholesome, open smiles. There were a few "hippie" types, but that was only to be expected at an experimental college in 1969: leaven for the bread. Nothing, in short, which should interrupt the cautious traditions of the University or the academic legitimacy so eagerly desired by Pres McCoy and his faculty.

Many of the students who ambled down from the buses simply could not be recognized from their photographs. Long hair, wispy beards and moustaches, worn boots and plaid shirts, peasant blouses and scruffy levis, pony tails (but only on the males): it was suddenly the few carefully dressed graduates who made the leaven. But as they milled around the mountain camp's main plaza, unloading guitars and backpacks, they looked much more at home. Someone began to play music, a tetherball game started up; most of the new arrivals went searching for their assigned cabins with new-found friends, or wandered off along the fire trails that led up into the mountains. Pres circulated among the group in his friendly, slightly abstracted way. The faculty and their families, arriving in cars, surveyed the scene with a mix of apprehension and excitement. It was really about to begin.

Pres called a general meeting and introduced Gene

Kuehl, "Minister of Camping" and the boss of Pilgrim Pines. A hefty, balding man who was used to ruling the 8-14 year old set, his drill sergeant manner and his readings from the strict camp regulations brought sniggers from a clientele that imagined it had left repressive authority behind. Freedom, self-exploration, new beginnings — these things were in the air, not the minutiae of fire regulations and food distribution.

Pres followed this introduction with his official welcome and gave an overview of the ten day schedule. Del Poling, the head trainer, made some remarks about the sensitivity groups that would begin the next morning, and the meeting was adjourned. People were free to pass the evening getting to know one another.

As one strolled through the camp in the gathering dark, folk music and young laughter and the heavy, sweet smell of pot all passed on the crystalline air. Pres, the faculty — everyone, really — felt a deep sense of dramatic expectancy, almost a sense of Edenic beginnings. Chances to form intentional communities are rare, and chances to form new learning communities rarer still. An unstated, ephemeral dream of salvation — personal, vocational, societal — was in the air. It was not precisely the saving dream that Pilgrim Pines was built to celebrate, but certainly one in a related key. American higher education seemed to be waiting for a new vision, and the new Johnstonians were ready to offer one.

The anomalies in the emerging community were striking. These freshmen, like all others, arrived at college in fear and trembling, anxious about whether they could perform academically and unsure of how they would adjust to living apart from friends and family. Such feelings were much in evidence at Pilgrim Pines. But this group of freshmen (and the few sophomores) had been told, in effect, that they had somehow already passed these crises and were ready — right now — to take charge of their education and organize their lives according to their own wisdom. They had been recruited not to consume an education but to *produce* one, not just to live on a campus but to run it as well.

The faculty's position was equally complex. Nearly all were disaffected with traditional authority roles and were eager to establish themselves on an egalitarian footing with the students. Departmental affiliations and scholarly titles were forsaken willingly. But at the same time they were nearly all very successful products of the system they wished to change, shaped beyond their knowing by its authority and discipline.

And a further anomaly: both these groups were, for the next ten days, to be unquestioning consumers of a program designed for them by strangers. Only a few Johnston faculty had been involved in planning the ten days of sensitivity training. The group of NTL trainers, nearly as numerous as the faculty, formed a shadow government overseeing each day's events.

This group in turn had its hierarchy. At the top was Del Poling, whom Pres had worked with in Georgia. Del was surrounded by a small inner circle — Tom Greening, Kouji Nakata, Dave Peters, all from UCLA, and Sam Farry from TRW — assisted by the new psychology faculty (Miller, Tubbs, Whitlock). The rest of the trainers were recruited from around the country; their job was to carry out Poling's program.

All the trainers lived together in their own cabin and met to review progress and tinker with the overall design. In effect, then, the new community was piloted by a group of affective experts who had no direct or long-term stake in Johnston and who for the most part would vanish from it in ten days, having revealed to faculty and students alike the mysteries of sensitivity training. Applying that to classrooms and community life was up to those left behind.[1]

This melange of people also had to contend with a number of visitors, most of them persons with ostensible authority over their lives. The Johnston Board of Overseers was scheduled to hold its autumn meeting at the camp on September 5; several of its members planned to arrive a day early to observe the groups in action. President George Armacost and his wife Verda were also slated to make an appearance on the 4th, and hoped to sit in on one of the groups. A writer and a photographer from *Time* magazine were also present.

A soupçon of expectations, then: nearly everyone was trying to learn new roles and to mesh these with their own dreams and histories. Authority was dispersed among everyone, yet at the same time couched with experts who were in the last analysis strangers to the project and with a Board that was literally invisible to nearly everyone in the community. The only person who bore both convincing authority and the clear will to dispense it was Pres himself. For that reason he was the center of everything.

The "statement of goals" drafted by the trainers' planning committee on August 5 set forth the purposes and priorities for the retreat:

1. Basic encounter experience as individuals, in T-groups; to build self and other awareness, sensitivity, trust, and interpersonal communications skills.

2. Build a "total learning community":

    • to develop relations of individuals and groups into a climate of belonging to and feeling a part of the community.

    • to aid in the process of identity-formation and "becoming."

    • to develop the college as an organic, problem-solving organism.

3. Task oriented and problem-solving experiences, in small groups and as a community:

- for linking process insights with the accomplishment of tasks.

- to develop skills of leadership and membership, conflict resolution and decision making.

- to make some decisions regarding:
  a. college dorm living rules.
  b. selection of future roommates.
  c. mechanisms for defining the curriculum upon return.

The statement shows how closely the plans for the ten days followed the rubric of the National Training Laboratory. Feelings were to be elicited and enlisted for the business of creating a learning community as sensitive to the individual as possible. Encounter and the resulting self-awareness were always in aid of specific political and educational tasks. The practical focus of the design shines through the jargon.

The specific schedule for the ten days also reflected this pragmatic approach. T-groups met for three hours every morning, with a fifteen minute break. During the afternoons, while the students and faculty were let loose, the training staff met to plan the next day's events and to discuss procedures for the next community meeting, held each evening at 7 p. m.

The principal subject of these larger meetings was the thorny problem of transition — how to convert self-discovery into educational designs, and feelings into curriculum. That presumed a sophisticated passage between affective self-awareness and politics, a presumption that was to be tested to the limit by the powerful emotions released by mass T-grouping. The method had worked well with established business and professional leaders and with technical experts working on specific projects. But Johnston was altogether different. An overarching purpose was there, to be sure, but it was still vague and inchoate. The people involved were strangers to each other, some had no educational planning experience, and many were overwhelmed by the impact of sensitivity training on their own emotions. Finally, all were in the grip of an intense feeling of sharing in the creation of a new world. Exhilaration married to emotional upheaval, and to inexperience and uncertainty, created an atmosphere of nearly unbearable intensity. It was an atmosphere that the trainers had not predicted and with which they did not really know how to deal. By the end of the second day many of the T-groups had moved entirely away from the pragmatic first-generation format to the expressive-therapeutic second-generation form. The night meetings had become extraordinary communal encounter-confession-celebrations, and Johnston had exploded beyond anyone's plans or expectations. It had a life of its own and everyone, trainers included, was caught up in something genuinely new. The college had been born.

A typical day at Pilgrim Pines had a special rhythm. It began with a few down-jacketed, toothpaste-fresh souls gradually emerging across the quiet camp — a quiet which never arrived until well after midnight. At that early hour only the faculty children were loud and lively. The camp crew was starting breakfast and the smell of eggs and coffee drifted through the trees. One almost morbidly healthy professor, theologian Doug Bowman, was up and running around the narrow, two-tiered parking lot. At eight o'clock the camp PA system would come alive to the strains of "Good Morning, Starshine" from *Hair*. The song became the celebrative hymn of the ten days. As it echoed through the camp students and faculty and families and secretaries — all dressed alike in rough clothes that made everyone look more like members of a commune — would straggle in to the dining hall. Many people never made breakfast, and the real wake-up was the call to the day's first T-groups.

At the 10:30 coffee break faces were enough to chart the progress of the morning. Some people would walk to the coffee urns alone, hands stuffed in pockets and heads down, surfeited with human contact or wrestling with private demons. Others would arrive hugging each other, gazing into each other's eyes, glowing with newfound love and friendship. There was always a mix of beatific smiles and wrenching tears. A few looked frightened; no one looked bored.

At lunch "Come on people, smile on your brother, everybody get together, let's love one another, right now" would call the faithful to their meal. Now everyone was present and the dining hall resounded with exultant yells and laughter and the general din of hungry people; as the meal ended many would stay behind to talk in small groups while others helped clear the debris and wash the dishes.

Afternoons were free time at first and people used them for less intense purposes: sports, letterwriting, long slow walks through the conifer forest or just desultory conversation under the great tree that formed the center of the camp. But as the feeling of being-at-Johnston took over, the afternoons began to fill with new meetings. Task groups, political meetings, and voluntary T-groups began to dissipate the leisure and add their urgency to the ever-increasing intensity. The relative quiet of the afternoon was then overcome by the sounds of the morning: laughter, crying, even agonized screams, and talk — intense, passionate, ceaseless talk. Just before dinner the sounds would change. Then there was always a vigorous volleyball game as people tried to work off the tensions of the day. There was no focused competition; everyone played in spontaneous rotation, nobody kept score, and soon the game became an institution. If you did not play, you watched. The game seemed a microcosm of the New Society

After dinner, which sounded and felt much like lunch except that it was held in the lovely dusk and was thus a bit more gentle, there were more meetings. These were the gatherings at which curriculum and political practices were hammered out, and they usually lasted until ten or eleven o'clock. Afterwards, exhilarated but exhausted people would drift toward their cabins, there to celebrate and relax at informal parties. Walking the camp, one could pick up the aroma of marijuana, or the sharper bouquet of cold beer or bourbon, and hear muted conversations in the darkness. People paired off, or played poker, or talked about the day; some just sat quietly thinking of home. Sometime after midnight the camp fell silent and the mountain was briefly given back to the raccoons, rabbits, and coyotes.[2]

There were seventeen T-groups at Pilgrim Pines, each with fourteen participants and a professional trainer. With one exception each group had a faculty member, and most also had a staff member or faculty spouse in their number. There were five groups in which parents participated. Every secretary and administrator took part, as did nine of the fifteen spouses.

It is hazardous to generalize about experiences in the groups. Most began with the inevitable mix of tentativeness and suspicion but moved quickly to an emotional outpouring — affection and relief for some, anger and frustration for others. From the first there were disaffected people. Several black students were scornful of what they considered the emotional self-indulgence of the whites; it seemed off the point when the business at hand was getting a college education. The few foreign students (two from Tibet) were understandably bewildered, and even some of the faculty found the process distasteful. Roger Baty labeled T-grouping a "disastrous institutionalization of premature disclosure...to me it was the extreme of throwaway culture, the temporary alliance culture, the built-in obsolescence culture."

But the effect for the great majority was one of release. There was a sense of vulnerable but liberating openness of needless barriers of age and sex and profession struck down. It was unity, spiritual awakening — above all, emotional freedom to be oneself, whatever that self might

be. Even people in those groups that went through terrible
internal confrontation, shouting matches and tears felt
transformed in positive ways — the release of anger was
cleansing. Nearly everyone was caught up, nearly everyone changed.

The trainers were used to this phenomenon and knew it
could not last, but they underestimated its permanent, if
ephemeral, effects. This communal, quasi-religious
feeling was enough to create a unified community which,
without clearly stated goals or established political
processes, was still cohesive enough to resist outsiders and
to found a tradition of near-mystical membership that
persisted for the whole history of the college. The community was elemental; it was invisible; and it expressed what
Johnston meant: to be in it was to live in the Johnston
mythos, to celebrate its values and to loathe its detractors.
Not to be in it was tantamount to being either a heathen or
a heretic.

This inchoate but powerful feeling of belonging, which
was born from the often painful crucible of the T-groups,
had to come to bear on serious issues almost immediately.
Classes needed planning and governance needed structure.
But before the energy could be focused on such matters a
confrontation occurred which left deep marks on
Johnston and the University, and which once and for all
made the University and especially its official cadres
"infidel." It revealed fundamental conflicts between
George Armacost, incarnating the University, and Pres
McCoy, who was by now the very flesh of the community,
and shattered for good any sense of shared purpose they
once might have held. The issue was both moral and
political; in that setting and at that time it could not but be
religious as well. The issue was the status of Jeanne
Friedman and by extension the relative power of the
Board of Trustees and the President to control the life of
the college.

Jeanne Friedman graduated from CCNY in 1963 and
enrolled in the political science department of Stanford

University, where she earned an M.A. the following year. She continued work toward her doctorate while employed as a researcher at the Hoover Institute and as a teaching assistant at Stanford.

Friedman was a committed East Coast radical raised by parents who had been associated with leftist causes since the Thirties. She was a dedicated advocate of social justice and, though hardly a full-fledged Communist, far more of a Marxist than had ever been seen on the University of Redlands faculty. At Stanford Jeanne joined the Students for a Democratic Society and worked with special interest on reducing international conflict and violence. This interest, and the fact that the Vietnam war was becoming a major source of international conflict, led to her association with an SDS sub-group investigating the involvement of Stanford University, and its subsidiary, the Stanford Research Institute, in war-related activities. SRI, as it was known, conducted biological and chemical warfare research and created counterinsurgency strategies specifically for the war in Vietnam.

Debates between student leaders and Stanford Trustees about the future of relations between Stanford and SRI began in October of 1968. The unsuccessful attempt by students to get Stanford to shut down the facility, or at least to divest itself of any interest in the place, led to the formation of a coalition among fourteen radical and protest groups, among them SDS. This coalition, later named the April 3rd Movement (hereafter A3M), demanded that all defense work at SRI be terminated and that the University *not* sell the Institute because then it would have no control over its work.

The Stanford Trustees finally voted, on April 8, 1969, to reject the coalition demands. On April 9 nine hundred students occupied the Allied Electronics Lab., also associated with Stanford, which did classified electronics research under Defense Department contract. The occupation lasted nine days and Jeanne Friedman was one of the occupiers. A second sit-in at Encina Hall was also sponsored by the A3M group; this took place on May 1 but Friedman was not involved.

These protests led the Stanford Trustees to announce, on May 13, that all chemical and biological warfare research at SRI would be stopped, but they also announced that they were going to sell SRI without including convenants that would forbid its future use for such research. The A3M responded by voting to shut down the SRI facility at Industrial Park in Palo Alto. On May 16 some five hundred coalition members blocked access to the Park. Traffic was obstructed for four hours as police orders to disperse were either not heard or were ignored — it is not clear which. The police then broke up the demonstration with tear gas, and students broke some of SRI's windows as they fled the scene. Jeanne was present at this event, and appears in police films linking arms with fellow demonstrators. There was a second, less troubled demonstration outside SRI on May 19th, at which Jeanne was also present....

Pres McCoy telephoned the head of the political science department at Stanford in early June, asking about potential faculty for Johnston. He was told that Jeanne Friedman was the best teacher among the candidates for the Ph. D. and Pres called her to Redlands for an interview on June 12. She was interviewed by Pres and John Watt, and hired quickly. Articulate, charismatic and aggressive — Friedman seemed a welcome addition to a faculty which at that point was all male and virtually all liberal. Pres recalls that at her interview she struck him as "highly intelligent." She told Pres that she had been in a demonstration but that nothing had come of it yet. McCoy thought to himself that Armacost would not like that at all but McCoy did not mind. "In fact, I thought it was a point in her favor. Little did I know how much it was going to cost us in terms of publicity and all." So he assured her that the demonstration was not an issue, but he did not explain clearly to her how conservative Redlands was and how unhappy George Armacost would be if he ever found out about her background as a political activist. So Jeannie Friedman agreed to a contract, more or less unaware that she had just signed on with one of the more reactionary universities in the country.

On July 25, about four weeks after Jeanne had signed her Johnston contract, she learned that there was a warrant outstanding for her arrest. She immediately turned herself in and was charged with disturbing the peace, trespassing, failure to disperse, obstruction of traffic and inciting to riot, the last a possible felony. She and two codefendants were tried between August 18 and 29 and convicted on all but the charge of failure to disperse. The "inciting to riot" charge was reduced to a misdemeanor. She received an unusually heavy sentence for a first offender: thirty days in jail and three years' probation.

Jeanne accepted the probation but appealed the jail sentence. She also got in touch with Pres and informed him of the outcome of the trial. Pres took no action against her but he also chose not to tell Armacost about either the original arrest or the conviction. On September 3 a reporter, from the *Palo Alto Times*, doing a follow-up piece on the trial, called George Armacost to ask him about the new radical on his faculty. He also gave the story to the *Redlands Daily Facts*, which ran a rather inflammatory article on *l'affaire* Friedman.

George Armacost, armed with this shocking knowledge, arrived at Pilgrim Pines on the morning of September 4 to take part in the retreat. Personal responsibility and curiosity dictated that he do so, and the information he had just received gave him more compelling reasons still. Since he wished to see the new college in the act of forming itself he asked to be "enrolled" in a T-group. Someone, who unfortunately knew nothing of the circumstances, put him and his wife Verda in the same T-group as Friedman.

Ed Williams, who was also in the group, recalled the incident: "...the great mistake in strategy was to bring the

Trustees and other people in after the T-grouping had been going on for two days .... We were really into it and then they came in. For Verda and George Armacost, I think that was the moment of undying hatred for the college. Verda was a person who prided herself on real, if genteel, relations with the Redlands students; she was famous for knowing the names of each new freshman every September. But here of course people were completely in the raw, so to speak.... It was kind of a confrontation." As was his wont, Ed tried to make the Armacosts feel more comfortable in this tight-knit, unwelcoming group. He asked Armacost, "Well, now, what should we call you?" Armacost replied, "My colleagues call me George...." And so George and Verda it was, not only for Ed Williams but for all the students and Jeanne Friedman as well. This had never happened before — but it got worse, and quickly. The students began berating their new "comrade" George with the fact that they had been promised living/learning autonomy in the Johnston catalog and had only learned after their arrival at Pilgrim Pines that they would have to live under the University's strict housing regulations. In the atmosphere of honest encounter generated by the group, and in the egalitarian setting of the retreat, students felt no compunction about accusing Armacost of being a liar, promising one thing in a catalog and delivering something quite different in fact. Not only that, they couched their disapproval and their questions in a language which so upset Verda Armacost that she rushed from the group, never to return. George, made of sterner stuff on that day, tried to respond with equal candor and feeling but he was no match; years of carefully cultivated civility could not be jettisoned in an hour. His inability to talk in the situation was interpreted as a sign that his resolve about the dorm rules might be weakening, and Jeanne pounced on the opportunity: "Get with it, George!" she demanded. Armacost left soon after, without responding, harboring the conviction that he had been led to that T-group by McCoy.

He knew now that McCoy had promised living autonomy against all University wishes and policy, and he suspected that McCoy had used the Friedman T-group to bully him into relinquishing control over the dormitories. By now he was thoroughly appalled at the directions Johnston seemed to be taking and felt that decisive action was called for. Armacost found McCoy outside the dining hall and brought up the Friedman case immediately.

"Pres, for the good of the University you've got to fire her. I don't care how you do it — just get rid of her."

McCoy responded: "No. For the sake of the University she's staying. There is no way we can or would fire her. What she did up there may very well turn out to be something that reinforces her role as a teacher." As McCoy spoke, knowing that his open refusal would bring serious repercussions, he thought of the defiance of German professors against the Nazi regime and of his own participation in CORE sponsored sit-ins in 1960 in Webster Groves, Missouri. Overdramatic? Perhaps, but fully in keeping with the religious energy of Pilgrim Pines.

Pres thought he understood Armacost's position: Redlands was a conservative University with a conservative constituency, and the addition to the faculty of a person who had broken the law in defense of what seemed radical ideas would only damage its image, especially when it was trying to drum up financial support for its underfinanced new addition. But such understanding could not change Pres' own adherence to principle. If McCoy gave in, then not only would Armacost have imposed his own conservatism on the college but any hope of proceeding with even relative autonomy would be gone. Pres could not accept this any more than he could accept what he felt was a deep injustice to Friedman. At this moment he understood: he and Armacost were "worlds apart" and the relationship between Johnston and the University would always be one based on mutual antipathy. So, even though Pres did wish that Friedman's acts had not been quite so public, he sympathized with her action and decided to protect her at all costs. As always with McCoy the deepest level of decision was personal rather than political. Even though he knew the consequences of backing Friedman he felt that she deserved his support — and he gave it without qualification.

Pres told George that he wanted to think about the matter and that they could meet after dinner to discuss it further. But when Armacost arrived at the meeting that night he found the entire Johnston faculty arrayed against him. Prominent among them was Jeannie Friedman who was more than willing to discuss the matter further. Armacost remembers the scene with anger that still flashes as he speaks: "It was the most shocking example of unprofessional behavior I ever encountered...he (Pres) broke confidence without batting an eye. If I'd been smart, I would have fired him right then." But George stuck with the unexpected format, defending his actions and listening to a moving apologia delivered by Friedman. In the atmosphere of Pilgrim Pines this direct confrontation, witnessed by a supportive group, made perfect sense. To Armacost it was a ruthless exercise of pressure tactics and intimidation, and he did not forget it.

Though both sides had been heard, nothing had been resolved by the time the Johnston Board of Overseers arrived on campus the following day. Nine of the ten voting members made the trip as did several *ex officio* members, among them Mr. Frederick Llewellyn, Chairman of the University Board of Trustees. Their morning session was workmanlike. Llewellyn even noted that his company, Forest Lawn Memorial Park, used sensitivity training in some of its management meetings. Pres distributed a hastily-composed list of six arguments for retaining Jeanne. The official minutes record only that a brief and very general exchange on "political activism" took place; much more time was spent on an issue that was potentially just as divisive as the Friedman case — autonomy in the dormitories.

As the morning wore on and T-groups disbanded,

restive students began gathering in the large community meeting hall. The Friedman story was abroad, and dissatisfaction about living autonomy rankled nearly everyone. The Overseers' meeting, closed to students, dragged on. Tension rose and rumors prospered. It appeared to the community that their leader was being called to account in the very first days of the school's life, and by a group of powerful strangers who might even be hostile to the enterprise.

The Overseers meeting finally adjourned; they had decided to come to the large meeting hall to discuss living/learning issues with the students. By this time almost the entire community was gathered in the hall or strung out along the path that led, across the camp's main plaza and under the oak tree, down from the meeting site to the hall. Pres led the Overseers, Armacost and Llewellyn across that charged space. Immediately he was surrounded by the faithful, two hundred strong, and literally borne into the hall. The religious analogy was exact; this was a community which had already shared an experience that no one else could understand, and Pres was the very incarnation of their bond.

McCoy's account helps recapture the intensity; he had been engrossed in his discussions with the Board and did not realize that a spontaneous mass meeting was developing in and around the main hall. Leaving the Board meeting and walking out into the camp plaza "was like walking into another world.... You want to be real humble...I had no reason not to be.... I wanted to communicate to people, 'Look, this isn't one person....'" He knew that such things happened but he had never experienced such an outpouring of heartfelt support: "...when you are the focus of so much energy you can't ignore it. And it does sustain you." The crowd's love charged him, "it tended to revitalize every cell...it increased my sense of responsibility.... I wanted all the more for it to succeed...."

McCoy knew he did not deserve the adulation and wanted to move that energy toward the construction of the college. He entered the meeting followed by the bewildered and understandably uneasy Board; this was not a typical college retreat but more like a politically charged and very unstable revival meeting. Yet there was a feeling of gentleness underlying the tension, as if the effects of T-grouping had imbedded frustration and anger in a willingness to discuss, to consider. The meeting went on all afternoon, adjourned for a quick dinner, and reconvened. Living autonomy and Jeanne Friedman's case were discussed. Dwayne Orton spoke; Jeanne spoke. Pres spoke but has no memory of what he said. But he does recall the feeling: "I wish it had all been on tape. I would love to hear that now. Those are unforgettable moments. There were a number of times at Pilgrim Pines that are just unbelievable...and the spirit of those ten days will always be vivid. It still stands out as something entirely different in my life. And I don't expect to find that again." Discussion raged, feelings were vented and the community coalesced for the first time around specific issues. A politics of feeling was born.

Jeanne Friedman was not fired but she did become the center of a continuing controversy that eventually involved the University's lawyer and the University Board of Trustees, as well as Ed Williams and Roger Baty. Armacost sent the lawyer, Charles Bierschbach, to Palo Alto to get more information on the case and on Friedman in general. To counter this McCoy sent Williams and Baty on the same errand. The lawyer did a rather superficial job but Baty and Williams were very thorough. They read all the police reports, viewed films of the demonstration and read the transcripts of the trial. Both Bierschbach and the two faculty members made reports to the Trustee Executive Committee. The Baty-Williams report was enough to cast serious doubts on the validity of the charge to "inciting to riot," the charge that Armacost considered most damning.

A few days later Friedman was called to a special Trustees meeting held at the Ontario Airport, thirty miles west of Redlands. She appeared with an attorney. It was, recalls Armacost, a "hot" meeting. Jeanne claims that Armacost and Bierschbach offered to buy out her contract for half her annual salary. When she turned them down she was offered her full year's salary, because she was from a "poor background." She refused this backhanded charity as well. Then (a report denied by Armacost but confirmed by other witnesses), she was shown a photograph of a nude woman, rear view only, dancing in People's Park in Berkeley. A Berkeley policeman had given the photo to a Palo Alto reporter who in turn passed it on to the University with the allegation that the woman in the picture was Jeanne Friedman.

Moral turpitude now became the issue. The ploy did not work because the photo was too dim to admit positive identification and Jeanne was shortly thereafter able to prove, through witnesses, that she had not been in Berkeley on the day the photo was taken. But the witch-hunt tone of introducing odd evidence of this sort into a Trustees meeting indicates the level to which relations between Friedman, Johnston and the University had sunk. The University was willing to go to great lengths to abort the introduction of radical voices on campus.

Though nothing ever came of the photograph incident and Jeanne was not fired, the pressure and humiliation of such confrontations made her lose faith in her future at Redlands. She began looking for work in the Bay Area. Even though she was an excellent teacher with a large and loyal student following, and though she contributed a great deal to the planning of the college, her loyalty to Johnston could not overcome her distaste for Redlands and she left in the second year.

She remembers. "I didn't leave Redlands: I fled. I came to Redlands a radical and left a revolutionary...my firing was blatantly anti-Semitic...." She asked for a part-time contract for her second year because she had found employment at San Jose State. This was ultimately denied by Pres and she was told she must either teach full time at Johnston or not at all. She considered this a subtler way of letting her go, but still saw it as a dismissal.

The remainder of the ten days, after the exhilarating defiance and intensity of the night meeting, was devoted to more sober pursuits. The new politics of feeling had to be given its day-to-day shape and marshalled to fight against dormitory restrictions. And an academic program had still to be created. A meeting on September 6 raised the fundamental question: "How do we decide how to decide?" What sort of politic could best preserve the heady openness of the T-group and the near-archaic respect for dissent and individual freedom that it seemed to imply, while at the same time fostering the communal solidarity that the same groups helped to create?

A few naïve souls argued for *Roberts' Rules* and ordinary representative government. But things had gone too far for that, though incongruous cries of "Point of order!" and "Call for the question!" echoed through our meetings for the next several months. Del Poling and his trainers were arguing for a consensus form of governance, which was also Pres' original idea. The faculty had used the method during their planning sessions in August and found it workable. The idea seemed foolish to George Armacost, who was still attending meetings despite widespread hostility. Armacost stated that consensual government was impossibly inefficient and slow-moving, and could itself become tyrannical. But one trainer, Tom Greening, argued that consensus was based on the presumption of the honesty and sincerity of each member of the community. It presumed that people would not capriciously object to proposals and that the majority would respect the sincere reservations of every member. Consensus assumed the best in everyone and often got just that. Such a system operating properly would never tyrannize, and though time-consuming could produce the most humane form of governance.

Discussion of this issue continued and mealtime approached without resolution. Then Tom Greening had an inspiration. He asked permission to teach everyone a game, and got it. You, as a group, he said, must choose one of the following five songs, which you will then play. You have only the fifteen minutes left before the next meal, and no decision will be accepted unless everyone agrees. First there was laughter, then attempts to evade the exercise, then a grudging agreement. Serious negotiation began as the minutes passed. The lists of songs was quickly whittled to three, then through vigorous negotiation to two. Time pressure mounted. Discussion became more frantic. Could it be done?

The frivolity of the exercise contributed to the passion with which it was carried out. With just seconds left before the dining hall bell would end the discussion one song was chosen by all. Shouts of victory went up. Consensus did work, and it did not take forever. "Let's try consensus!" someone shouted — and he got an immediate consensus. Everyone cheered again. Thus consensus was consensually adopted. The group went to their meal with a new form of governance; the politics of feeling had its form. That day a large sign hastily painted by Cat Chapman and other students appeared over the dining hall: "A painful birth doesn't make the baby any less beautiful."

A political system of the most hopeful and imprecise sort was in place. Now there was at least a forum for discussing how to resist the University's insistence on imposing dormitory rules. But for the moment other business took precedence. There was still an academic program to create!

This process was excruciatingly difficult and quite wonderful. Two hundred people operating by consensus tried to shape an academic world in which all they had felt and learned in the mountains could invigorate their daily lives as students and faculty and college staff. The inefficiency of consensus was soon apparent but so was its corresponding strength; it made possible complete ownership of the college by nearly every community member and created a sense of mutual responsibility for the school quite removed from the paternalistic model favored at the

University, and especially by George Armacost.

The plans sketched by the faculty in August were not entirely forgotten. But they were reintroduced tentatively, as possibilities rather than necessities. A Johnston catch-phrase, almost the school motto, entered common usage: "Everything is negotiable." In keeping with that spirit graduation requirements disappeared, to be replaced by graduation "guidelines." A common seminar topic, "Quest for Meaning," was adopted after three hours of discussion. It was agreed that all students would enroll on one version or another of this class, though no provision was made for achieving uniformity.

An ingenious method for building curriculum was invented by Jeanne Friedman. Students and faculty wrote their course ideas on 3x5 index cards, signed them, and handed them to a small committee which then organized the cards under some general headings. Cards expressing similar interests were then tacked to the walls of the main hall in various locations and community members would circulate among the cards looking for proposals that sounded interesting and seeking out people whose interests paralled their own. Since each card was signed, exchanges of ideas were easy and soon class groups began to form around a finite number of course proposals. The more popular topics emerged as seminars. Faculty then expressed a willingness to lead such groups, though the topics were often not of their proposing. Less popular offerings became tutorials or independent studies, and cards that could not be used at all were saved to be reintro-duced as a beginning point for negotiation in the spring semester.

Thus nearly everyone found at least one, and often more, courses that they had helped to create. Consensus, leavened by negotiation and compromise, had easily infiltrated class planning.

The "Quest for Meaning" seminar was the Johnston equivalent of a general education course. It began with the premise that the combination of affective and cognitive learning should be the central subject of at least one seminar. Every student (there were three stubborn exceptions) took a "QFM." These formed around faculty members or around topics; typically the group emerged out of the original T-groups but there were important exceptions. Several of the QFMs were taught by teams of faculty. Titles for this seminar ranged from conventional-sounding courses in "Existentialism" to seminars built around each member's personal quest; in the latter there was no shared booklist or topic and each member opted to pursue a separate goal. Naturally a few of these groups failed dismally under the pressure of their centrifugal energy but some succeeded brilliantly. One, which managed to combine a heavy dose of T-grouping with a respectable academic format, worked together for two full years. Thus T-group training paid off in largely successful seminars. They were the first and perhaps the purest illustration of McCoy's original vision.

The last few days at Pilgrim Pines were upbeat, with only the uncertainty of what awaited in Redlands to mar the idyll. Armacost, too deeply committed and too shrewd to surrender his influence, no matter what his reservations, gave a rambling speech of support for the college at the community meeting of September 9. Since Armacost was already, in a perverse way, a full member of the community, he got a great round of friendly applause. John Kerr, one of the more far-out members of an already far-out community, rose from his place on the floor, strode up to Armacost, held out his hand and said: "Dr. Armacost, you've taken a great risk tonight in speaking to us and I want to take one too. Here's my part of the bridge between us." He clasped Armacost's hand in both of his and everyone cheered. Reunion of the opposing camps seemed to have been effected. Even Gene Kuehle, the gruff minister of camping, was finally won over to the new community. As we left he told us, almost wistfully, "you were all a great gang to have around."

The final morning came. Bags were packed, cabins

swept and aired, the last meal eaten. The old yellow school buses returned and packs and guitars were thrown in. Slowly, reluctantly, the community disbanded to descend from their magic mountain to the less alluring world below. Problems abounded — but so did hope. Issues were unresolved — but we had a college. And even though some of that original community spirit was forged in reaction against outside threats, much of it derived from more positive sources. The descent from the mountain was sad but promised the fulfillment of a dream. Like BenSalem, its sister college at Fordham University named for the island that welcomed Bacon's seafarers in *The New Atlantis*, Johnston saw itself as a missionary outpost in an alien land.

NOTES:

1. It should be noted in passing that Pilgrim Pines was expensive. The camp rented for $20,154.30 (room and board for students, staff, family and guests that averaged about 275 people a day). Each trainer was paid $100 a day plus travel expenses — another $20,000 plus — with higher stipends for the lead trainers. Buses and other miscellaneous expenses brought the total to just short of $50,000 for the retreat. Given Jimmie Johnston's founding grant, such a program could not go on indefinitely.
2. See Appendix.

CHAPTER 3

The First Academic Year

After the mountains came the dorms. Square, air-conditioned, hermetic, the two three-story buildings with their carpeted hallways would have seemed luxurious to students in 1959. But, as Pres had feared, in 1969 they were a disaster. Johnstonians who treasured their new-found freedom suddenly found themselves penned in buildings with sealed windows, small interior lobbies, and bourgeois decor that cut against their dreamy liberalism. Worse, there were hours posted for women students. Worst of all, they quickly confirmed that they had no power to do anything about it. McCoy, who had devoted himself to the academic legitimacy of his new college, knew that the living side of the living/learning equation was out of his hands for the moment. He had had nothing to say about the design of the dorms. They were far from perfect, but they seemed a relatively minor flaw in the overall design. He was sure students would tolerate the inconvenience to keep the academic experiment going. But McCoy was not eighteen, and he did not live in Kofap or Fokat halls. [1]

The dorm situation remained at the center of college politics. As we have noted, the University had reserved to itself decision-making power in the areas of finance and student life. Armacost had given assurances to the Board of Trustees that the rules governing University housing would apply equally to the Johnston community. He reaffirmed this position in a two-page directive issued to the Johnston community on September 23.

At issue initially were women's — or as all the documents then called them — "girls" — hours. The regulations in force in the fall of 1969 stated that freshmen women could stay out until midnight on fourteen nights of their choice during each semester, and could stay away overnight six weekdays. Otherwise they had to be in their dorms by ten o'clock. Upperclasswomen had automatic midnight hours on weekdays and could stay out until two in the morning on weekends. Since nearly all Johnston "girls" were freshmen, Fokat Hall had to be locked at 10 p.m. each weeknight. Locking the dorm did not bother students; they enjoyed the security that provided. What maddened them was the fact that they were supposed to be *in* the dorm when it was locked, plus the fact that the regulation was not negotiable. So the living-learning autonomy promised in the Johnston literature was a fraud. As they had at Pilgrim Pines, the students protested vigorously; they felt a principle had been violated.

One plausible political strategy for Johnston women might have been to make common cause with university women who suffered under the same controls. Indeed, a campus newspaper poll indicated that University students had a positive attitude to Johnston students, largely because they felt that Johnston students would work with them to liberalize dorm policies. But in the fall of 1969 such cooperation did not materialize. The gap between the cultures of the two campuses was too great. The Johnston Commons was still not finished, thanks to a plumber's strike, and the tight-knit Johnston community was forced to eat meals for the first two months in the University Commons. But there was little mixing: long-haired, sloppy, outspoken Johnston students were threatening or repellant to the more conservative Redlands undergraduates, who in turn looked hopelessly straight to the Johnston group.

Redlands women tended, in those days, to dress in neat

skirts or dresses; their hair was carefully done and most wore makeup. There was a dress code on the campus: no shorts or curlers or bare feet in class. Johnston women tended more to the fashions of the Age of Aquarius: most wore jeans, and those who did wear dresses showed unshaven legs, bare feet, and a notable disinterest in bras. Their hair was usually very long and hung free, and makeup was all but unknown. And the differences went far beyond dress: Johnstonians often looked down on the "poor souls" from the University who were not participating in the Johnston experiment. It was so clear that the Johnston way was superior that students often openly condescended to their University fellows. Under such circumstances concerted political action was all but impossible. Johnston students soon withdrew all fiscal support from the University-wide student organization, thus abdicating any role in the public life of the institution.

The faculty, beset with pressing academic problems, were suddenly faced with students who found the repressive dorm situation academically paralyzing. Given the much-heralded promise of living-learning autonomy, the students were right. Accordingly, the faculty voted to teach "under protest" against the violation of a central Johnston tenet. Though some Board members and administrators saw this vote as scornful of agreed-upon arrangements, most did not take the vote seriously because it had no practical effect. But the faculty and students were getting a bit uppity, and pressure from the University began. On the morning of September 15 George Armacost called Pres and asked him to report that day on the following items[2]:

1. Sensitivity groups: are they satisfactory? How do you plan to evaluate the results?

2. What decisions have been made regarding the curriculum, and in what way is it working?

3. What has been decided about the living arrangements at Johnston College?

4. How are students going to participate in decision-making?

5. What procedures have been adopted to resolve the question of appointing to the faculty a person whose previous behavior seems to be contrary to the University's policies?

This is a verbatim transcript of the Armacost question. Nor did the President wait for a response; the same list of questions was proffered to the Board of Trustees Executive Committee that same afternoon.

The bombardment continued. On the 19th an Armacost memo informed McCoy that a meeting had been set up with the Chairman of the Board, Fred Llewellyn, "to gain agreement relative to lines of authority which are delegated to the Chancellor...and the way in which accountability is provided for in the(se) relationships..." "Accountability" was a buzz word in higher education in the early 70's, and was particularly popular with University staff and trustees. In fact, accountability would color nearly every contact between Johnston and University administrators over the next eighteen months. The long memo on student life, noted above, appeared on the 23rd. By the 24th, Armacost felt there were "sufficient concerns" to justify a meeting between the faculties of the two schools. On the 25th came an outcry against students who were smoking and hanging pictures in the Johnston office complex underneath the Library. The final paragraph of this memo reveals much about Armacost's attitude at this time:

I wonder if it is going to be necessary to allow things like this to happen before the community takes any preventive action through the establishment of some guidelines to help students whose values are so different and, if values exist, do not practice them in relation to an Honor Code. I feel that we have the right to ask that issues of this kind be anticipated and be resolved with some promptness. Am I being unreasonable to suggest that a catalog of things of this nature might be developed for your community to react to and to decide how they are going to handle situations of this kind? I would like to have a definite answer before the Student Life Committee meets on October 3. Please reply.

Most college presidents do not write memoes concerning student violations of smoking regulations; they rarely know or care that such violations have occurred. But for Armacost everything that students at his university did was of interest, and Armacost read small signs as symbols of a more general moral laxity in the wild-looking Johnston students. They seemed to embody all that he and his Board dreaded.

Armacost's fears were not groundless. Johnston people *did* use drugs (though probably not any more than students at other colleges) and they did sleep together, and they were not particularly discrete about either activity. They did have the audacity to smoke in the University's administration building; a casual search unearthed nine memoranda dealing with this heinous offense during the 1969-1970 academic year. They were also guilty of some vandalism; from the first the rather expensive furniture in the dorm lobbies suffered a good deal of damage. (The first vandal, according to legend, was the unknown student who apparently clipped the wires of the intrusive intercom system in the dorms while they were still under construction). They also decorated the sterile rooms and hallways with murals, built wooden lofts to increase floor space and painted Monopoly murals on the large squares of the Johnston sidewalk that framed the quadrangle between the dorms. Nude sunbathing on the isolated dorm roofs was not unknown. Finally, they filled the dorms with loud music; this was the age of the stereo and noise pollution was an early and persistent problem. But student behavior was not anarchic. Both they and the faculty worked hard to develop sets of rules for dorm life consistent with *their* ideas about good behavior. They were eager to promote two values: maximum respect for individual self-expression, and mutual consideration. University rules were illegitimate and above all irrelevant intrusions on the real business at hand, which was to develop a *modus vivendi* for communal existence.

The conflict was fundamental. Armacost could not believe that human beings, especially those of college age, were capable of deciding how they would conduct themselves on a campus. Moral common sense demanded rules which would curb adolescent passion. He did not believe that Johnstonians took *any* rules seriously, and he interpreted student resistance to University rules as evidence that they came to the school in order to indulge in excess rather than to learn. After all, the University saw itself clearly *in loco parentis*, and there were sufficient numbers of parents who agreed with this to make the University's parietal stance plausible for most University students. So political encounters were adversarial from the first. They even had a conspiratorial tone; the University was trying to police behavior, while Johnston students wanted to be responsible to and for themselves alone. The University had little sympathy for such strivings for freedom, and the students had none at all for University policies and their rationale. Johnston students simply did not wish to live in a world of courteous, well-groomed people conducting chaste lives on a quiet, safe campus.

The outcome was predictable. On one side students began to scheme to live off-campus; on the other they began to develop strategies in the dorm to protect themselves from University regulations. There was a certain cynicism in all this; Johnston students acquiesced, as they had no real choice but to do, to the outer forms of the rules, but they also devoted a good deal of ingenuity to circumventing those rules. Unfortunately, the entire apparatus of student life governance at Johnston grew up in this Janus-faced way and never overcame its divided character.

Even the Deans of Students and the Hall Managers at Johnston were compelled to live something of a double life. They had to appear to enforce University rules but they also had to win student confidence by mitigating the effect of such rules as much as they could. Of course this ambivalence is found in any institution with stringent rules, but at Johnston the gulf between University rules and real behavior took on vast proportions, and the ideological conflict acquired virtually metaphysical significance.

The only areas in which Johnston students agreed with the University were ones that they themselves came to recognize as serious problems. Thus Johnston and the University cooperated in developing and enforcing animal control rules; in setting up procedures for decorating rooms and public areas; in the establishment of counseling services in the dorms. But other areas which the University considered serious problems — cohabitation, drug and alcohol use and vandalism — were never regulated in a serious or consistent way.

The most extreme — and therefore most revealing — attempt to develop case-specific rules at Johnston came in response to the actions of a single student, freshman Jan Hoffman. Jan's behavior was admittedly sometimes strange, even by Johnston standards. She unilaterally integrated the single-sex dorms during the second week on campus; she simply moved herself and her possessions into the men's dorm, much to the chagrin of the authorities, and of Pres. When she was evicted, she set up her belongings in the middle of the quad between the two dorms and lived there for several days.

Jan came under more intense official scrutiny because

she had "unacceptable pets" — namely a dog which had a litter of pups during the course of the first semester, and a pet rat, Alice, which Jan carried about to class and meals. One faculty member recalled seeing Alice at an open faculty meeting, poking its nose and tail out of Jan's long, rather frizzy hair, and quietly relieving itself. "My God," he said to himself, "is this what I went into college teaching for?"

Jan's refusal to move her brood of dogs out of her dorm room, when added to her other misbehaviors, caused understandable anger in both Johnston and University officials. The University's Dean of Women, Mary Brown, called for serious action.

The action taken by the community now seems a parody of the therapeutic philosophy which underlay much of Johnston's communal life. Jan was assigned a special T-group, composed of students and a professional trainer, to consult with her regularly and monitor her behavior. Nearly a dozen of her peers, in other words, were watching her every move. Jan's cooperation with this group was made a requirement of her remaining at the college. The group agreed also to keep Mary Brown informed of Jan's "progress." And Jan did meet with the group for several weeks, though, predictably, Brown was not kept privy to their discussions.

This seems a wildly intrusive, punitive overreaction to a relatively simple problem. When a community member irritated other members, as Jan clearly did, Johnston outdid the University in imposing sanctions and even enlisted the T-group mechanism to implement a system of surveillance and correction. And all this was done in perfect seriousness.

As it turned out, Jan did get rid of the dogs and did enroll in the second semester (again to the dismay of Mary Brown, who was not informed of the decision). Gradually, Jan became a powerful political force in community governance. After graduation she went on to law school and a highly successful career as a public defender in

Boston, and now a private attorney in Portland, Oregon. She returned to campus on March of 1982 and gave a brilliant and moving lecture on a woman lawyer's defense of accused rapists. T-group surveillance, let it be said, gets no credit for any of her success.

The troubled character of the University-Johnston connection took an even darker turn after a public relations meeting which took place in late September. A panel of Johnston faculty and students appeared before members of the University in the student center. Led by Lee Tinnin, whose imposing presence gave the new college special respectability, panel members made short presentations and then responded to questions. Most asked for information or clarification. But there were hostile inquiries as well. The most notable of these came from a man seated at the back of the room. He wanted to know, in a slightly sneering tone, "Well, if you people are all equals, why don't you get equal salary?"

The questioner was George Armacost. Here was a man, concerned to the point of obsession with public image, making public fun of his new college in front of an audience that was, at best, neutral. Armacost's complaints about Johnston snobbery and his concern over his "negative image" on that campus produced even less sympathy after that outburst.

Pressure continued unabated. Both the Student Life Committee and the Educational Policy Committee of the Board of Trustees met on October 3rd. A September 26 memo from the Board had asked McCoy to prepare written responses to a series of questions about the academic program: curriculum design, faculty and student loads, class enrollments and the like. McCoy's careful responses were well received; the Board committees seemed content on the academic level, at least for the time being. But on that same day the good effects of the McCoy report were erased by the appearance of an article about Johnston in *Time* magazine.

Flip in presentation, making snap judgments, the

article seems more harmless today than it did in 1969. Entitled "The New Eden," it began cautiously enough with an historical note on educational reform and a casual biographical sketch of McCoy. But its real focus was T-grouping and the total freedom it supposedly empowered. Reporter Tim Tyler included a voyeuristic account of John Watt to illustrate the Point: Watt, attired in "funny blue sneakers and shorts, [was] sitting on the ground under a spreading oak tree, surrounded by young girls with blond hair and Levis." Then another pretty coed rushed up to John, wrapped her arms around him and started discussing her course of study. The *Time* article confirmed the worst fears of parents and Board members. Their daughters had been delivered into hands of lecherous, lazy professors; their sons were now free to shout all the words of derision at authority that they had been forbidden to use at home.

Armacost received cries of outrage from conservative alumni. Selected telegrams and letters were forwarded to McCoy. One mother began her angry letter thus:

> To think that twenty-seven years ago I chose another college over Redlands because Redlands was so conservative it didn't have any dances on campus. If I had been born three decades later I could have enrolled at Johnston and spent four years running through the San Bernardino Mountains with my boyfriends.

Reactions at Johnston ranged from irritation to amusement mixed with gratitude for the publicity, whatever its nature. But many in the Redlands community thought that the devil had been named at last. So, at the very moment that Johnston students were clamoring for more control over their lives, University officials were increasingly determined that control should remain in the hands of duly constituted authority.

Amid these upheavals classes had begun. The Quest for

Meaning seminars and a few eccentric tutorials were not in full operation. But many other courses were well within the traditional academic disciplines. Indeed, what is striking about the first semester course list is its academic conservatism; arguably, the Johnston curriculum even in its wildest days was less bizarre than that of many a large university. Even the most outrageous titles — "Explosions," for example — turned out to be very tame. This course was a serious practical chemistry seminar assisted by a University of Redlands professor. It was singled out for attention in part because of a damaging fire-bomb thrown into the University's Dean of Students office during the spring semester. Despite the fact that class members *looked* like archetypal anarchists, they were not responsible; there was no budding revolution here. However deeply built on feeling and however communal it was, Johnston was always self-consciously serious and careful about academics. It was a school which had to prove its excellence to a skeptical world.

This pleased McCoy. The methods of learning at Johnston were different, but subject matters were not. The fewer far-out courses, the easier his job of selling the new design. Since his first year budget called for him to raise a quarter of a million dollars for direct program expenses, his pleasure and relief are understandable.

The dynamics of classes, however, certainly were different. Class purposes, projects and assignments were all negotiated at great length in a prevailing spirit of shared responsibility. The main weight in seminars fell on the *experience* of learning together, rather than on the content being learned. In successful classes shared responsibility worked to great effect. Students badgered peers who cut class, or who did not bear their fair share of the work. Both students and faculty were devising, together, a new way to teach and to learn.

Alumni reviews, twelve years later, were mixed. Rustee McCain, for example, felt that she was robbed of her education by the emphasis on process and experience. "I was a loner, impatient with the interminable community meetings and do-nothing politics. My life at Johnston was one long identity crisis; Johnston was a haven for people who couldn't quite do what they were expected to do." In the middle ground were students such as Peter Michelsen who, with his father, had taken part in the Johnston planning year. He felt strong pressure "to be free, and to become yourself fully and completely — right now." "To be exotic, hipper-than-thou, was a benchmark of success among many students," he said. Peter discovered his academic vocation during his first year, and was able, indeed, to "become himself." And for some others Johnston was nearly a form of salvation. "For the first time in my life I was learning what I wanted to learn." "I didn't just go to school at Johnston, I lived my entire life there." (Diane Sabin) "The intensity was almost overwhelming; nearly everything was a peak experience."

Beyond question, not everything went smoothly. Perhaps the most embarrassing academic event of the first year occurred when the father of freshman Steve Gielow came to campus in early November to visit his son. Kevin O'Neill still reddens when he recalls the event.

"I got a call in my office from Pres. 'You're Steve Gielow's adviser, aren't you, Kevin?' he asked. I thought hurriedly. 'I think so,' I answered, 'but I haven't seen much of him lately.' 'Well,' Pres continued, 'his dad just dropped in. Steve's on his way over from the dorm. Can you come over and talk for a few minutes?'

When I got there Steve had already arrived. His father was a friendly man, happy to see his son and genuinely interested in the college's program. 'So, Steve,' Pres began, 'how are your classes going? Which ones are you taking?'

Steve, curly-haired and handsome, grinned a boyish grin: 'None, right now.' 'What?', asked Pres, leaning forward slightly. 'I'm not taking anything.'

I started sliding down in my chair. Pres glanced quickly at me, a desperate look in his eyes. 'Well, Mr. Gielow,' he said, 'we like to give our students a lot of freedom in designing their own program. Instead of taking regular classes, Steve must be working independently with...'

Mr. Gielow was genuinely interested and did not seem the least bit angry. He asked, 'Well, how many credits are you enrolled for, Steve?' 'None,' Steve replied.

'It's sometimes difficult to find yourself when you're in a new educational environment,' I offered lamely, thinking of the full tuition that Steve's father had paid out.

'I'm sure that's true,' said Steve's father, still a paragon of patience. 'So what *are* you doing, Steve?' 'We talk a lot about things in the dorms,' Steve answered brightly, his face a study in innocence. I slid down a little further in my chair.

It went on from there. Steve had simply slipped through the cracks entirely. He wasn't doing anything. Yet somehow Mr. Gielow felt he'd gotten satisfactory answers. He even sent Pres a supportive letter ten days later. After all, his son *did* seem happy! I think it was the worst academic moment I ever experienced at Johnston. Thank God it wasn't typical!"

Seminars were scheduled in ninety minute slots. They usually met twice a week, on a Monday-Thursday or a Tuesday-Friday schedule. A few met once a week, at night, for three hours. Tutorials and independent studies were arranged around these times. Wednesdays were kept free for meetings, and these occurred in plenty. At first, in fact, the faculty met every day. This evolved into a longer meeting(s), 10 a. m. to 4 p. m. every Wednesday, with the Community Meeting following. Community Meetings were deliberately scheduled late in the day so that the time pressure of the approaching dinner hour would make them more expeditious. Even with this, some meetings still lasted well into the night.

Long meetings were caused, and fueled, by intra-faculty and intra-student differences, which gradually emerged as the communal ecstasy of Pilgrim Pines began to wear off. Conservative faculty such as Lee Tinnin spoke repeatedly and with increasing sharpness about what seemed to them shoddy courses, unclear requirements and a general disrespect for professional standards. Radical individualists such as chemist Paul Corneil were beginning to chafe at McCoy's distrust of unproductive students and his occasional authoritarianism. Under constant pressure to "normalize" Johnston, McCoy grew impatient with the continuing student restiveness about living conditions. On October 22, for example, he supported University of Redlands' faculty member George Derfer's offer to negotiate between Johnston College and a group of students threatening to withdraw over the issue of living autonomy: not much community solidarity in those politics.

Other faculty were restive with T-grouping. Roger Baty had always scorned the "instant intimacy" of such groups. Jeanne Friedman felt they led to narcissistic self-involvement and smothered political awareness. Sporadic but stubborn student resistance to obligatory T-grouping was also surfacing.

But none of these difficulties, in academics or in social arrangements, seriously challenged the euphoric high spirits of those first months. For all its problems and its wholesale lack of organization during that first semester, Johnston was a happy place.

But it was also an extraordinarily busy place as the real process of setting up a college began to go forward. Agenda for faculty meetings was staggering. Each meeting had to deal with five or six major items: on October 22, for example, the group had developed plans for the January Interim semester, for a more effective advising system, and for the nuts and bolts of graduation contracts. In addition they had to contend with long-range planning! Slowly, and with almost infinite deliberation, the faculty began to make decisions about the future shape of the school.

This first evidence of effective planning met with unexpected resistance. Students felt that faculty were arrogating too much power to themselves and thereby undercutting the ranking authority of the Community Meeting. Enough faculty agreed that it was decided, in March, 1970, to rename the faculty meeting the "Faculty Forum." Such fora might discuss issues but would not take votes or make decisions. At most, faculty would offer recommendations to the community, which it would discuss and vote on at its meetings.In addition a small set of ad hoc student-faculty committees, creatures of the community meeting, was emerging. By the end of the first year these bodies were doing much of the planning work. Hence, the faculty meetings ceased to be foci of academic decision-making, though they continued as forums for discussion and as a valuable morale-booster for faculty.

This did not mean that faculty abdicated power. They made up half of every committee and were almost always more vocal and more influential than student members. So powers of persuasion, and acuity of ideas, replaced official position as the means by which faculty exerted control. The committee structure as it emerged paralleled, in fact, the power distribution in most classes. Authority was shared, as was responsibility, but the most articulate and thoughtful people, students or faculty, assumed positions of leadership. Nearly ever visitor that came to study the college during its first year — and there were over two hundred — warned that faculty would burn out from the overload of teaching, governance and planning. But by and large they did not, because they felt a proprietary commitment to the institution. Faculty saw themselves as the "owners" and makers of the college, not as employees, and so seemed able to expend great amounts of energy without suffering exhaustion.

And the expenditure of energy, by both faculty and students, *did* produce a viable academic program by the end of the first year. Even though the college opened without any real plan, and did so by design, it did acquire a remarkably stable character by May of 1970. By October 6 a "graduation plan" was set down by the faculty and approved by the community. Students were asked to form an individual graduation committee consisting of an academic adviser and two other faculty members, preferably from different academic areas. They were to negotiate a plan for graduation which addressed a set of eleven "guidelines" — and the word "requirement" was assiduously avoided — as presented in the catalog. These were largely predictable (statement of professional objectives; reference to post-graduate education; state requirements; foreign languages; integration of knowledge), but some bore the Johnston stamp. One should indicate master of several "methodologies"; demonstrate "personal integrity," or integration of academic and personal growth; and show substantive evidence of awareness of "contemporary problems" — a faint trace of the original purpose to train people for international business and service. While the individualized committee was replaced by a standing Graduation Contract Committee in 1970, the design remained fundamentally the same throughout the life of the college.

On other fronts, resident standard boards were established in Fokat and Kofap. Surprisingly cautious proposals to liberalize the dormitory rules were approved by the community and forwarded to Don Ruthenberg, Vice President of Student Life. The campus planning committee was, quixotically, developing models for a school of 600 students. And a plan for evaluating courses, students and faculty was in rough but workable shape by January. In retrospect, the faculty seems every bit as traditional as they were innovative, and there was enough structure to support the new institution without stifling it. But it was not a structure that looked exactly like typical academic bureaucracy; it was not a structure that blocked loopholes or guarded against the exceptional case, and hence was not easily recognized by University officials.

If there was a slippage in the academic design, it came in the translation of general design into daily practice. For as we have seen, Johnston in the Fall of 1969 was as much a commune as a college. Students were there to go to school, but they were also there to live a Rousseauian vision of the free life devoted to self-discovery. The graduation contract idea was still terribly abstract to many; the majority were interested in lifestyle and personal identity, with politics a distant third. When academic courses touched these concerns, great; when not, they tended to drift out of sight. This was not helped by the fact that faculty-student relationships were so friendly; it was sometimes difficult for young faculty to combine friendship and academic rigor.

Meanwhile, student life continued to distract Armacost and the Trustees. They believed deeply in the appearance and the symbolic value of order; a campus which did not meet their standards of thoroughgoing academic structure, dress codes and obedient behavior automatically meant a campus where little of merit was likely to take place. Nor was this belief applied only to the Johnston side of the street. Representative is Armacost's two-page letter to his top administrators and the University chaplain deploring the showing of "The Graduate" in the campus chapel on November 7, 1969. The letter, in typical Armacost style, poses a list of five increasingly rhetorical queries about the "value system" of the movie. As he dictated, his anger (we presume) increased until he came to query six:

> Are we ready to abandon our Judaeo-Christian concept of the relationships between men and women before marriage, and during marriage in favor of a humanitarian concept based on humanism, in which what comes naturally and what does not apparently harm other people because there is mutual consent before performing the act — is this the concept which you are now ready to recommend to the Board of Trustees as the procedure to be followed when students are found guilty of performing pre-marital sex acts on campus or situations where we bear the responsibility to

parents for what takes place?

Few paragraphs could be more revealing of the man. His Board of Trustees looms behind him as a many-headed judge, ready to denounce the University's irresponsible complicity in the unrestrained sex acts of its ersatz children. The pressure is from the Board, the center of corporate theology, and the parents, the real (because paying) customers. Natural things are dangerous; orderly things are best. Everyone — even his chaplain who permitted the movie to be shown in the chapel — is carelessly (or deliberately) letting order and control slip into the hands of the morally flabby humanists. Armacost's letter winds down in a slightly garbled sentence: "I realize that my ideas and concepts are quite out of step with the current thinking but I don't see that it is getting much better as a result of acceding to current thought so, maybe if we hold on to some of the things that are more or less sacred to our tradition, we may not be any worse off then we are and might have preserved something as well." Once again, a Protestantism of control and constraint clashes with the wild, tent-meeting enthusiasm and "naturalness" of young libidos running free.

Given these attitudes and the era itself, it might be expected that open political confrontations over local and national issues would also be regular occurrences between such philosophically divergent schools. But this was rarely the case. The most telling example was the nationwide Vietnam Moratorium which took place in May, 1970. At that time the University concurred in a three-day voluntary suspension of classes in order to run discussions about the American invasion of Cambodia.

Marches were organized and faculty and students joined with outside speakers to hold meetings all over campus about the morality of the war. George Armacost, to the surprise of some, energetically endorsed the plans for such discussions, though he insisted that "both sides" be represented. A student proposal that students be permitted to miss classes for the last few weeks of the semester (though they would complete assignments and take finals) in order to maintain study groups on the war, was seriously considered by the Faculty Senate and in a few places (Johnston!) even approved. So in this instance the University not only acquiesced in student desires to make political protests, but even approved the suspension of classes for a short period.

Incidents like this revealed a complex side of the problem. Armacost was not a simple conservative and he did not object to either political activity or protest as such. Rather he, and others in the Administration and on the Board of Trustees, feared disruptive protest that gave the public appearance of being discourteous or radical, and thus anti-democratic. The anti-war moratorium might have stirred protests from conservative townspeople and alumni, but Johnston was not automatically blamed for the event, and Jeanne Friedman, to everyone's surprise, was not singled out for special attention even though she played a prominent role in the moratorium meetings.

There was a second, more important reason for the unruffled appearance of the Redlands campus. Johnston itself was not an activist campus. There was a small and dedicated group of political radicals during the first year of the college's existence, but it soon became obvious to them that Redlands was too isolated to offer much opportunity for radical political action. The ironic truth is that Johnston College was essentially bourgeois in its political structure and aspirations. No school so solidly grounded in the individual could provide a permanent home for people whose categories ran more to class struggle and the oppression of groups. Johnston implicitly made such groups secondary in the scheme of things, appendages to the all-powerful individual. The small minority of true radicals gradually left for such organizations as Venceremos or went to work among the laboring classes. Johnston was never a very fertile ground for Marxists, and remarkably few ever attended.

Johnston's real political problems stemmed from internecine differences between divergent types of moral and political liberalism. As we have seen, Armacost was by ordinary standards of the time an educational liberal. He, like McCoy, expressed a deep belief in the value of individual freedom and felt that higher education needed to free itself from unproductive attachments to departmental structure, inert bodies of knowledge and the life. But his vision was also grounded in the Christian belief in moral absolutes, and in a deeply serious conviction that neither learning nor citizenship could survive without propriety. To him such qualities were a large part of what Christian liberal education was designed to produce: civilized, thoughtful and above all well-behaved citizens. He feared the antinomian tendency in Johnston's structure that threatened to jettison the forms of civility and to free passions which could only lead to excess and degeneracy. Even Friedman's "alleged communism" fell under this rubric. What disturbed Armacost the most was his perception that she was an apostle of disorder.

It is interesting that early faculty and community meeting minutes suggest that both bodies spent a good deal of time discussing order. Johnston was always more middle class than Armacost realized, and exerted remarkable energies, in its slow and somewhat untidy way, to hammering out a set of political and academic rules.

On the academic side the most embarrassing gap between theory and practice occurred in December and January when faculty wrote their first-semester evaluations and submitted them to the registrar. The results were in large part inept and in some cases hilarious. Some faculty, caught up in the mood of the T-groups, wrote what amounted to clinical case histories of students' psychological progress. Others read like intimate confessions of friendship meant to be read exclusively by the student. Still others cavalierly omitted any description of the course that was being evaluated and many never got written at all because of faculty overload, poor scheduling and lack of clarity about what evaluations should look like. This collection of gaffes was not reviewed by either the Chancellor or the Vice-Chancellor before it went to the "Hill."

The "Hill," in the person of Vice President for Administration Dr. William Umbach, responded. A shocked registrar sent the offending documents to Umbach, who professed in a letter to Ed Williams that he had been looking forward to reading the evaluations. But when he did read them his response was "utter dismay." He found the sample he read "totally inadequate."

Umbach's memo to Williams on February 6, 1970, was the first direct attempt of a University administrator to influence the Johnston academic design. The intervention was wholly justified. An admittedly extreme example of the "confessional style" in evaluation helps explain Umbach's reaction. The course being evaluated was a "Quest for Meaning" seminar and the evaluation ran as follows:

> Life, it appears, is for you rather crazy (sic). Almost not to be made sense of. You have an uninhibited, almost a bizarre attitude sometimes about the world around you. This doesn't bother you as long as you are prevented from getting into trouble. You are suddenly not carefree when you are put up against something and made to account for yourself. When you can fail and not lose face or reputation, you are (like others of us) carefree. So in your poem: "What's wrong with the Alice world/So long as we can catch ourselves in mid-fall?/" which is, I feel, a tremendous expression of your real feelings. You can be proud of it.

And so on for two more paragraphs. Never mind the incomplete sentences, the content alone was enough to call down the critics. Faculty excused their performance on the grounds of "experimentation." Ed Williams replied to Umbach with an atypically aggressive letter, pointing out that the evaluations really weren't in his province. The fiasco culminated in a February faculty meeting with Armacost and other administrators in attendance at which especially inept examples were read aloud by Umbach. There was clearly no defense, and several people started to laugh.

What followed demonstrated that the college could organize itself as tightly and quickly as a situation demanded. A faculty task force recalled the abortive documents, laid out a timetable, organized a rewriting session, and within a month presented the registrar with a much more accurate and professional set of evaluations. The farcical experience clearly benefitted the institution; everyone had to learn how to write thoughtful evaluations under time pressure. Faculty became very good at it indeed. The college also began keeping and controlling the quality of its own records. Within a year a Johnston registrar was appointed "from the ranks" (Sally Hickok).

But wider problems of evaluation did remain. From the beginning Pres had been anxious to employ some "outside" evaluating agency to review his experiment in progress, and to keep any biased University evaluators at bay. University officials, for somewhat different reasons, also wanted such an agency. Accordingly, the Wright Institute of Oakland was hired in October of 1969 to evaluate the Johnston program. Its director, Nevitt Sanford, prepared an elaborate and impressive research design. But the implementation of the design became hit-and-miss because Sanford farmed the project out to assistants, most of whom were graduate students. By May of 1970 both Johnston and the University were unhappy with the rather banal (but by no means negative) results, and the final Wright Institute Report, issued in 1971, proved all but worthless.

A final note on evaluation. The most impressive document George Armacost ever produced about Johnston College was his report to the Board of Trustees, presented on January 15, 1970. The college took up the lion's share of the report. In this lengthy essay Armacost demonstrated familiarity with theoreticians in experimental education and made astute comments about problems facing the faculty in experimenting colleges. He is particularly surprising in his temperate comments about publicity and public image: "The larger community is only too ready to attribute addiction to LSD and sexual laxity to any unconventional youth group." He also cites the need for a "much longer period of operation before any definite and final conclusions can be reached." Granted that Armacost wanted to placate his Board, this was still a promising new note.

There are a few lapses in logic, and the Armacost method — praising faintly and then attacking — is in evidence: "While the Utopian design has merit, it also had disadvantages. Moving in the realm of ideals and fantasy rather than realistic...." Consensus, sensitivity training and the absence of a fixed curriculum come in for predictable knocks, but even these are restrained. The document, in other words, had a statesman-like tone which rarely appears in Armacost's inter-office memoranda and seems to show some inclination towards compromise with Johnston. It shows George Armacost at his best. But Pres felt on the defensive. His marginalia on the report indicate that he saw the document too narrowly as an attack.

Dedication ceremonies, with their inevitable optimism and bonhomie, fall into self-parody even sooner than most official academic ceremonies. There is a gap between public sentiments and private wrangling on such occasions, but the contrast was particularly acute on January 20, 1970.

The day began with a cheerful procession which combined (or tried to combine) the traditional academic festival with the new-sensed spirit of the age. Faculty self-consciously wore academic regalia, and students were somehow cajoled into dresses and suits. They resembled nothing so much as tribesmen quaintly dressing up in borrowed clothes to please the local missionaries. There were the requisite local dignitaries, representatives of other schools and learned societies, and most delightful of all, James Graham Johnston himself.

There was an investiture ceremony in the morning for the entire campus community, then a luncheon, followed by a program of dedication in the afternoon. The tone of each was distinct. The investiture was held in a two-masted circus tent erected on the quad between the dorms. With its broad striped sides and pennants, it seemed just the sort of festive place from which to launch the college. And the tone of this event was appropriately affirmative and visionary.

Armacost offered an opening speech that sounded more like McCoy than McCoy. He scrupulously used Johnston terminology like "living-learning," "experimental," and "interpersonal" rather than the new-abandoned terminology of international business. He even added that "We shall be patient and shall avoid premature judgment of results as you experiment with new ways of learning.... Your leadership is a position of trust to be mutually shared."

Pres' response was really a summary of the college's beginnings and life to that point. He made clear how much of the design he had in mind before ever meeting with University officials. His ideas were by now canonical, inseparable from the institution. The "central focus of the college shall be the growth of the person"; interdisciplinary dimensions shall replace "rigid" departmental structures. The necessity for sound institutional research and careful evaluation of the experiment, for small seminars and tutorials, for focus on methodologies, and for interest in values, were all reaffirmed. Whitehead's "I care, and it matters," was his motto. "Openness," "constant growth" and "social conscience" — his voice had a ritual tone. It was not unlike the reading of familiar scripture at a gathering of the faithful. His call for "a prophetic quality in our inquiry and commitment with the courage to take a stance" perfectly evoked the New Eden. Everyone believed....

McCoy's evangelical tone was supported first by student Mike Nixon, who gave the salutation for both students and faculty, and then by the keynote speaker, Alvin Eurich of Stanford and the Academy for Educational Development. He presented a view of what education would be like in 1980. He saw Johnston as shaping that decade: You are deciding what the future should be, and then inventing that future for yourselves." Eurich was especially confident that student involvement in classroom negotiation and campus governance would grow. He even cited Johnston evaluator Nevitt Sanford's forecast, in *The American College*, of an increase of diversity and activism as the predominant trends in student life in the 1980's. So much for prophecy.

The luncheon was highlighted by the unveiling of Joy Buba's commissioned bronze bust of Jimmie Johnston, and by his simple and heartfelt response. He spoke of his birth in Galashiels, Scotland in 1887 and of his lonely arrival in the United States in 1916 with his "hand tools," mechanic's skills and little else. He began working with IBM on March 16 of that year, in one of the first research laboratories in American business. He soon invented the first printing mechanism for the automatic printing of tabulator results, an invention which helped launch the primitive stages of the computer revolution. He concluded his remarks in a sweet voice, the burr of Galashiels still fresh: "...individuals make their best production records and finest human relationships when they are stimulated and encouraged to develop themselves.... Our work as sponsors of the college is to create an environment, to secure the facilities, to provide the guidance and assistance our students need. It is a privilege, for which I am deeply grateful, to be associated with a college dedicated to such ideas and ideals."

The dedication that afternoon sounded more like business as usual. First, George Armacost made a lengthier and more pointed address than his introduction of McCoy that morning. In it he mixed more assertions of Johnston's value with thinly veiled warnings against the dangers of educational self-indulgence. Then, Jimmie's homey marriage of capitalism and human sensitivity took a more aggressive cast in the entertaining remarks of Dan Seymour, president of the J. Walter Thompson advertising agency. Science and business, he declared, "all those so-called bogeymen, actually contain every possibility of peace and prosperity that we know." He challenged his audience with the flexibility of the "Establishment" and the inevitability of the triumph of technology ("We have the means to do anything."). The recessional was Handel's "Hail the Conquering Hero," whose sentiment was not sustained much past sundown.

Draining daily squabbles offered jarring counterpoint to the official festivities. An Armacost memo dated the day after the dedication was a sharply worded critique of a Johnston proposal for a community house, a project which Pres and the Overseers felt was a purely academic matter. Armacost claimed, however, that this was a student life matter and took an aggressive, even hectoring tone. Yet he ended with a sincere question: "I confess I feel now that I can no longer be honest and frank for I feel I'm not trusted by your community...what can be done to change this feeling? I am deeply troubled." McCoy offered him little consolation.

Armacost justified his frequent complaints by arguing that Johnston's "bad image" was costing the University the support of alumni and donors and thus costing it money. But this was a one-sided view. Johnston *was* roundly and continually criticized by some people but it had a large number of admirers, even among allegedly conservative circles. The editor of the *Redlands Facts*,

Frank Moore, who could hardly be counted a radical, wrote on the day following the dedication: "Rudyard Kipling said, 'Prophets have honour all over the earth, except in the village where they are born.' This may have some application to Johnston College in the village where it has been born...." And commenting on Eurich's speech Moore remarked: "his whole appraisal is an indirect message to Redlands to refrain from judging Johnston College too soon and standing too closely. It may be that Johnston is now a prophet of education that in time will bring more honor to Redlands than the people of our town imagine in its first year of life."

But Armacost's worries about finances were justified even if his claim that they were caused by Johnston's image were not. By the spring of 1970 the precarious financial position of the new college was coming clear. As we noted, only some $300,000 of the founding grant of $1.5 million was available for use. And the University had borrowed heavily to construct the dorms, commons and library. Consequently McCoy, working with the University's Development Office, was supposed to raise $250,000 in grant support during the year 1969-70 to help balance the budget and help pay off the new mortgages. By May he had secured $23,000 in donations, plus a three year, $75,000 Danforth grant which was earmarked for paying the salaries of additional intercultural staff. The Development Office proved to be of little help. So, money had to be cut, even though there was not a large deficit. The dimension budgets were the main target, and some tension developed among faculty trying to protect their small portion of the pie.

There was a lengthy T-group, on March 16, to wrestle with the budget and the feelings it provoked. There followed, on March 26, a singularly fatuous action on the part of University officials. Facing new financial difficulties arising in part from a slumping stock market, Armacost and the Board decided to increase the charges laid upon Johnston for "administrative and academic services" from 6 percent of the total University budget to 16 percent for the coming academic year. The rationale for this hike was that since the Johnston student body would then constitute some 16 percent of all University of Redlands students they should pay their fair share of the overhead. In return Johnston would receive an enhanced share of endowment income. Since library and student services cost $78,000, and charges for Johnston students taking classes at the University totalled another $28,000, the total cross charges equalled $166,000, while the endowment yield only reached $73,000. However paternalistic and controlling Armacost wanted to be, when it came to finances he treated the fledgling school as though it were a separate institution merely renting space on the campus.

The above also reveals that University officials expected Johnston to be a paying proposition. There was no leeway for the inevitable period of losses which marks the founding of any institution of higher learning. And even though Johnston produced very small deficits until it began to suffer serious enrollment declines in 1976, the University began to produce and use the fiction that Johnston was ruining the University with its extravagance. The first-year shortfall of about $100,000 — a modest loss considering start-up costs — became a bone of contention and a source of blame for years afterward.

The first casualty of financial pressures was the Swiss economist René Françillon. In addition to his full teaching load, Françillon was also the unofficial budget officer of the college. He had volunteered for the onerous work during the 1968 planning year, and was now a victim of his own success. He spent hours during February and March negotiating the budget with the University business manager, Larry Hendon. Hendon was as forthright and supportive an administrator as Johnston had encountered but he had no power to make policy.

Hendon told Françillon that he had been instructed to cut at least $100,000 out of the budget and to raise the allocation percentage. The 16.2 percent charges were imposed. Several hours after the March 26th meeting Françillon, 34, suffered a major heart attack. He remained on the critical list until well into April before slowly recovering. It would be sentimental to blame Françillon's illness solely on budget frustrations but they were clearly a factor. It also had the effect of leaving Johnston without its most able budget negotiator at a time when these punitive new rules should have been challenged. The issue of Johnston's "drain" on University funds moved toward center stage, a place it would occupy for the remainder of the college's history.

The first year also produced an addition to the original dimension model. The three scientists, Paul and Isobel Corneil and Allen Killpatrick, organized the "Environmental Dimension." Since ecology was a vital part of 1960's liberal politics, students gravitated toward such non-laboratory courses and began to design graduation contracts in the area. The idea had been discussed and affirmed at Pilgrim Pines, but not seriously developed for several months. This was viewed by both Bill Umbach and Armacost as yet another affront to the original plan for the college.

That plan, to repeat, called for "laboratory science courses" to be taken at the University, thus avoiding the enormous costs involved in duplicating facilities. The key sentence read, "The courses offered by Johnston College may be supplemented by courses in art, music and speech and in laboratory sciences...provided by University college." Armacost and Umbach took this to mean that no science concentration should be undertaken by a Johnston student using Johnston faculty. If a student wished to major in the sciences he or she should transfer to the University.

Johnston people naturally argued with this reading. The Environmental dimension was primarily geared to "interdisciplinary programs..." allied to careers in "urban development and public service," and did not intend to compete with University pre-med or pre-graduate programs. But the University typically saw this as an assertion of further independence and several sharp memos and phone calls followed. But the Johnston faculty prevailed. The Environmental dimension got its final touch of respectability through the voluntary transfer to Johnston of Dave Bragg, a University mathematician in fall of 1970. This was virtually the last vigorous attempt by University officials to shape Johnston's academic program, which was already proving itself sufficiently formidable to resist such inclusions.

But by far the most ominous of all the events of the spring semester was going on behind the scenes. Pres had been under direct threat of dismissal since an October memo from Board Chairman Llewellyn ("you've had two chances already."). The Friedman case and the sheer difference of Johnston students were the central issues. McCoy had supported the radical Friedman and he seemed incapable or unwilling to control the odd behavior and appearance of Johnston students.

McCoy kept all this from the faculty and students. He saw his job as protecting the experiment and its members from anything which could disturb its purity. But the new development — an official Board inquiry into the operation of the college — was another matter, and one that could not be kept private.

This in-house evaluation team began its work early in the spring semester. Whatever fitful patience George Armacost had demonstrated in the earliest days of the college's founding had vanished. A special "Ad Hoc Committee of the Board of Trustees for the Evaluation of the Administration of Johnston College" was called into being specifically to evaluate the progress of the first year's experiment.

This Committee did not limit itself to administration but reviewed academic progress as well. It is one of the more intriguing documents in the Johnston archive. Had its recommendations been followed, it is possible that the catastrophic events of the following January would never have occurred.

The Committee was composed of five persons. Two were supporters of the college (Frances Willis and Arthur Willis); two had serious reservations about it (Lee Launer and Fred Llewellyn); one was a neutral outside observer (Bernard Hyink, an academic administrator from Cal State Fullerton). Armacost's charge to the Committee covered five single spaced pages. It is a rather disorganized litany of charges against the college and especially against McCoy. The academic program is faintly praised ("The contract plan...is good," followed by three sentences of critique) and the faculty even more faintly lauded ("The faculty is competent. Does it have the balance needed? Are Faculty properly in balance in viewpoints?").

Everything else in his sixteen point bill of particulars is negative. The Friedman case is raised again, long after it had apparently been settled. Students are criticized for bare feet, for being "fringy," for seeking to live off campus and for hostility toward University administrators. And these "behavior problems," in Armacost's view, come back to the Chancellor. A second document dated May 15, "Questions to direct the evaluation of Johnston College" (just so there would be no confusion as to who was doing the directing), covered the same ground, though in a more coherent way.

The Committee's first report (issued June 3, 1970) was drafted by Lee Launer. It gave high praise to the academic program, warning only that faculty might be so involved in the college that their scholarly pursuits could suffer. (This generally proved correct.) Armacost's various charges against the students were simply ignored. But the Committee did agree with the President on his main contention: "Administration" was considered entirely ineffective, and a straightforward proposal was made to improve it:

A Vice-Chancellor for Administration be hired (paralleling the University structure). This person would report to the Chancellor and be responsible for the following items:

    a. student affairs
    b. fiscal affairs
    c. admissions
    d. inter-college relations
    e. all non-academic functions

The Chancellor would henceforth devote most of his time to fund-raising and public relations. That was it: very simple, very clean. The crucial items in the proposal are (a) and (b). Had these matters been left in the hands of a person who was a day-to-day member of the community, two of the greatest problems that beset the college could, conceivably, have been eased. Item "d" could well have had the greatest long-term significance; Johnston people had, myopically, done very little to build relationships with their peers across the street. Participation in the bi-weekly meetings of the advisory Campus Council did not suffice. Consequently, the college had no politically active allies at the University in its struggles with Armacost and the Trustees.

The recommendation implies that the new Vice President would have significant authority in student life, potentially resolving the year-long wrangle over autonomy. Neither McCoy or Williams was consistently strong on administrative detail; a person in charge of all "non-academic functions" who would keep an eye on the minutiae of administration would have eased the impatience of University administrators. The reasons why that proposal never bore fruit gradually emerged during the fall of 1970.

Finally, the year spun threads which stretched into Johnston's future. Glenn Whitlock initiated conversations with Bill Umbach concerning an M. A. in psychology; Umbach was supportive. Ed Williams made initial contacts with the Western States Accrediting Association. He also introduced the idea of "external degree" work for working adults. Approval was finally granted for a community project in the Mexican-American barrio; students, male and female, would share a house and work in the community. These moves prepared the way for Johnston's separate accreditation, for the University Without Walls program, and for much larger involvements in off-campus internships.

Some students ran a weekend coffeehouse in a University-owned building on the edge of campus. Simple entertainments were offered and the "Green House" attracted enough student business to break even. Other students developed plans for increasing minority admissions; these were adopted by the Admissions office and worked for a time to raise the percentage of black and Mexican-American applicants.

And other first year battles were shortly to be resolved. In May of 1971, thanks largely to the subtle nudging of Arthur Willis, the Board of Trustees passed a new housing code. Women's hours were all but abandoned and a type of coed dormitory was approved. This type of dorm was called a "correlative" arrangement. It meant that men and women could inhabit the same dorm but must live on separate floors, or on different lobbies in the case of Johnston dorms. Willis made use, in his presentation, of a research paper on coed dorms on American campuses prepared at Lyle Thompson's urging by four Johnston students (Jane Creighton, Nikko Schoch, Jeanne Woods and Casey Jones). Correlative dorms were still conservative but it was a giant step toward the free-for-all policy that Johnston desired and which was in fact practiced there from an early date in blithe defiance of University policy.

But, the old conservatism about sexual morality never altered in George Armacost. In the last days of his twenty-five year reign as President, in the spring of 1970, he spent

considerable time and energy trying to find out the names
of a Johnston couple who had shared a sleeping bag in the
Johnston quad and who were discovered by an earlybird
maintenance man.... It seems somehow an indecorous
finale to such a long and distinguished career.

NOTES:

1. In September the halls were unnamed while donors were being
sought. The students "took possession" of the buildings by holding a
random drawing of letters to name the men's dorm — "Kofap" was the
result — and then (roughly) transposing them (obscene pun intended)
for the women's dorm ("Fokat"). The Trustees' Executive Committee
responded in October by "officially" naming the halls, neutrally, "East"
and "West," and affixing bronze letters to the entryway. For years
afterwards the "East" and "West" were regularly hidden behind banners
proclaiming "Kofap," or spray painted, or simply stolen, only to be duti-
fully replaced by the maintenance crew.
2 This is a verbatim transcript of the memo Armacost sent to McCoy
to confirm their conversation.

CHAPTER 4

The End of the McCoy Era

The Fall Term, 1970

Once again, it was Pilgrim Pines. Superficially, the program was the same: concentrated T-grouping punctuated by political meetings, volleyball and late-night parties. But for the returning students and faculty comparisons were unavoidable. The budget was smaller, so the time spent in the mountains was shorter. As a further economy some psychology faculty doubled as trainers. And not everyone felt compelled to join a T-group. Since forms were already in place, the magic of world-building was hard to recapture. There was no Friedman case to serve as a galvanizing agent for community togetherness. The same songs were sung but the old hands knew all the verses.

Back in Redlands these differences blossomed into political tensions. The integration of new students and faculty proved impossible to do quickly. No matter how hard they tried to overcome it, the founding members felt a deep proprietary urge; against all reason they wanted to exclude the newcomers from *their* college. A second-year student said that the powerful figures of the original class

— Kathy Davis and Toby Greene and Marylou Morelock, to name a few — seemed like "gods" to her when she first arrived. "And sometimes they acted like it," she added. Dan Gilbertson, himself a newly arrived faculty member in sociology, organized a survey of attitudes. It showed a strong emotional adherence to the communal side of the college, but a dispirited attitude toward both political and academic work. "And the trust level just wasn't the same," remarked second-year student Peter Michelsen, "People started locking their doors all the time."

The faculty proved particularly intransigent. Old faculty were perceived as unwelcoming and new faculty were sometimes critical of "traditional" methods of decision-making and record-keeping. Uncertainty about the real intentions of the new president, Eugene Dawson, and a growing disaffection among faculty with McCoy's unevenness in sharing power added to a general malaise. This was abetted by a certain dissatisfaction with the fact that Johnston had developed fixed forms for getting things done. Bureaucratic forms seemed to be undercutting the trust that characterized human dealings at Johnston, and the growth of such forms was both consciously and unconsciously resisted. Ironically, then, the standardization of Johnston added to the sense that both faculty and school were drifting off-course.

To meet this mood the faculty held an all-day meeting on October 23rd at a nearby retreat center in Cherry Valley, which was run by an order of Catholic sisters. Students held similar "let's clear the air" meetings on campus. At Cherry Valley the morning was given to T-grouping. New faculty confronted old faculty with their intentional or unintentional snobbery and Pres made temporary peace with his critics. The afternoon was devoted to problem-solving meetings and, though nothing specific was accomplished, a tone was set which produced important decisions during the next few weeks.

During this fertile period additional necessary forms were established: a graduation review committee to determine whether candidates for graduation had in fact fulfilled the terms of their graduation contracts; Roger Baty's guidelines for screening applicants for off-campus projects; a Chancellor's advisory group to break down Pres' isolation and to alleviate some of his workload; a determined effort to call in unfinished evaluations — some 20 percent of the total by the end of the first academic year. All but the last act were effective; overdue evaluations proved a chronic problem. The Johnston style was too respectful of persons to become punitive; persuasion was the only weapon and it was only partly successful.

On the student life front the big issues of the new year were animal policies and off-campus housing. The former problem was ludicrous, yet serious. Though the University clearly forbade cats and dogs from living in the dorms, Johnston students imported both in large numbers. These proved all but impossible to eliminate. The student life committee spent hours forging regulations which were then routinely ignored. Students insisted on seeing their dorm rooms as private apartments, and felt that they should have the right to decide whether to keep cats and dogs. As a consequence the dorms and the quad were afflicted with dog and cat droppings, most of which were not picked up by their owners. Carpets were ruined and an unpleasant odor often permeated the lobbies. Despite these irritations, the animal problem persisted; it was a clear instance of self-indulgence overriding community values.

The off-campus housing issue was also chronic. Students knew that they could rent more spacious and charming quarters in the older sections of Redlands for less money than they were paying to live in the infamous block-house dormitories. The University knew that it had to keep the dorms full in order to pay the mortgage. So the fight was joined. Students came up with all manner of excuses from doctors and psychologists explaining why they *must* move off campus, and complicated priority systems were developed to let some upperclassmen leave the dorms. Sophomore Mike Lavender is generally credited with inventing the concept of "deals," in which a student would pay for a double room on campus then move off to cheaper quarters, splitting the fee with the on-campus student who got an otherwise unavailable single room. But there were always *more* people aspiring to escape the dorms than there were off-campus slots, and the dorms were never quite full enough to satisfy the University.

A part of the original vision which languished during the second year was the inclusion of faculty spouses (all women, not surprisingly) in college activities. This had worked wonderfully well at Pilgrim Pines in 1969. Faculty wives were freed from joining an innocuous Faculty Wives Club and T-grouping made them feel a real part of the community. Many participated in all the August planning sessions and had as great an emotional investment in Johnston as their husbands did. Two lived on campus as co-counselors with their faculty spouses, a third taught German, a fourth became a student herself. But most had no continuing role to play in the school and their erstwhile devotion understandably faded.

In the second year several wives began to take a more active professional interest in the college. Solange Landa went to Europe during Interim to investigate opportunities for study abroad. Urmila More worked as a consultant with the international dimension. But difficulties arose when several students decided to set up a day care center and enlisted faculty wives to help them staff it. The idea quickly evolved into that of establishing an interracial "Creative Playschool." Here students could learn how to teach preschoolers from a variety of cultural backgrounds and in the process help low-income parents keep their jobs. They could also test new ideas in education.

Anne Watt, John's wife, became a moving force in the project. She had a Master's Degree in education as well as teaching experience, and she was willing to volunteer her services as seminar leader and school organizer for the sum of $750 per semester, the going University rate for part-time instructors. But other faculty whose wives also had professional credentials raised the issue of nepotism. Anne was aggressive in pursuit of her goal and angry at what she perceived as prejudice and jealousy. She was offered $550 and turned it down. It was a long time before another faculty wife offered a course at Johnston. The idea of a "Johnston family" withered.

Eugene Dawson, the new president of the University, seemed a perfect appointment for Johnston's purposes. A Baptist and a minister, he was also a student of Carl Rogers, and hence sympathetic to the humanistic psychology that was fundamental to the college's program. He was also an old friend of McCoy's. Pres had invited him to lead seminars at the Danforth teachers' conferences. He had played tennis with Dawson and been a guest at his home. He had written Dawson a recommendation for the presidency of another college — and Dawson had given Pres a positive recommendation for the Johnston job. In fact, it was McCoy's idea to nominate Dawson to replace Armacost. He followed Orton's advice and engineered the nomination through a third party so that Armacost would not know that Dawson was McCoy's candidate.

In any case, Dawson was contacted by an executive search firm retained by the University. He almost turned the job down because of what he perceived as volatile campus politics; "Johnston College was like a hurricane on campus," he observed. But he did take the job, and arrived on campus in the fall of 1970 to replace George Armacost.

Dawson was hired partly for his religious background but more pragmatically for his ability as a fund-raiser. He had secured a very large grant for the college at which he was then president, Colorado Women's College. Redlands' financial position was not perilous, but deficits were starting to make regular appearances in the budget and a Baptist who had landed a multi-million dollar gift seemed very attractive indeed.

Dawson attended the Johnston dedication. A photograph of the occasion shows McCoy leaning toward the President-elect, giving him what almost seems a conspiratorial smile. When Dawson visited the campus that spring the two men went to breakfast together. McCoy was a bit unnerved by his old acquaintance's formality but passed it off as unimportant. As McCoy dropped Dawson off at the administration building, Dawson turned to him and said, "You know, Pres, I have to confess that I have some concerns about the governance arrangement here. I really much prefer the Santa Cruz model of a Chancellor (President) and a provost. And I just wanted you to know that." McCoy recalls the scene: "And then he just got out of the car and walked away...and I'm left there and I thought, 'Well, he's talking theoretically.' I just didn't believe what I was hearing."

The President made his first official appearance on campus at the annual opening picnic on the Johnston quad; he seemed a bit reserved, but was cordial. He attended portions of several Johnston faculty meetings during September and early October. He listened carefully but said little. His first formal remarks to the community on September 6 dealt with fourteen "Indices for Creative Behavior." The talk was as Rogerian as the title suggests. One funny moment occurred during these early contacts. Dawson, eager perhaps to show his solidarity with the students, self-consciously tried to swear along with them. But as Mark Twain told his wife after she failed at the same venture, "My dear, you have the words but not the tune." And his characteristic posture at the meetings — legs and arms tightly crossed, head held slightly back, lips thin — suggested a cautious and even secretive personality. For psychologically sophisticated Johnstonians looking for evidence of openness and inner calm, the posture was distressing. Dawson looked more like a college president saddled with a problem than a man willing to support the experiment.

It was Ed Williams' explicit policy to co-opt Dawson, hoping to forestall any tampering with the experiment by convincing Dawson of Johnston's potential greatness. But since it was McCoy's style to bristle at any show of authority, this more subtle policy did not have much chance to work once Dawson began to assert presidential power.

McCoy's uneasiness was evident during that Fall semester. At least two Johnston professors visited Dawson in secret and complained to him about McCoy's authoritarian administrative style and about Ed Williams' person-centered but sometimes inefficient manner. Pres learned about this meeting and felt it was an act of treachery. He called an *in camera* meeting of the whole faculty at a local restaurant and demanded confessions of loyalty: "Otherwise, they'll pick us off one by one." The faculty voted confidence in his administration but the vote was not unanimous.

At a subsequent community meeting in October, where opinions were aggressively divided, Pres once more called for a show of unity. This angered Yasuyuki Owada, a veteran of student-institution struggles at the International Christian University in Tokyo. Typically a cool, even bemused speaker, Owada's voice, on this occasion, shook with emotion:

> Pres, I think you owe the community an apology for forcing us out of our natural academic business into this business of trying to be unified behind you. And I think you're disrupting the community. And I think you owe us an apology.

Stung by this, Pres answered with an assertive speech in which, carried away by his own vision, he said something like "We have brought Dawson to his knees by showing our unity so far. So let's not quit now." There is little doubt that within hours this outburst had reached the President. Dawson told us he was "always well-informed about community meetings." Williams' dreams of co-optation began to fade.

Whether because of McCoy's ill-chosen phrase or for other reasons, Dawson became even more reserved in his relations with Johnston. He began to chafe at Johnston's administrative organization and at McCoy's "inflexibility." "Pres understandably wanted me to run interference for him with the Trustees," Dawson said later, "but I had the feeling that Pres would bite the hand that fed him. He expected me to be his friend and supporter, but I expected the same of him as well."

Dawson began to say publicly what he had said to Pres privately months earlier. He felt that the two Boards and confusing lines of authority were a mistake, and he much preferred the more hierarchical arrangement of one Board, one President, and a Provost for each of the member colleges of the University.

Another incident in October did little to bring the two men closer. Ed Reinecke, incumbent candidate for the office of Lieutenant Governor, came to speak at a University convocation. The meeting was held in the Student Union and was attended by about 250 students and faculty. A bevy of some 25 students sitting in the front rows engaged in exaggerated applause, cat-calls and other forms of interruption. These people, among others, asked hostile questions about Reinecke's part in the non-renewal of Angela Davis' teaching contract at UC Berkeley. They asked for his views on the Black Panthers and wanted to know where he stood on the Owens Valley water rights controversy. He was also asked what he thought of student protest.

Reinecke answered all the questions, admitting ignorance on some points, and his answers — middle of the road to conservative — got lively negative responses from some of the audience, especially the front row group. But he was not prevented from speaking and he himself had set the session up as a question/answer period specifically to solicit student response. When he left he received a mixture of mocking and real applause.

The visit was reported in *The Redlands Daily Facts* and the *San Bernardino Sun*. In both, the impression was given that the encounter between Reinecke and the students was spirited but orderly. It was noted that Reinecke expressed pleasure about the session as he left. But certain University officials saw the meeting differently. Bill Umbach was visibly agitated. Immediately after the meeting he confronted Ed Williams and told him that he thought the behavior of the "Johnston" students was outrageous. He was especially exercised over the fact that Jeanne Friedman was among the dissident group and that she seemed to be egging the students on.

Ed tried to explain to Umbach that as far as he (Ed) could tell, fewer than half of the students at issue were from Johnston, and that most of the hostile questions had in fact come from black students at the main University. Undaunted, Umbach told Ed that he was going to write a strong letter of protest to the Board of Trustees and to the Johnston Overseers. Ron Kibby, then director of public relations for the University, also wrote an angry letter to McCoy in which he deplored the behavior of the students he assumed to be Johnstonians.

But Don Ruthenberg, the Dean of Students, while admonishing some of the more sarcastic students, asserted that their behavior was not particularly outlandish by contemporary standards. He at least realized that only a few of the students involved were from Johnston. At Dawson's request Ed Williams investigated this claim. His findings essentially confirmed what he had told Umbach at the meeting: Johnston students were not in the majority. McCoy, nonetheless, asked the Johnston dean of students, Lyle Thompson, to provide him with a list of names of the Johnston protesters. He apparently took the complaints at face value.

This incident is important because it shows so clearly

the state of Johnston-University relations. University administrators automatically assumed that students engaged in protest *must* be from Johnston; they also assumed vocal protest was *prima facie* bad behavior. And such behavior was bad for the University's image, despite the fact that Reinecke himself wrote a letter to Ruthenberg in which he stated "I am not unhappy or critical of the incident.... "Yet even after this letter was received, Director of Development Gil Brown was telling people that Reinecke complained to a Trustee that he had never been more poorly treated. Whatever Reinecke might have thought, it was evident what many people at Redlands thought: political protest did not belong on *their* campus, and if it did occur the fault must be laid at Johnston's door. In the context of the times it is interesting to see what deep reactions a relatively trivial incident such as this provoked.

Dawson's reaction to this incident was mercurial, and indicates how uneasy his position was. At an Advisory Council meeting on October 13 he was clearly upset by the students' behavior and announced plans to write a letter of apology to Reinecke. Yet on October 19 he wrote a note to Dwayne Orton in which he accepted the students' behavior as normal and reported that he had chastised Bill Umbach for over-reacting. But at a Council meeting on October 20 he was engaged in a lengthy discussion about whether the students involved should be suspended! In any case, the incident did not improve Dawson-Johnston relations.

Dawson's fall report to the Trustees, however, gave no hint of a worsening climate:

In general I have found the administrative officers, faculty and students of Johnston College quite co-operative. I have sensed a growing cooperation between the representatives of Johnston College and the administrative staff of University College. You will recall that last Spring the Board of Trustees appointed a special Ad Hoc committee to study Johnston College and that in late spring this specially appointed committee reported and recommended to the Executive Committee that among other things a Vice Chancellor for administration be appointed...in the very near future the University administration expects to involve designated members of the Johnston community in...recommending a person for this position.

While this was not an enthusiastic vote of confidence in Johnston administrators, it was not particularly ominous. Dawson's "business as usual" tone seemed reassuring. And McCoy was, by this time, resigned to accepting the administrative Vice Chancellor. He *was* suspicious that any appointee would be loyal to Dawson and the University rather than Johnston, and that the position was a perfect training ground for a new Chancellor, but if the right person were chosen the position *could* benefit Johnston. On November 1, in this relatively positive mood, McCoy left on fund-raising trips that would keep him off campus for all but four of the next twenty days.

Dawson's official pronouncements, however, did not reflect his real thinking. Even before he gave his report to the Trustees Dawson contacted James Hester, religion professor at the University, and sounded him out about becoming not the vice chancellor at Johnston, but the provost. Dawson told Hester that he had known from his first visit to the campus that the problems at Johnston would have to be dealt with quickly, and that Trustees had told him informally about their dissatisfaction with both McCoy and Johnston. In a later interview Dawson confirmed that during his first semester as president Board members would "drop by" his office and tell him: "...If you get rid of McCoy..." or "If you get rid of that school...," then "I'll be able to do this for you...." He also said that various University administrators offered themselves as replacements for McCoy and promised that they could "clean up the mess" at Johnston.

Hester was shocked at first by the offer but he did accept, and he asked history professor Richard Andrews to be his administrative vice chancellor. Andrews was definitely interested and the two men met soon after with professors Larry Harvill and Howard Hurlbut, at that time Dawson confidants earmarked for high administrative positions at the University.

So by early November there was already a shadow cabinet for Johnston, one asked to serve without the knowledge, let alone the permission, of anyone at the college. The question in Dawson's mind was not whether to dump McCoy and Williams — the question was when. In early December Dawson again contacted Hester and told him that the Board had decided not to appoint either him or Andrews but had instead chosen Gene Ouellette of the Communicative Disorders department as the new Chancellor. Hester speculated that he and Andrews had been voted down because of their age and relative inexperience. Ultimately, Hester was appointed Assistant to the President in February of 1971.

When McCoy returned to campus on November 20, the plan to appoint a Vice Chancellor for Administration had been all but scuttled. Now Dawson was up in arms about more than a dozen "offenses" at the college, and talk of Johnston "reorganization" was common. What had happened during McCoy's absence?

The first weekend in November was reserved for Homecoming and Parents' Day. At both occasions some Johnston students were perceived as misbehaving. Especially galling to loyal alumni was the Johnston Kazoo Band, an irreverent entry in the Homecoming Parade. Johnston students were also unruly at the football game, making light of school spirit. The Director of Public Relations, Jack Cummings, reported that "we have never had so much negative reaction from alumni." The week preceding these sophomoric events had been tragic. One

University student had committed suicide and another had been raped and murdered in an orange grove adjacent to the President's house. The mood on campus was tense and the Johnston antics only exacerbated the tension.

The President's Advisory Council meeting of November 10 was troubled. More problems were in the air. The meeting began with a discussion of alleged racism against both latino and black students. This issue was handled well, for the time being, by Dawson, but it would erupt later in more virulent form. There were also problems with the University food service, and complaints about drinking at football games. A proposed article on suicide about to be published in the campus newspaper was discouraged, for obvious reasons.

Then came Johnston. Everything — tragic deaths and offended alumni and angry minority students — conspired to increase the tension. The result was a list of six charges against Johnston over which "extreme concern" was expressed:

1. attitude at the Reinecke speech
2. attitude at the Schwartz speech
3. general disruptive nature of the Kazoo Band at the Homecoming Parade
4. general attitude on Parents' Day
5. divisive materials mailed from Johnston College to parents
6. attitude at Homecoming Game

This bill of particulars sounds like the complaint of an angry father to a teen-age son. Five of the items have to do with what can be called, quixotically, "deportment." As we know, the majority of hecklers at the Reinecke speech were not Johnston students and Reinecke explicitly denied being upset about the incident. The "Schwartz" incident refers to a speech given on campus by the leader of the ultra-conservative Christian Anti-Communist Crusade. He too later wrote that he found the interchange with Redlands students "challenging, stimulating and informative"; again, there was no reason to believe that student questioners were from Johnston — but they *looked* as if they were. And Dawson reported that after the speech "people came to me with fire in their eyes, saying, 'What are you going to do?'" The complaints about Homecoming and the football game have already been detailed. The misbehavior on Parents' Day consisted in the refusal of some Johnston students to stand during the playing of the National Anthem.

The only non-deportment issue — the letter to parents — was actually more of the same. In this case a group of students had sent parents a letter asking them to put pressure on the Administration to liberalize dorm policies. No one in the Johnston administration had any connection with the letter, which was innocuous in any case and certainly within the rights of students to compose and send.

One would like to think that it was the tensions of the moment that led adults to take such matters so seriously.[1] But taken seriously they were, enough so that at a special Johnston faculty meeting on November 20, called at Dawson's request and attended by all the University's top administrators, the list was repeated. First, Dawson elaborated on his position. Johnston and the University did not seem compatible and the incompatibility was causing serious defections among alumni supporters. The "structure of governance is almost impossible; it is awkward, cumbersome, and contains the seeds of self-destruction," said Dawson. "We are getting too many problems too fast and they are not helping either school. They are growing more and more serious even if they sound facetious."

There followed an expanded version of the Advisory Council list; this one had thirteen items. To the old list were added: the use of the word "shit" by Johnston students in the presence of the University controller, retired Colonel Joe Wogen;[2] "complaints of smugness and piousness by Johnston and University students against each other"; ignoring presidential advice on procedures in seeking twenty-four hour visitation privileges in the dorms. Dawson's administrative team added still other charges to make the full thirteen: disorganized reception for prospective students on the Johnston campus; messy and unkept dorms; University students transferring to Johnston to avoid work; lack of response to criticisms of Johnston student dress. Again the criticisms were geared almost entirely to real or imagined student behavior in public.

Dawson mentioned only one point that could be construed as academic: criticism of the sloppy narrative evaluations (which were justified but rather out of date). But as the meeting dragged on through late Friday afternoon ominous conclusions began to emerge from this discussion of violated decorum. President Dawson:

> I acknowledge that innovation entails risk, and that the frame of reference for innovation here is unusual. When I accepted this presidency I was wished well by friends because of the conservative climate in Redlands, and also because of Johnston College, and not given much time. The climate of the University College faculty and their social philosophy is, overall, different from yours. The seeds of self-destruction are here. *I knew this six months ago.*

Dawson went on to say that the "package had not been made clear" when he took the job. "The form of the new college has undergone a variety of changes between the original concept and its actual development, and others have never been sold on this. Its development has been too fast...too ambitious, too soon." He then announced that the Ad Hoc Committee had been revived and was undertaking another study of Johnston.

He went on:

I am not really critical of dress and long hair, except pragmatically. I could even defend it, though it would be an uphill battle. But I can't defend some of the other things or have the chance to defend them much longer. The issue comes down to what Johnston College can salvage and what it must relinquish. I want to save what is best — and I will put myself on the block for it. But I will not defend what should go.

What should go?

The structure, the situation now, is schizoid. I have asked the Trustees if they want Johnston to be autonomous and they have repudiated this. The College's future now rests with the academic statesmanship of its leaders...the present two-headed situation is untenable. If anything goes down it has to be Johnston College, not the University of Redlands...the Board of Overseers is cumbersome and almost impossible.... Both Colleges should have provosts

Kevin O'Neill asked, "Are you reorganizing for greater control over student behavior?"

Dawson answered, "Reorganization is coming anyway. Having a Vice-Chancellor for administration won't solve the problem. I want greater conformity to overall life-style." Stunned, Pres responded, "...to talk about reorganization and discontinuance of the Board would involve bad faith." McCoy still thought that the three-year grace period for experimentation was taken seriously by everyone.

The meeting broke up soon afterward.

The logic of the meeting was acrobatic. Two very distinct issues blended in the minds of Dawson and his staff. First, the administrative structure is unwieldy, and second, student deportment is unacceptable. That the first could somehow be a cause of the second could survive a moment's serious examination, yet this seems to have been the implicit argument of Dawson's speech. Better to say that for these men Johnston itself was the problem: everything from radical students to angry minorities to budgetary problems managed to find its way back to this gadfly institution. Perceived disorder in the administrative structure — which was primarily a problem for University people rather than Johnston people — coupled with perceived disorder in student behavior — added up to one thing: Johnston was a general source of chaos for the University, and must be brought to heel.

A more Machiavellian reading of Dawson's behavior on November 20 is that he was tossing out rationalizations for what he had already decided to do: fire McCoy and reorganize Johnston to suit himself. The secret offer to Hester supports such a reading. But this interpretation presumes that Dawson had a detailed plan for Johnston from the beginning, and there is no evidence for this; subsequent events indicate that he had no plans for Johnston beyond firing McCoy. Most of his decisions in that fall smack more of *ad hoc* attempts to protect his own position. Even the "appointment" of Hester looks in retrospect like a provisional move; if it became necessary because of Trustee pressure, Dawson could fire McCoy and install Hester without upheaval.

We must remember that Dawson's position with the Board was less than secure. He had inherited the great majority of that Board from Armacost and had to fight to establish his own legitimacy. They were Armacost's men, and we know what the former President thought of Johnston and McCoy. So we can speculate that it was Board pressure, combined with some real irritation at student gaffes and some serious questions about lines of administrative authority, that combined to turn Dawson against McCoy and make him willing to fire Johnston's founder. Whatever the accuracy of these speculations, it is a fact that relations between Dawson and McCoy deteriorated sharply after the November 20 meeting.

Elaborate attempts to head off a showdown failed. McCoy met with Dawson five times between November 30 and December 18. A special committee from the college sat in on some of the meetings; T-group specialist Del Poling even attended one. Dawson recalls that some of these meetings with Pres "were very personal, dealing with the intimate details of Pres' life." By December 16 Pres believed that the Vice President for Academic Affairs plan was still in flux, and he left for a much-needed Christmas vacation in Hawaii.

Even the vacation proved another mark against him. Llewellyn had commanded Pres to attend a special Executive Committee meeting on budget during that time. Pres refused, pointing out that a vacation was long overdue. This was seen as another sign of his dereliction of duty.

On January 6 Pres received a call from Dawson summoning him to Forest Lawn Memorial Park in Glendale for a meeting. Llewellyn was General Manager of the cemetery. No specific agenda for the meeting was announced; Pres thought it would focus on the issue of the administrative vice chancellor. He spent the morning reviewing the case for his off-campus candidate and against Dawson's man, Development Director Gil Brown.

He drove through the majestic iron gates of Forest Lawn, past the lush pond with its stately swans, to Manager Llewellyn's office in the large pseudo-English administration building. The office itself was immaculate. No papers or pencils cluttered Llewellyn's massive glass-topped desk. The atmosphere was, to Pres, gothic: plush carpets, red velveteen walls. The three men sat around a glass coffee table. Comments on the lovely January weather followed.

Then Llewellyn gave the meeting a different turn: "Well, Pres, while you were away the Executive Committee met and decided that your contract would be terminated at the end of this year. And we hope you will choose the gracious way out."

McCoy turned quickly to Dawson, who was sitting across from him, arms folded across his chest. He said: "Oh? Has the Johnston Board been consulted? Does Dwayne know about this?"

"Oh, no," Llewellyn continued, "they have nothing to do with this. The Board of Trustees hires and fires you, and the President is responsible for that." McCoy said: "I think the Johnston Board should be involved in the discussion, don't you?"

"No," replied Llewellyn, "it doesn't concern them."

McCoy recalled Llewellyn's opening remark. "Well," he said, "what is this 'gracious way out' you have in mind?"

"Here's what we would like you to do," said Llewellyn. "We would like to appoint a Vice-Chancellor who would report directly to the President. And you will go on the road for the remainder of your contract. You can plan for the future of the college. And raise funds, which you are very good at. In the meantime you can be looking for another job. And we'll enthusiastically recommend you for whatever it is you decide you want. We're sure that there are opportunities out there for you. And no one will know."

Pres replied. "Let's see if I get this straight. You want a Vice-Chancellor who'll report directly to the President. So he's going to bypass the Johnston Board. And They're not going to know this. And the faculty aren't going to know it. So all I've got to do is deceive the Board, the faculty, the students, and the people I'm raising funds from."

"But you're protecting your professional future," countered Llewellyn. "You don't want a mess."

"That isn't even a choice," McCoy answered, "I think Dwayne Orton should be consulted on this."

"No," said Llewellyn, "we don't think so. And furthermore, there will be a letter terminating you on your desk by noon Monday." (January 11, 1971)

Pres said, "I just don't think that there is a choice. What you're asking me to do is impossible."

Pres then turned to Dawson, the man whom he had

recommended so strongly for the job. "Gene, I don't understand how you can do this to a friend."

"It isn't as easy as you think," Dawson replied. "There's not much more to say." It was his only contribution to the meeting.

Pres paused. "Well, there have been some beautiful moments, gentlemen."

He left the room with the two men still sitting at the table. He walked to his car, his composure crumbling, sat down, and turned the key. Forest Lawn kitsch lay everywhere before him. The radio came on; it was playing "To Dream the Impossible Dream." He sat and cried.[3]

The Lone Mountain Schism

When Pres recovered he drove to a phone booth and called Orton and two other Overseers, David Guyer and Anne Stephens. The latter two offered support while Orton counselled delay until the Overseers' meeting on January 15. When he finally got home there was another call from Llewellyn requesting a follow-up meeting the next evening at the Holiday Inn in West Covina. Pres had no choice but to go.

The two men sat together uneasily. Pres figured it was his last meal and ordered the biggest steak on the menu. Llewellyn turned to business. "You know, Pres," he said, "Your future is very important here. We hope you'll do the reasonable thing. However if you don't...we'll brand you a trouble-maker and do our best to see that you don't get appointed to anything. We won't recommend you for anything either."[4]

"That's interesting coming from a Presbyterian elder," Pres said to himself. Out loud he said, "Well, I have my instructions from Dwayne that I am not to give you an official answer yet. But I think you know what my answer is."

Fred replied, "I'll tell you what. You can talk to Dwayne if you want, but I want your answer by ten p. m. tonight. That's it. Yes or no."

When he got home he called Orton, who again advised delay. Llewellyn called just before ten. "What's your answer?"

"I'm under instruction from Dwayne not to give you my answer yet."

"Then I have your answer," said Llewellyn. And he hung up.

The next day, shortly after noon, Llewellyn and Dawson appeared in Pres' office just before a faculty meeting was about to begin. They handed him the letter of termination and then walked next door to the conference room, where faculty meetings were always held. Unaware — or unconcerned — that Pres could hear every word through the wall, Llewellyn brusquely announced the firing to the faculty. He made much of the fact that it was an accomplished fact, with no appeal or recourse, and that the faculty would simply have to accept it. No explanation beyond "administrative insufficiency" was given. The faculty was stunned.

Then Pres came in. He offered the first account of his understanding of the firing — that the University wanted to control the Johnston experiment more closely and that his stubborn defense of the experiment's integrity and of decentralized power stood in the way. His firing therefore meant, must mean, the end of the Johnston experiment. That perception was not shared by Dawson or Llewellyn. Despite their hostility to McCoy and their serious reservations about certain aspects of Johnston, both men were committed to continuing the college. They really believed that firing McCoy would reduce intra-University friction and benefit rather than harm Johnston.

Not all the faculty were surprised. Years later it was learned that Dawson had offered Pres' job to three people. First, as we have seen, was Jim Hester. Second was Roger Baty. Baty looked and sounded more conservative than most other faculty at Johnston and Dawson felt that he would be a strong, reliable candidate. Baty pondered the offer overnight then turned it down, realizing that no "in-house" replacement could succeed McCoy.

Dawson then turned to Gene Ouellette, chair of the Communicative Disorders and Drama departments. Ouellette was running that year's Interim program. He had impressed Dawson with his quiet efficiency. He had taught communicative disorders at the University since 1964, and he had graduated from Redlands years before after he was discharged from the Marine Corps following the Korean War. Even though he had never held another administrative post, Dawson offered him the job.

Ouellette was silver-haired, strikingly handsome and soft-spoken. He was an astute politician, veteran of any number of skirmishes with Armacost. Dawson telephoned him in Santa Barbara, where he was attending a professional conference. The President offered him the job directly, telling Gene he had only five minutes to decide. Ouellette pleaded for a bit more time, called his wife Anne, thought hard for an hour, then called Dawson back and accepted.

He returned to Redlands for a Sunday morning meeting with Dawson and Llewellyn — a "very calm meeting," he recalls. "There was no talk about big changes." But the following Tuesday he thought he had accepted the leadership of Bedlam:

My first community meeting was an angry one. Pres' termination was announced officially. People were hostile and hurt. They looked on me as a company man, and I could understand why. Dawson and Llewellyn were there with me, but not Pres. I got up to speak — and for a speech professor I'm not a great public speaker — and I was standing with hostile people all around me. Frankly I was scared to death. I remember that one student, Nikko Schoch, offered me a seat. I was always grateful to him for that. People were asking me questions and I had no idea what they were talking about. They were using Johnston jargon that I'd never heard before.

One outcome of the meeting was a statement, dated January 13, signed by ninety students and ten faculty. It denounced Pres' firing, suggesting that it was not an act befitting people who professed the Judeo-Christian ethic. The document tried to respond to the charge that McCoy had been an inefficient administrator by citing the already-functioning structures which organized the Johnston community. It concluded by asking that the Board of Overseers not accept the action of the Executive Committee or its ad hoc evaluating committee. The community approved this statement by consensus and it was duly presented at the Overseers' meeting on January 15.

Both the discussions which preceded it and the document itself were notable for their restraint. Reaction was muted and great care was taken not to alienate the Board of Overseers or to appear to be demanding action. Several faculty emphasized that the document was meant to support the Board in its struggle with the Trustees. It was definitely not an independent manifesto from the community to the Trustees. Direct confrontation of this sort was avoided.

On a wider front, there was an article on Pres' firing in the January 14th edition of *The Facts*. Comically, it reassured readers that Johnston students were not planning violence! The Trustees' action shocked and frightened Johnstonians; these emotions predominated at first over anger, let alone violence.

The January 15th Overseers meeting took place. The original agenda had changed, of course, especially the Chancellor's Report slated to be delivered by McCoy. Instead Ouellette gave a truncated report devoted to faculty appointments. Other ordinary business was conducted as

if no crisis existed. Finally the issue of McCoy's termination was addressed.

David Guyer proposed a resolution that directed the
Trustees to appoint McCoy as "Chancellor for Academic
Affairs" and Ouellette as "Chancellor for Administrative
Affairs," with both responsible to the President. As
Bizarre as such a proposal was for a college with fewer
than three hundred students, it was passed and forwarded
to the Trustees, who predictably rejected it on January 21.

The next community meeting on January 18 discussed
the Overseers' action. They decided to send their January
14 statement to the Trustees and to support the Overseers'
"Two Chancellors" proposal. Ouellette stated that he
would be willing to serve as co-chancellor; he also
reported that McCoy was considering the idea. The next
meeting was called for January 22, the day after the Board
of Trustees Executive Committee meeting that would
consider the proposal.

From all this we conclude that the community was
incapable of decisive protest action during the week
following the high-handed firing of their founder. What
dominates the documentary record is a spirit of almost
timid conciliation and willingness to compromise.
Perhaps people at Johnston felt that they were powerless
in the face of the Board's *fait accompli.* And it is true that
the Johnston style of governance, with consensus and
decentralization of power, inhibited the development of
strong leaders who might have rallied the community into
a more stubborn political resistance.

Although the community did display remarkable flexibility by carrying on normal business during the crisis,
this flexibility did not offer a solid base for united protest.
The power of the community to unite against outside
pressures did not extend to a situation in which several
sorts of real interests were at odds. Many of the faculty
immediately reacted against any strong protest because
that might entail leaving the University. That, frankly,
was too great an economic price to pay. Others did not feel

much loyalty to McCoy — at least not enough to give up their jobs. Still others were outraged, but since they lived by consensus it was difficult to articulate their feelings in a politically effective way. The same can be said of students. Many wanted to stay; some did not like McCoy; still others were angry but had no way to express that anger in the absence of leadership.

During this period of uncertainty an absurd variation on the "Two Chancellors" proposal was being acted out in the Chancellor's office. When Gene Ouellette walked in, for his first official day on the job, Pres' papers still covered the desk and McCoy himself occupied the high-backed chair. "This is all going to be reversed, and my contract will be renewed," Pres told Gene in a friendly, confident tone. In a display of tolerance — a tolerance that would mark Ouellette's chancellorship — Gene urged McCoy to stay right where he was. "I'll work over here," he said, nodding toward a small conference table in a far corner of the room.

Ouellette knew that the only way for him to learn about Johnston was to read everything in the files. So he started in. As questions arose he asked McCoy, who obligingly answered them. Ouellette read for a solid week, and asked for summary reports from all standing committees. During that time he and Pres continued to share the office. There was some question about the Chancellor's University-owned car. Gene asked for the keys but Pres told him that since he was getting his job back he'd keep them for awhile. Ouellette didn't push it.

Faculty and students would walk in to see both men busily at work. Privacy was impossible but hardly seemed necessary. Poor Marilyn Prihoda did have a hard time routing calls through the single phone. "To whom do you wish to speak?," she would ask. The answer, "the Chancellor," didn't help much.

The Community Meeting of January 22 proved crucial. The scene was this: the meeting area of the Orton Center is a large room, some sixty feet by thirty. The ceiling with inlaid fluorescent panelling and modern Danish beam-work, is nearly thirty feet high. Tall plate-glass windows open south toward the open-ended college quad. A rect-angle of recently new but already rather battered couches and chairs form their own large rectangle centered on the deep blue carpet. The seats are all jammed, with large numbers of students and faculty standing behind them, or sitting on the floor in front, or pacing around along the room's walls. In the center of the room is an oversized foot stool used by the two chairpersons of the meeting, pre-med student Mike Wynn and religion professor Doug Bowman.

The meeting began with a report from Gene Ouellette stating that the Trustees "could not accept" the "Two Chancellors" proposal. Copies of the refusal were handed around and a few were fixed to the walls, where they remained long after the proposal was a dead issue. McCoy was present, with his wife Doris Lee. After the Ouellette announcement was read there were a few cries of outrage — though no one was really surprised. For a moment nothing was said. Then Pres raised his hand, Mike Wynn recognized him, and he spoke:

> I want to thank all the members of the community for their support. I trust that this latest action of the Board of Trustees, which Chairman Llewellyn communicated to me this morning, will be com-municated to those community members presently off campus. Even though the highest priorities of the Chancellor's office have been met, some of those further down the line, in my mind, were evidently more important to those in power. The action of President Dawson and the Board of Trustees in repudiating the Overseers' initiative breaks their pledge of a three year period without significant structural change for our experiment. The Board appears to have broken their own principles of 'good faith and credit' in substance and in method. By their action they have done a

great injustice to me personally, to Johnston College and to their own University. The whole incident should be an example to us of how vicious, violent and unscrupulous those in power in institutions can be. Their actions violate a basic principle of Johnston — that the individual is of the highest value — that personal growth is most important.

Note the secret way in which the firing was carried out. Note the timing (during Interim), while many of our members were away from campus. Note their refusal to allow the Overseers to hold a hearing on the issue...these actions do not speak very highly of the Board of a Christian college.

Next came a recitation of the litany of charges against him; these are familiar by now to the reader. "I even brought him a present from Hawaii," he added pathetically. McCoy moved toward his conclusion:

Johnston College is not built on this campus. It is the living embodiment of a vision which we've brought into being, and which other colleges have emulated. One of our administrative problems has been the great number of visitors on campus. We perhaps should have foreseen this. But all of these administrative problems are not the real issue. The real issue is centralization versus decentralization.

His voice began to tremble:

Johnston College exists where the people are. I promise never to desert you. If the majority of Johnston faculty and students (supported by their parents in writing) wish to relocate, I stand ready to serve you. You can individualize education.

Don't deceive yourselves about centralization. The erosion may be slow but don't doubt it. It's happened in other colleges, due to the nature of decisions not involving people. There is no arm-twisting behind this. I am stating it out of commitment. On vital issues we of Johnston College have been together. At Pilgrim Pines last year it was stated that if at any time there was a threat to our academic autonomy, we would fight it. If not here, then let us leave and form a truly integrated philosophical program of living and learning. It is my conviction that what we want to do is impossible here. Centralization eliminates the conviction of individual worth on which we are based.

It will not be easy to relocate. This will be interest-ing but difficult. I feel it would be a mistake to delay this response. But I want it fully discussed by you. If you choose to remain here, so be it. This statement has been motivated by hope, promise and a vision of things to come. This has been a wonderful learning experience for me at Johnston College, probably the greatest of my life.

There were shouts, tears, a standing ovation.

McCoy's proposal instantly empowered political action. A task force was formed which drafted a letter to Johnston people who were off campus for Interim. This letter, along with an official letter from Ouellette, were sent out that night.

There was discussion about withholding tuition payments and about getting control of the Johnston grant. There was talk about applying parental pressure on the Hill to reverse its decision. The faculty met immediately after the community meeting to form planning commit-tees of its own.

At the next community meeting on January 26 McCoy

discussed possible relocation sites. These included Loyola Marymount in Los Angeles, Pitzer College at Claremont and Lone Mountain College in San Francisco. Pres claimed that these institutions had all contacted him. Each had problems, but Lone Mountain seemed to have the fewest. It was ideally located on a large, under-utilized campus in the heart of San Francisco, where Johnston could have its own dormitory facilities and access to the city. This was appealing despite the fact that Lone Mountain was beseiged by financial problems and the fact that it was a Catholic college run by sisters. Not even Rene Francillon's estimate that at least $250,000 would be needed to finance just one hundred students dampened enthusiasm.

By February 7, when the rest of the community had returned from their off-campus Interim projects, Pres was able to announce the support of two Overseers, Dave Guyer and Anne Stephens. Both had resigned because of the firing and were willing to serve on a new Board. By now, though, some practical problems were making inroads on the initial enthusiasm. Scholarships, faculty salaries, McCoy's salary, moving expenses — such economic questions were difficult to answer with assurance. Pres had, at least initially, only secondary interest in such questions; the injustice of the firing and the vision of a new Johnston filled his mind.

The faculty, as well as the students, were beginning to take sides. Doug Bowman and Don Miller were the first leaders of the Lone Mountain group. Six others — the Corneils, Landa, McDonald, O'Neill and Watt — joined them, for a total of eight faculty leaning toward the move. Vice-Chancellor Williams, who had not been fired, decided after much soul-searching to remain behind as leader for those committed to staying. This included historian Bob Treacy, political scientist Vishwanath More, philosopher George Derfer, and psychologists Glenn Whitlock and Walter Tubbs. Several faculty remained undecided. Though this division of faculty was painful and caused some animosity, Bowman argued convincingly that the personal decision of each faculty member should be respected and that any "us vs. them" confrontations should be avoided. Remarkably, they were.

Nor did the split in the faculty prevent united action on other issues. On February 2, during semester break, the full faculty issued a statement asking that the Trustees approve clarifications and revisions in the rules governing college-Trustee relations. The new rules stipulated that the faculty would be responsible for "generating...educational policies in consultation with the students and in concurrence with the Board of Overseers" and that "termination or alteration of existing academic policies and practices of Johnston College require formal concurrence of the Johnston College faculty." The policy statement also stipulated that faculty hiring and firing and "any personnel changes with regard to the positions of Chancellor and Vice-Chancellor must be enacted with full faculty consultation," and further that both officers "hold dual administrative/faculty appointments." Last, the statement announces the creation of the position of Chairperson of the Faculty, "who shall sit as an *ex officio* member on all administrative and academic committees and who shall have access to all information regarding academic policy and other matters of faculty concern."

This statement was designed to protect any new Chancellor and to give the faculty more power in making administrative personnel decisions. It was also intended to guarantee academic autonomy to the faculty. The statement was passed by the Board of Overseers at their February 5 meeting, and, to everyone's surprise, by the Board of Trustees on February 16. A little reflection, admittedly, made the Trustees' move much less surprising. The statement gave the faculty no new powers except that of consulting with the Trustees on the appointment or firing of administrative officers. Faculty still lacked any control over such appointments. In approving the statement the Trustees managed to placate the Johnston community without the loss of any significant power.

Meanwhile, Gene Ouellette had moved past his initial bewilderment with the ways of Johnston College and was beginning to find the place intriguing, even seductive. He was impressed by the friendliness and candor he encountered almost everywhere. The initial hostility evaporated quickly. Ouellette was also compelled to adapt in another way; like his predecessor, he was almost immediately embroiled in a dispute with Dawson.

The issue was faculty contracts. Ouellette was shocked to discover that 80 percent of the Johnston budget was already spent by the end of January. Dawson wanted Ouellette to rescind several raises and salary adjustments that McCoy had negotiated with individual faculty and to wait until September to issue any faculty contracts at all. Ouellette reluctantly agreed with the first request but refused to delay the issuing of the next year's contracts. He avoided a major confrontation by offering to spend more time in fund-raising than he had originally agreed to. Unlike McCoy, Ouellette was capable of political compromise. This ability kept him out of a full-blown adversarial relationship with the Hill, at least for a little while.

Dwayne Orton appeared at the February 8 community meeting. He reviewed his relationship with Johnston, noting that he had failed to educate the Trustees sufficiently about what to expect from an experimental college. He also acknowledged McCoy's central role in founding the college, and praised the students for their constructive reaction to the firing. But he ended his speech by affirming that Johnston could survive and even flourish on the Redlands campus. He announced that he was remaining on the Board of Overseers.

The meeting was opened to questions. Bowman felt that if people did stay at Redlands, after having declared for Lone Mountain, they might suffer recriminations from the Trustees. Several students discussed the question of whether Trustee perceptions of Johnston could be changed. Orton answered that one Trustee, Arthur Willis, *had* changed his perception. Mary Lou Stuart, a sophomore asked why Johnston students had to wait so long for alleged adults to "come up to our level" — a question which perfectly encapsulated student frustration and Johnston arrogance.

Orton was then asked whether he thought McCoy's dismissal had been a "power play attempt to get control over Johnston." Orton replied that he did not think so. All he had been told was that McCoy had not consulted enough with Redlands administrators and that he hadn't developed a good working relationship with them. Orton's answer conveyed something more: he had clearly separated himself from McCoy's cause and adopted the University position. The relationship which had begun so well three years before with the sharing of a dream was effectively over. The major outcome of this critical meeting, then, was not renewed enthusiasm for moving, but the further isolation of Pres McCoy.

Llewellyn took exception to Orton's appearance at a community meeting. Apparently basing his reaction on second-hand information, he wildly accused Orton of sowing further dissension. Orton replied sharply, indicating that his presence was anything but divisive. He made it clear to Llewellyn that however much he disagreed with the fact and the manner of Pres' firing he was still casting his lot with the University, not with the break-away group.

At the February 15 meeting of the Overseers Ouellette made his first full-fledged Chancellor's report. "Morale is low and there are feelings of unease and distrust," he said, "springing from an apprehension that the experimental nature of the college will change or that there will be a loss of academic autonomy." Ouellette acknowledged the activities of the Lone Mountain separatist group but noted that the great majority of new transfer students had elected to remain at Johnston and that ten faculty were definitely committed to remaining at Johnston-in-Redlands. He now believed that some 16 of the faculty eventually would decide to stay. He also noted that all faculty were conducting business as usual. In the same vein Ouellette characterized students as "looking for reassurance" rather than as disaffected.

Beginning on January 22 a series of meetings took place between McCoy and those students and faculty who wanted to move the school to Lone Mountain. The membership of the defecting group varied from meeting to meeting but there was a core of "schismatics" who worked hard on the project all through February and well into March. This entailed repeated visits to San Francisco to negotiate with the administrators at Lone Mountain. Kevin O'Neill recalls one such trip, which was typical:

In early February five of us headed north in Pres' late-model Oldsmobile station wagon. Pres was a very fast driver who paid little attention to maintaining his car. It shimmied badly at highway speed. McDonald was riding in front with McCoy. I was in the back seat with Doris Lee and Michel Landa. Heading north toward Boron on old Highway 395, the wave-like rise and fall of the two lane road was hypnotic. Conversation, which had been animated at the beginning of the journey, died out as we crossed the endless expanses of the high desert. The day had grown warm.

McDonald looked over, somewhat anxiously, at the speedometer. It was hovering just past 100. Then he looked at McCoy. Anxiety blossomed into panic: Pres was asleep. Three, four, five terrible seconds passed; miraculously the car still hugged the road. What could Bill do? He obviously couldn't let him sleep at that speed, no matter how much he needed the rest. But if Bill woke him up, one jerk of the wheel at that speed and the Lone Mountain movement would end right there. Bill finally eased his hand onto the wheel and whispered to Pres. He did awake with a start, but the wheel remained firm.

When we stopped for gas — and coffee! — an attendant at the station pointed out that the car shimmied because it had four bad tires. While the rest of us went to a restaurant Pres was somehow persuaded to buy four new tires at a cost of well over three hundred dollars, which he paid in cash. With supernatural disdain he ignored the shocking expense as a minor irritation. Drawing inferences was hard to avoid....

As we turned west on the Interstate on the last leg of the journey, conversation was once more lively. For three of us it would be the first visit to Lone Mountain. But we had to wait a little longer to see the promised land. Pres ran out of gas on the traffic-clogged Oakland freeway: a long walk to a Chevron station and a long walk back. We reached Lone Mountain after a high speed ten hour drive to San Francisco. The trip normally took eight. More inferences were inevitably drawn....

At the San Francisco campus we were met by Dean Fred Hudson. After an hour of negotiation it was clear that Hudson was more interested in his own future position than in the future of Johnston College. But meetings the following day with Sister Patch, Lone Mountain's president, were much more reassuring. Her courtesy and fairness through the long weeks of negotiation earned her the respect of everyone she dealt with. After dealing with Redlands administrators she seemed a paragon of wisdom and understanding.

The beauty of the site alone — a park-like hill with imposing buildings in the old Russian section of town near Golden Gate Park — was enough to keep negotiations moving. There could be no more lovely or versatile setting for the new Johnston. Pres and his followers drafted detailed terms of an agreement which stressed living-learning autonomy; that mistake would not be repeated. The Lone Mountain community seemed ready to accept us. On February 26 the students voted more than 2 to 1 to approve the merger, and a March date was set for the final vote of the Lone Mountain Board.

Back in Redlands a February poll of students published in the *Daily Facts* showed that nearly half were ready to move. But by March the number was dropping. Seventy-four students were pledged to move, but those committed to Redlands or undecided now numbered 215. And rifts began to develop over Fred Hudson's ambiguous promises, financial uncertainties, and perhaps most important, over Pres' relations with the faculty.

Glenn Whitlock dropped out of the Lone Mountain movement very early in the game. This happened a day after a long faculty T-group at Pres' house, on January 17th. Whitlock recalls that Pres agreed to several things at that T-group, but reneged when he sensed strong student support for his original views the next day in the January 18 community meeting. That was enough for Whitlock. McCoy did not appear to be willing to stick by his promises. Allen Killpatrick went with Pres on his first trip to Lone Mountain but quickly became disenchanted with the financial complications of the plan. He too dropped out.

The most dramatic loss was Doug Bowman, early leader of the defectors, who left the Lone Mountain group after a bizarre incident which came to be known in Johnston legend as the "Meeting of the Three Deans." There are at least two versions of the tale, and we will relate both, since the honest memories of the principals differ significantly. First, here is Bowman's account. He and Pres flew to San Francisco on February 18 to continue negotiations. During the flight Pres asked Doug whether he would like to be the academic dean of the new Johnston, since Ed Williams had elected to stay in Redlands. Doug accepted.

The next day, after talks with Lone Mountain staffers, Doug renewed his acquaintance with Malcolm MacAfee, father of a Johnston student and an avid supporter of experimental education, and Robert Greene, the organizer of the Johnston Parents Association and father of two students. As Doug remembers it, Pres asked the three of them to wait for him while he attended to another matter. They went into one of the Lone Mountain classrooms, with their traditional rows of chairs facing front. As they talked a Johnston student walked down the hall outside the room singing a slightly scurrilous folk song about the Virgin. Conversation turned to the structure of the new Johnston.

"I'm willing to accept the deanship," said MacAfee. "I think that with my experience I can help both the students and the faculty."

Bowman looked at him, incredulously. "But on the plane up here yesterday," he said, "Pres offered *me* the deanship — for the time being anyway."

And Robert Greene chimed in: "Wait a minute! Pres gave me to understand that...."

The three men looked at each other. The Dean's office, they realized, was going to be very crowded. Bowman remembers the haunting song about the Virgin wafting down the hall. It was the dirge of his participation in the move to Lone Mountain....

Both Pres and Robert Greene recall a different, less arresting set of events (we could not locate Malcolm MacAfee). Greene does not recall the conversation in the classroom. McCoy did approach him about his interest in working for the new Johnston in San Francisco, but no definite offer was made. And McCoy insists that Bowman, at least, mistook an inquiry for an offer: "there was no offer as such put in writing with salary. I should have been clearer as to the distinction between inquiry and offer...I wouldn't have done anything as crazy as that." Bowman's account, however, entered Johnston's oral history, and further discouraged several faculty about the prospects for an orderly move to Lone Mountain.

There were other problems. Some students and some faculty wanted to make the new Johnston more egalitarian than the old, in effect undercutting McCoy's authority as Chancellor. This was an extension of feelings that had been expressed in the Cherry Valley Retreat the previous autumn, and Pres' position remained the same. He would willingly listen to advice but he would not relinquish his position as leader. And part of this position was that he wanted to receive the same high salary (approximately $30,000) at Lone Mountain as he had at Johnston. Given the financial risks attending the move such a demand seemed unreasonable to many, and led to more defections.

But it was the "Three Deans" fiasco which had the most damaging effect. It made faculty doubt Pres' good sense; worse, it made them question his mental stability. The incident seemed a desperate attempt to maintain support at any cost.

On February 16 the faculty issued a statement which affirmed faith in the University and pledged support for Johnston College in its present location. This statement, which the University welcomed, was composed by the group of faculty who had chosen to stay, but since it appeared as if it were a resolution passed by the whole faculty it further demoralized the Lone Mountain people.

Despite all this the movement continued into the second week of March. A Lone Mountain Board meeting was scheduled for March 13; this would decide the issue.

At Redlands life was returning to normal. The University had done nothing to the college beyond firing McCoy. Even defecting faculty took leading roles in working on governance proposals and academic procedures. On April 6 several Johnston faculty were awarded University research grants for which they must have applied some weeks earlier. Among the winners of the grants were four who had been involved in the Lone Mountain project.

Everyone, it seems, had begun to hedge their bets.

Suddenly, on March 12, it was revealed to the press that the Lone Mountain movement had come to an abrupt end. Doug Bowman was the spokesman even though he was ill and had missed the crucial meeting in San Francisco. He stated that financial problems, "difference of opinion," and "an inability to work out compatible relationships" had combined to kill the move even before it was voted on by the Lone Mountain Board. Two faculty, Don Miller and Michel Landa, countered in a *Daily Facts* article that the Lone Mountain project was still alive. But their optimism was unfounded. The Lone Mountain Board cancelled its March 13 meeting because the Johnston group had failed to submit a final proposal setting terms for the move. When that Board met in May it formally rejected the Johnston initiative, though by that time there was no formal plan to reject.

Thus Lone Mountain died, and with it McCoy's effective connection with the Johnston community. It can be understood as a last show of loyalty to McCoy, and as an attempt to relocate Johnston in an atmosphere more conducive to its survival. It can also be understood as a protest against the manner in which McCoy was fired. But in the meetings on Lone Mountain, which were in effect the hearing that Pres never got from the Trustees, his colleagues and students ultimately rejected him as their leader. The heart of the failure was not Pres' administrative ability. It was a combination of fear and mistrust, fear of financial risk on the part of faculty, and mistrust of McCoy's need for authority on the part of many students.

The break with McCoy was very painful but can be seen as a maturing process; faculty and students overcame McCoy's charisma and gained a certain independence in the process. But this process left McCoy unemployed and bitter, and it left some faculty and students with a guilt that could not be easily assuaged. That June Pres said: "I would have put my job on the line for Jeanne Friedman if she had chosen to fight for a full-time job. I would any-time, anywhere, for any faculty I felt deserved reappoint-ment. And frankly I felt the faculty would do the same for me." But they wouldn't, and didn't. The founder had been discarded.

The erstwhile defectors rejoined the community without recriminations. Gene Ouellette helped the healing process by welcoming the Lone Mountain people back, even as he had supported them during their attempt to leave. Just as he had been able to share an office with Pres, he proved capable of sharing the college with the Lone Mountain group without the slightest hostility — an attitude which certainly influenced the potential defectors not to leave. This, combined with the shared trust and sense of mission forged during eighteen months of T-grouping and meetings and struggle, made the reintegra-tion of faculty and students virtually effortless. Johnston rejoined itself and went on.

The remainder of the spring semester of 1971 was anti-climactic. The community was exhausted. It did little more than tinker with established procedures. And it concentrated on academic work, which had suffered during the crisis. On May 19, Carl Yetzer of the *San Bernardino Sun*, who had attended many of the stormy community meetings in February (and had been thrown out of at least one), wrote an article entitled "Johnston College Resigned to Dismissal of Chancellor." He noted that despite Ouellette's efforts and the reintegration of defectors, a deep resentment still festered among the students. They felt that "they had been...lied to and...cheated." Twenty-eight withdrew as a direct result of the firing, and a projected enrollment of 400 for the Fall semester dwindled to 350; in September only 298 students actually enrolled. Word about the firing had spread to the high schools and students were afraid that Johnston had lost its experimental character.

McCoy made his final public statement in Yetzer's article. He attributed his firing to his refusal to "make the Johnston College students knuckle under to the more conservative living restrictions imposed by the Trustees." Yetzer added the inflammatory suggestion that Llewellyn had applied pressure to the Lone Mountain Board to make them reject the Johnston proposal. Gene Ouellette denied this charge in the same article, and we found no evidence to support it. Frankly, there was no reason for Llewellyn to apply any pressure; the Lone Mountain project unraveled on its own.

On the day the Yetzer article appeared Ouellette was officially named Chancellor (rather than acting Chancellor) with the unanimous endorsement of the faculty and the majority of the students. The McCoy era was at an end.

The legacy of the firing and the Lone Mountain movement was of mixed value. The entire series of events had strengthened the siege mentality at Johnston and produced a permanent skepticism about the University's intentions. Ironically, the University officials seem to have lost interest in Johnston after this and restricted themselves to attacks on the college's financial position. Significantly less was heard about student behavior, life in the dormitories or academic accountability. It was as if, having gotten rid of the man who symbolized all the supposed countercultural defiance at Johnston, and having assured themselves that they could exercise power without fear of violent student uprisings, the powers-that-be concluded that Johnston was no longer a great threat. The cat had been belled. Johnston mistrust was now met with Administration lack of interest. This gave Ouellette a short grace period in which to establish himself as Chancellor and to re-establish, if he could, a healthy Johnston.

The grace period would not be ended by ideological or political tensions. The era of protest was nearly over and Dawson was much less interested in student behavior than Armacost had been. What began to preoccupy the

Administration was money. The postwar baby boom was over; students were harder to find and the upheavals of the sixties had ended the long American enchantment with Higher education. Students were less interested in college and parents trusted colleges less.

The University's deficits continued to rise. Enrollments stagnated or dropped. Johnston failed to grow. The Age of Aquarius was over, and Johnston seemed permanently wedded to that era. Students were less and less interested in such an atmosphere, and enrollment figures reflected this. Naturally, as enrollments stagnated or decreased budget problems increased. The new decade would be a long, losing struggle against diminishing enrollments and growing deficits, accompanied by constant University pressure to break even and little University support to make Johnston more marketable.

But increasing problems with enrollment and budget did not prevent Johnston from flourishing as an academic institution and as a community. Even as it became less appealing to potential students, Johnston became a more and more effective college. The Ouellette years were the zenith of the college's development, the coming to fruition of the institution which McCoy had founded but had not been permitted to nurture into its maturity.

The next section of this book will tell the story of Johnston's coming of age and its demise as a separate institution. We have chosen to do so by focusing on two periods — 1974-5 and 1978-9 — using material from other years as necessary to give a coherent account of developments.

NOTES:

1. Pres, unwittingly, had committed another major administrative *faux pas*, this time while absent from campus. Between fund-raising appointments in New York City, he contacted Orton about a candidate for the vice chancellor for administration position, a man with Danforth

connections who had been highly recommended to him. Orton asked for a letter confirming the information, with a copy to Dawson. On the day when Pres returned to Redlands he received a blistering memo from the President. He was outraged that a mere carbon copy had been sent to him, the head of the University. McCoy, understandably, had trouble taking this offense seriously since he had simply followed the instructions of his Board chairman, but the infamous 'carbon copy' returned to haunt him. He apologized in writing to Dawson, but noted in the same letter that Dawson had sounded out a University administrator for the job without consulting McCoy.

2. Colonel Wogen, in a burst of tactical brilliance, perpetrated an infamous fire drill that fall. Wogen directed that the fire alarm in East Hall be set off very early in the morning so that he could count how many male students stumbled out of the women's dorm. There were several. There were hearty guffaws and loud comments from the onlookers. Prisoners were not taken, but congratulations for the colonel for this statesmanlike operation were certainly in order.

3. Gene Dawson recalls a night meeting just before this, attended by the same three people, at which Pres was "all but told" that he was fired. "Firing Pres," he added, "was a necessary surgery to save the patient." McCoy's shock indicates that the "all but told" message had not been received.

4. It is Pres' understanding that Llewelllyn denies saying these things to him. Since Llewellyn was "too busy" to be interviewed for this history, we cannot be sure. The above conversation is based entirely on Pres' recollection.

Section Two

1974-75:
Johnston at Its Zenith

History ought to work its subjects to their
imaginative limits.

— Irving Howe

First we make our experiments, then they
make theirs.

— Virginia Woolf, *The Years*

CHAPTER **5**

"The System"

A student entering Johnston College in the fall of 1974 enrolled in a notably different institution from the one which had attempted to flee to Lone Mountain two and one half years earlier. Johnston was still an experimental college but the ways in which it was experimental were largely established. There was no serious sentiment that the fundamental design should be scrapped; the great majority of Johnstonians felt that the experiment had succeeded.

Johnston students of this era were less radical, more willing to accept established tradition. A "typical" student in 1974-75 was female (always a majority at the college), from out of state, white, and a consistently good performer in high school (though her SAT scores were slightly lower than those of the founding class). She was more career-oriented and less wary of taking classes at the University than her predecessors. But she was still a leftist politically and a feminist like her predecessors; even in an era when students were growing more conservative Johnston people remained "counter-cultural" in these respects. She was sexually active, used drugs about as frequently as her peers in other colleges, and valued her friends enormously.

We have chosen one student to represent the class which entered Johnston in 1974. We call her Sherry Austin — not her real name. She was not a freshman but, like many who came to Johnston, a transfer; she had completed two years at Simmons College in Boston. The oldest of three daughters, she had lived in a small manufacturing city near Cape Cod all her life and loved the Cape's beauty and culture.

She had enjoyed her two years at Simmons, but felt that she needed to escape the Northeast. She learned about Johnston from a student who spent a semester at Simmons as part of an ongoing exchange program between the two schools. She applied to Johnston and was immediately accepted. Her father, a middle-management banker, tried hard to dissuade her, but with the inevitable results. For the record, Sherry had good grades at Simmons and had also done well in high school. Her SATs were 630 verbal, 510 quantitative.

Sherry arrived on campus in the same late afternoon dry heat and smog that had greeted the first Johnstonians. The trees ringing the quad were taller and the sidewalk bordering the lawn now sported a giant Monopoly board, but no buildings had been added. The planned classroom complex, and with it the projected 600 member student body, were now subjects for humor, not fund-raising. There was a student-built geodesic dome just east of East Hall, and a large platform for a second one stood in the open field to the south. A sign on its frame proclaimed, optimistically, "Women's Center."

The dorms were by this time co-ed, a change that was now taken for granted. Sherry had a choice of "interest" lobbies: "cross-cultural," "quiet," "women's" and others. She could even opt for the increasingly popular single-sex lobby.

A complete student life staff greeted her. There was not only a Dean but an Associate Dean of students as well, plus student hall managers (three per dorm). The once-sealed windows could now be raised and there was a brisk market in sleeping lofts, new and used. The walls of lobbies and stairwells were covered with murals, and the dorm had a lived-in look — including stains on the carpet from various animals and a good deal of gratuitous damage to lobby furnishings.

Sherry's roommate, a shy freshperson, arrived in the same style: faded jeans, backpack, and stereo. Both were surprised that the entering class had only fifty-five members.

Sherry's first academic experience was "curriculum building," an event which usually followed some days of new student orientation. Year-opening college-wide retreats were a thing of the past; they had been replaced by the "GYST"[1], which took place in mid-semester. As she walked into the dining area of the Orton Center, she saw columns of paper all along the south wall. Each was headed by a faculty member's name. Taped under each name were descriptions of proposed courses together with sign-up sheets. Some of these were already nearly full. At the end of the list, after "Williams," she found a potpourri of student-proposed courses. At twenty-seven of the round dining tables placed randomly in the large room she saw her new faculty members. She was slightly relieved to see that indeed they looked like real faculty types; her father's warnings had left their mark. In 1969 there were seven professors under the age of thirty. Now there were none.

Some of the faculty were sitting by themselves, or talking quietly with a single student. Others were surrounded by students lobbying for a course or negotiating class contracts. Knots of people studied the class proposals on the wall. Armed with the name of her assigned advisor, Sherry quickly located him at a table and, after introducing herself, asked "What do I do now?"

"The courses listed over there, under the faculty names, are the tentative offerings for this semester. Nothing is absolutely set, but it's likely that most of the courses offered by faculty will be taught in one form or another. In fact, a lot of those courses were actually proposed by students last semester who have graduation contracts to complete. They have to make sure that certain classes are taught."

"I thought that everything was negotiable at Johnston. This looks pretty settled."

"Well, things aren't as spontaneous as they once were — but we need to order books beforehand, and people do need certain classes. Usually about a third of the classes are really spur-of-the-moment."

"So — what do I do?"

"Go over to the wall, move down the row of proposals and see what's being offered. Take notes if that will help. Then go to the area meetings."

"Area meetings?"

"Starting this afternoon, groups of faculty from different areas — humanities or psychology — will meet in the alcoves in the next room. Each faculty person will describe his or her proposed classes and answer questions about them. Students who are teaching classes in that area, or who want to get classes in that area, will also speak. You're a transfer, right?"

"Yes."

"Okay, then, after you look over the class listings and go to the area meetings and negotiate with faculty, come and see me. We need to get started on your graduation contract."

"Okay. By the way, how many classes should I sign up for?"

"Depends on what kind of classes you pick. Some require a lot more work than others. It used to be that people took three courses per semester, plus one more during Interim. The idea was that Johnston classes would be hard enough so that three per semester would be a full workload. But that was idealistic. Now most people take four classes a semester and do well. But I wouldn't take more than that, if I were you. So, why don't you look at the listings and go to the meetings, then check in with me?"

Eventually Sherry picked seminars in "International Political Economy" and "Philosophy of Law"; she also signed up for a student-taught course, "The Psychology of Women," and a tutorial in "Myth and Symbols." She also indicated interest in participating in the activities of the Wilderness program, one of Johnston's physical education options. Classes began two days later.

Sherry first encountered the theory and practice of course contracting in her "Philosophy of Law" seminar. The contract was the bedrock of the course, indeed the academic life of the college. It was a document negotiated — the operative word — between individual faculty and students in a class. The quadruplicate form itself contained three segments on each sheet. First came the listing of necessary information — the semester, the names of the student and the instructor, and the class title, with meeting times and places. The second section was a "Course Description" which cataloged resources (e.g., faculty, special research materials, laboratories, field trips), a reading list, the level of difficulty and, most important, the general purpose of the class. Each of these items was subject to negotiation.

The third section was the body of the contract. Here Sherry specified what she hoped to learn in the seminar and the means she would employ to achieve her goals. This section included information on what sort of papers she would write, how many reports she would present, and what academic skills she would try to perfect. She then noted, as best she could, what bearing the class had on her graduation plan and estimated the percentage of her study time that the course would consume. She stipulated her commitment to attend regularly and to participate in class discussions. She also had special expectations of the faculty member — her philosophy background was thin and she wanted extra help — and said as much here. Finally she agreed to evaluate herself, the seminar, her peers and the faculty member in writing at the end of the term. She kept a copy of the contract, signed by both herself and the faculty member. The faculty member also kept a copy, while others went to the registrar and her adviser. This document was negotiated and filed during the first three weeks of the semester and constituted her official registration for "Philosophy of Law." She went through similar negotiations for each of her other courses.

Sherry soon learned that her contract also formed the basis for evaluation at the end of the term. Sherry's professor would write an account of her work which addressed the points specified in the contract. These evaluations were now typed on standard forms and typically ran between 200 and 400 words. These evaluations eventually made up the major part of Sherry's academic transcript. The amateurish, impressionistic evaluations of the college's first days had disappeared entirely.

In preparing the evaluation the faculty author would, ideally, pay close attention to the "Course Evaluation Form" which Sherry had written. Typically she and the instructor would share impressions of the class at a face-to-face meeting. At that time she also handed in her written evaluation. This form had three sections. The first, "Self Evaluation," urged Sherry to take "a couple of hours" to complete the form because a thoughtful self-assessment could give her a valuable overview of her learning. Specific questions included the amount of time she actually spent in preparation for each class meeting, the usefulness of the course for her overall educational plan and her candid estimate of the strengths and weaknesses of her performance.

The second section posed a series of questions about the course itself, including queries about the contributions of her fellow students, the extent of her influence on the course design, and the overall academic quality of the seminar. The third section, evaluation of the faculty member(s), had political as well as academic significance. It began with the sobering information that "student evaluations of the faculty are used by the Personnel Committee as a major component of overall faculty evaluation. What you say here will have an effect on the future make-up of the Johnston faculty." She was then asked to evaluate her instructor's availability, enthusiasm, preparedness, knowledge and the like. There was even the option of submitting a separate sheet, anonymously, to the registrar, if she feared reprisals for her remarks. But here, as in her self-evaluation, Sherry soon learned that anonymity was rarely invoked. Open, and surprisingly honest evaluation was the order of the day. This was a legacy of T-grouping. Though such groups were no longer a required part of Johnston education, the ethos of expressing, and encountering expressions of, feelings lived on.

This ethos of honesty extended to an informal honor code: cheating and plagiarism were almost non-existent at Johnston. Such acts ran so counter to the spirit of the place that they just did not happen: socialization to the "Johnston Way" was swift and efficient.

Everyone, Sherry learned, took class evaluations seriously. While students tended to be too harsh on themselves and too lenient with faculty, most evaluations were thoughtful and some were acute. A proof of their seriousness was the fact that they were almost never brief. While faculty evaluations of students ran to one or one and a half pages, student evaluations of classes typically filled all three pages of the form and ran over onto the back of the sheets. Professors also took them seriously and ignored what they said at their peril. Indications that a faculty member was not connecting with students usually presaged mass desertion from that person's classes.

Sherry and her roommate spent time complaining about all the paperwork, and about having to deliver copies of all these forms to different people. But such records were made and delivered with surprising regularity; despite its cumbersome nature the contract/evaluation system was something students recognized as among the most valuable components of their education. The contract form made it clear that a Johnston class was a negotiated experience entered into freely by faculty and student alike. Student evaluations confirmed the fact that the class was a shared enterprise, not one produced by the faculty member and consumed by the student. Responsibility for the class and for candid evaluation of its results lay with both parties.

Classes were usually defined operationally: the class entailed the doing of certain tasks by both parties to the contract. Fulfillment of the contract meant the completion of the stipulated tasks. However, the faculty evaluation of the student indicated that though contracting was essentially democratic, the faculty member did have the final say in evaluating student performance. In the long run a student's evaluations could influence whether a faculty member kept his job, but in the short run the public judge of student performance was the faculty member. The system mitigated the faculty's power, but stopped short of revolutionizing it.

These academic forms had important consequences in the classroom. After two years at Simmons, Sherry was especially pleased with the egalitarian feel of her seminars. She found that both her professor and her peers challenged her to do her best work. Though skeptical at first, she soon discovered that she *could* learn a great deal from her fellow students. At Simmons she had listened to the professor and largely ignored what other students said. At Johnston she found that her peers felt that they had a responsibility to make discussions work. They not only read the assignments, they thought about them. On days when they were unprepared they were apologetic, especially in those classes which they valued. Students who regularly failed to complete assignments were looked down on; there was serious social pressure to work hard.

Sherry found that the Johnston seminars covered somewhat less material than her teacher-centered classes at Simmons, but the material was covered more thoroughly and she knew it more fully. Scope was traded for intensity.

One factor contributing to the lower "efficiency" of Johnston classes was the fact that class process was always open for review. If discussions were not going well it was standard procedure to "stop action" to determine what was going wrong. And it was common for classes to have lengthy mid-semester evaluation sessions in which the progress of the course was at issue.

Halfway through the semester Sherry developed a strong interest in the topic of "Space Law," which was also a special interest of her professor in the "Philosophy of Law" seminar. So Sherry renegotiated her class contract; she dropped one of the original readings and substituted a set of articles on this new topic. She and the professor also worked out new paper and report topics to reflect her new enthusiasm.

But Sherry quickly learned that the Johnston system had consequences as well as flexibility. The responsibility for her education, she discovered, rested almost entirely on her shoulders. Although help was always available when she asked for it, her success or failure in classes was purely a function of whether she lived up to her contracts. She found this out at the end of her first semester when she failed to complete one of her papers — the one on space law. She asked the professor for an extension, which he gave her because, as he said, learning could not always be confined within the arbitrary time-frame of a thirteen week semester. So Sherry took her first "W. I. P." (Work in progress). Even though her reasons for not finishing were good ones and even though her professor supported her, she was surprised at how guilty she felt about the WIP. There was no person or institution on which she could place the blame except herself. This was an unexpected — and painful — consequence of taking charge of her own education.

Sherry also found that WIPs created severe practical problems. New demands came with the new semester, and since there was no external pressure to complete the WIP it was easy to keep putting it off. She finally dragged herself through the writing of the paper the following summer. She eliminated the WIP, but Sherry knew that her work had not been nearly as good as it would have been if she had done the work on time when the topic was still fresh and exciting. She never took another one.

Unfortunately, not all students followed Sherry's example; some virtually made a career — or a noncareer — out of WIPs. A few accumulated WIPs in double figures, though this was rare. But a number of otherwise very good students began each semester haunted by three or four unfinished classes. In most cases they had done all the reading and much of the writing for the class and lacked only a final paper to complete the contract. Frequently this happened not out of laziness or indifference, but from a desire to write the "perfect paper." Sadly, too many talented people were lost to the college because the number of WIPs they accumulated discouraged them from every completing their degrees.

WIPs also created bureaucratic chaos. The registrar's office was responsible for collecting evaluations once WIPs were completed, and for keeping a record of which WIPs were outstanding. Since WIPs were most often completed months, even years, after the class ended, contracts were misplaced and faculty forgot details of the student's performance. As a result they often wrote vague, cursory evaluations, irritated that past generosity was costing them later work. Some evaluations for completed WIPs just did not get done. Registrars had to keep records of unfinished classes and were forced to hound faculty to complete evaluations for classes long past. Students suffered from the WIP system, faculty found it annoying — and the registrar's staff hated it.

In 1975 the Graduation Review Committee became so unnerved by the number of students barred from graduating because of WIPs that they unilaterally stipulated that WIPs should no longer be permitted. Though the Committee had no right to make such a stipulation, exasperation made them bold. The matter went to the Academic Policy group which, after much debate , backed the Graduation Review proposal with the alteration that "addenda" could be added to contracts if work was not completed and/or evaluated on time. This proposal, which denied WIPs on one hand and granted them on the other, passed the community meeting shortly afterwards. But the rule was inconsistently applied because, despite the problems WIPs created, the flexibility and trust on which they were based were elemental to the Johnston system. People respected student freedom too much, and faculty strongly believed that nearly everyone who failed to complete a class did so for legitimate academic reasons. No administrator was willing to enforce a policy which, whatever their motives, most community members disliked. The gap between regulations and actual practice — always a wide one at Johnston — was enormous here. Faculty simply kept giving WIPs and the registrar did not have the wherewithal — or the backing — to do much about it. WIPs were the worst consequence of an open academic system, and they were never successfully redesigned. The college did a serious disservice to many of its members by perpetuating them.

In October Sherry met with her adviser to discuss the second crucial portion of her academic program — her graduation contract. She was just on time. Students were urged to get a contract on file during their fourth or fifth semester, and they were required to do so a calendar year before they graduated.

Her adviser explained that, as with class contracts, negotiation was the cornerstone of building a graduation contract. First the two of them would hammer out an overall plan for her degree, and then they would present this plan, in writing, to the Graduation Contract Committee, which was composed of equal numbers of faculty and of students with contracts already on file. When that group approved her contract she had only to complete its terms in order to graduate. Finally, Sherry would meet with the Graduation Review Committee a few weeks before graduation to verify that the work stipulated in the contract had been completed.

"So — how should I begin?" asked Sherry. "I've read the

catalog, and since I'm interested in pre-law I looked at catalogs from some other schools to see what they require for that major. And I talked to my law professor Vishwanath about it. What's next?"

"Well, some people suggest that you study completed graduation contracts to get an idea of how they look. They also tell you to read through the graduation contract guidelines in the catalog and follow those closely. But I have a different approach. This is your contract, Sherry, and your degree. So don't begin with other people's contracts. What I'd suggest is that you start with *your* dreams. At some point the law took on some special magic for you; it became an academic passion. Start with that.

"Why is law so special to you? Why do you want to study it? What do you want to do with it? And how do you want to prepare yourself in it here at Johnston? What would your *ideal* B. A. look like? We'll get to 'reality' soon enough, but let's start with your dream. Think hard about it, write it down and then come back and talk to me. I think you'll be surprised how much of that dream we can make real."

Sherry listened, reflected and decided that the advice was worth trying. So, curled up in a chair with a pad of paper and a glass of wine, she wrote her dream and brought it back to her adviser. First, she wanted a generalist degree, with study in a number of different areas. But she also wanted to have the skills to qualify for the best law schools. She wanted high LSATs, and she wanted to learn to speak Spanish so she could open an affirmative action practice in a major city. She wanted to try her hand at teaching a course, either on her own or, preferably, with a faculty member. There were other interests. She was afraid of heights and wanted to learn rock-climbing to overcome that. She had always had a curiosity about history and wanted to know one period of it really well. She wanted to work in a legal aid clinic. She wanted to study or live overseas — and she wanted to sail around Cape Cod by herself. "And I want to show my mom and dad that coming to Johnston wasn't a mistake!"

"Okay," responded her adviser. "We can't guarantee law school, of course, but we can help your chances. We can also help with the language learning and the overseas experience. You could take a review course in spoken Spanish next Fall, then spend Interim in Mexico with one of Roger Baty's homestay projects. He places you in a rural Mexican home in a small town or small provincial city, and you live that life for a month, among people who know little or no English. Or you could enroll in one of the intensive language courses in Cuernavaca, do an Interim there.

"There's a rock-climbing course that Bob Treacy organizes for the Wilderness Program. They have equipment and expert teachers. Talk to him about it. As to history you could work on a period in American history with Treacy, or on the Renaissance with Barney Childs, or on the ancient Greeks with Bill McDonald and Kevin O'Neill. But you have to go and talk to them to make sure they'll be willing to work with you. If they're not offering a class you want, you can try to interest enough students and lobby for it — or arrange an independent study or tutorial."

"What about the legal aid deal?"

"I don't know. You've got three semesters left after this one, and an internship might take up a lot of time. There is an Action program — as I'm sure you know — and they do sponsor a legal aid clinic. But that is a full-time one year commitment, and it might not be compatible with your law school plans. You might work *with* the Action people though — they're always looking for part-time volunteers. Go and talk with Carol Cespedes and see what you can work out. But you've got to be careful with your time."

"And I mentioned that I might like to help teach a class...."

"Yeah — sorry, I forgot that. What course?"

"Well, something in law, maybe affirmative action law. I could either just do it myself or maybe co-teach with

Vishwanath...."

"Right. Well, you'll have to talk with him about it. It's a good idea. You seem to know a lot about the subject and I'll bet he'd be glad for some help. So, there's another person you have to see...."

"Wow! This could take until I graduate! I've gotta see Baty, Treacy, O'Neill and McDonald, Cespedes and Vishwanath More. Anybody else?"

"Not that I can think of. But you *do* have to decide what area of study you want to concentrate in. What will your degree be *in*? And, once you've decided that you have to start thinking about whether you should do a senior project in that area."

"Senior project? But what would I do it in?"

"Well, let's say that you decide to concentrate in law, or legal studies. You might combine teaching a course and doing a senior project. Say you teach a class in affirmative action law, with special reference to women. Okay, you get a group of students and you stake out your topic or topics. Then you research it and give a group presentation to the school.... Anyway, think about it. It's a good experience to do some capstone work in your field — and it might make an impression on some law schools.

"As far as the rest of your work goes, you've already got a pretty good general education — I mean, you've got a nice spread of courses in different areas. And you already have five classes in political science and law from Simmons, so you'll need several more, upper division of course. I think you'll need something in constitutional law...."

"Wait a minute! That all sounds too cut and dried to me. I want to combine experience with all this. You know, work in a legal aid clinic so I can see whether I even want to go to law school. I could combine theory and practice — maybe do a project on that for senior year. And I could call my degree something a little more interesting like 'Legal Institutions in America,' or 'Law and Politics' — I don't know, something less everyday than 'Pre-Law.'"

"Well...Okay...what if we change the degree to...um...let's

see...how about 'Political Theory and Legal Practice'?"

"Hey! That sounds more like it! Yeah, that's perfect! Can we do it?"

"Well, let's see how it works in terms of courses, and the guidelines in the catalog. Let's look at those first. First, you have to master certain academic methodologies, examine contemporary social and political problems, and integrate academic learning with affective living.... I think you've done a good deal of that already. Now, you're doing PE with the rock-climbing, and you're going to study Spanish and you will live in another culture...and you have a concentration. Looks pretty good, so far. Now all you have to do is write your narrative."

"Narrative?"

"Yes. The Committee asks you to write an autobiographical statement as an introduction to your plan. You address the guidelines we just went over, talk some about your interest in the law and about your future plans and, if you like, about how you got interested in the law in the first place, and even about how education fits in your life as a whole."

"But do I have to tell my whole life story?"

"Not if you don't want to. My rule of thumb is, tell the Committee what it needs to know to help you develop a good contract. Some people think that requires a complete autobiography; some people think it takes a page. That's up to you. In any case you can always rewrite if you don't like it, before your file gets sent to law schools."

"You mean the narrative is part of my transcript?"

"Yes, of course, because your class list makes no sense, in our eyes, without it. It tells why you've taken the courses you have; class evaluations only tell what you've done and how well you've done it. So, since it does go out, sometimes it's important to 'clean it up' for outside audiences."

"Is that it, then?"

"Not quite. Once the narrative is done you have to make up two lists: one, a chronology of classes and activities;

two, a typology of classes according to areas or disciplines, so that people can see just what this concentration in 'Political Theory and Legal Practice' really is, and that you have a good distribution of courses in other areas."

"So, who's on my Committee?"

"We have no idea of that until a few days before the meeting. Membership rotates among faculty and students so it is impossible to tell beforehand exactly which people you'll be dealing with. By rotating faculty and students in and out of the Committee we spread the workload and prevent the standardization that a permanent Committee might produce. I'd advise you to go to a couple of meetings before your contract comes up so you get a feel for how they operate. And keep in mind that this is not an adversarial system. Your contract will be judged, but the primary job of the Committee is to help you refine your contract to make it the best possible plan for you."

Sherry's meeting was scheduled for early December, right before Christmas vacation. Even though she had gone to one meeting where three contracts were considered, she was still nervous because each hearing had been so different and none of the contracts looked like hers. She began to appreciate just how sophisticated the contracting process was: individuals with highly idiosyncratic educational plans were making proposals to a group which did two things. First it applied certain general standards. At the same time the Committee had to understand each contract on its own terms and judge it accordingly.

In the meeting immediately preceding Sherry's several difficulties arose which finally made the meeting acrimonious. A student wanted to graduate in December of 1975; this did not give the Committee much room to negotiate. There were only nine possible courses still "open" and the student had very strong ideas about what he wanted to do with all of them. He resisted negotiation. His major was psychology and he'd devoted himself to that field. He had studied a bit of religion and literature, and there was one course in sociology, but other humanities, and mathematics and the natural sciences, had been wholly neglected. He had an open aversion to experimental psychology, not to mention physics or calculus.

He was pressured, mostly by student members of the Committee, to open up and take courses in more fields. He countered with the argument that the Johnston catalog promised him freedom to plan his own education and the Committee was denying him that freedom. Only he could know what was best for his education. Besides, he was planning to study psychic healing and massage after graduation, and that did not require background in ancient history or quantum mechanics.

His adviser, unhappily, saw himself as an uncritical advocate for the student. Whatever the student wanted the adviser supported. And the student had brought a claque of friends, who joined in the discussion, as was their right, and supported his position energetically. Finally, after several heated exchanges, the meeting broke down. The Committee did not officially reject the contract but said that it could not pass it in its present form. Another meeting was set for January and the student was advised to re-think his attitude to science and history; there was even talk of adding a semester to his plan. The student was still adamant, and by now both hurt and angry. A meeting scheduled for thirty minutes had taken well over an hour. The committee members were irritable and tired. Sherry's was their third contract and it was late afternoon.

The meeting followed a standard form. First the adviser presented Sherry to the Committee, and spoke briefly about her work and her future plans. Then a resource person spoke. The resource person was a faculty member who had gone over her file carefully. He reported on Sherry's academic performance to date, mentioning the WIP and asking several questions about her Simmons courses and grades. Then the convener of the Committee asked Sherry if she would like to say anything.

"Not really," she answered, "I only want to say that I am

serious about studying the law, and that I care about my education — and I'm very willing to negotiate!!" Everyone laughed and the sour flavor of the previous meeting dissipated. Suggestions were made and adopted; course lists were modified slightly. The possibility of a senior project comparing Mexican and American civil liberties law was broached. Sherry liked the idea and promised to think about it. She was encouraged to organize a course under faculty sponsorship as part of her senior project. There was one "stipulation" (i.e., negotiated requirement): Sherry was to take at least one course in sociology to enrich her program.

Sherry accepted that but resisted a strong suggestion that she take a lab science. She persuaded the Committee that her Simmons course in astronomy was sufficient to fulfill the guideline of studying a science. After forty minutes of discussion a vote was taken and the contract passed unanimously. Everyone applauded and congratulated her in the traditional Johnston way — with a bear hug. As she was leaving, the convener reminded Sherry that if she wanted to renegotiate any part of the contract she should file an addendum with the Vice-Chancellor's office. If the proposed change was considered a major shift away from the contract just approved, a new meeting would be held.

Sherry left with a buoyant feeling. She had been treated as a full partner in designing her education. She couldn't wait to get on with it.

Through these two media — the class contract and the graduation contract — Johnston institutionalized both individualism and the academic community. The contract system was vital because it supported both the centrifugal and the centripetal momenta in the college. Contracts were centrifugal in that they defined individual student programs. Each contract was unique, irreducible to any other. But contracts were also centripetal because the defining of individual plans was done in public meetings which established the identity of the college as a community of learning. Contract committee meetings were the most productive community-building events in the middle and later years of the college. They created a common law tradition of what Johnston education should be, and they gave students both a personal and a public identity.

NOTES:

1. Get Your Shit Together. For more genteel publics, "Stuff" or some other euphemism was substituted.

CHAPTER **6**

The Programs

The academic year 1974-75 was the third in Johnston's five year Federal grant from the University Year for Action (UYA), a program administered by VISTA, the domestic Peace Corps.

The idea behind the program was simple. Students would spend a year in community service, working with local agencies to help fight poverty and discrimination. Local agencies would supervise and evaluate students' work; the sponsoring universities would offer faculty support to integrate in-service learning with each student's overall academic program, and to meld practice with theory. Students would provide services; in return UYA would pay them a stipend to cover their living expenses and award the college a grant to fund academic services. It was hoped that some of the projects would prove so valuable to the community that they would be funded locally after the UYA grant ran out. And it was hoped that the UYA stipend would help minority students attend college while assisting their communities at the same time.

Volunteers were to live and work in the target communities. They were not to take regular college classes, but rather work full time at their jobs and do supplemental academic work on-site. Students would learn by a combination of experience and study; supervisors and faculty

164 A HISTORY OF JOHNSTON COLLEGE

would provide technical and theoretical training.

There were several keys to the success of this program. Volunteers had to be high quality people who were well trained for their community service. Universities had to provide preliminary training, and on-site supervisors had to continue that training while the schools offered additional academic back-up. Most important, the academic and experiential components of the work had to be integrated.

The Johnston UYA program was a mixed bag. Dramatic successes were counterpointed by near-comic mismanagement. Student dedication and student irresponsibility were both highly visible. With one major exception the program suffered from a chronic inability to wed the academic with the experiential components of student projects. This was an ironic failure for a college with self-proclaimed expertise in this area. Yet for all its difficulties the Action program made a deep, positive impact on a number of students — and their story bears telling.

The first Action grant was obtained in late 1971 and the program launched in early 1972. The grant funded thirty volunteers and provided money for faculty and administrative support. It was clear that a school as small as Johnston could not easily provide that many volunteers, so from the first year University students were recruited. The initial group had sixteen Johnston people; the percentage of Johnston volunteers never surpassed this and was often much lower in later years.

There were three segments of the Johnston Action program. One group of volunteers worked as probation counselors for juvenile offenders in Indio, an agricultural center in the Coachella Valley about sixty miles southeast of Redlands. Another group tutored in the Redlands and San Bernardino school systems. A third took part in a variety of community development projects — a drug counseling center, a legal aid clinic, and a job counseling facility. Of these, the Indio project was easily the most important and the most successful. Its history began three years before Sherry Austin enrolled at Johnston.

Johnston program administrator Bernie Fisken made the first contacts with the Riverside County Probation Department in Indio, but the development of the program belonged almost exclusively to Dan Gilbertson, a Yale-trained sociologist who joined the Johnston faculty in 1970. In the Fall of 1971 he made the first of what would be hundreds of trips to the desert community.

The Indio branch of the Riverside Probation Department was facing a crisis. Increasing numbers of juveniles, mostly runaways, passed through Indio on their way to Los Angeles. Arrests for vagrancy, shoplifting, drug possession and burglary were up dramatically and the options for dealing with minors, many of them 13 to 15 year olds, were severely limited.

The director of the intake center for juveniles in Indio, Bert Van Horn, wasn't sure what do with the flood of detainees, or with the seven Johnston Action volunteers that he'd agreed to take on as helpers. At first he thought he would herd the juveniles into large holding cells while parents were contacted or arraignments drawn up. Action volunteers would be posted in these cells and would provide activities until the juveniles were either released or moved.

Gilbertson realized that this was little more than crowd control. He made a counterproposal. "What if a team of students talks with each kid before the kid is put in jail?"

"Are you kidding?", said Van Horn. "Do you have any idea who handles intake interviews and counseling? It's always the senior probation officer, a person with at least six years' experience. My staff would hit the ceiling if I told them there was a bunch of college kids coming in to take over that job!"

"But it would be a perfect arrangement," countered Gilbertson. "The students would have some real responsibility, something to challenge them. I don't think anyone wants to come out here for a year and be playground director in a holding facility. And the juveniles would have a person close to their own age to talk to, someone they might even listen to."

"But — how would you like it if one of your students wanted to teach a class that you'd been trained to teach and had been teaching for six years?"

"I'd like it just fine," said Gilbertson. "I'm sponsoring a student-taught course next semester."

Negotiations went on for nearly a month and finally Van Horn agreed to try Gilbertson's approach "on an experimental basis." Volunteers arrived in Indio in January, 1972. Soon after they arrived the Department hired Larry Bloom, part of whose job was to supervise the program. Gilbertson helped interview Bloom and knew he would be ideal. A dynamic, even inspiring man, Bloom gave the volunteers a sense of mission as well as first-rate training for their jobs.

Gilbertson himself drove to Indio every Thursday night. He offered a seminar which combined theoretical study of the justice system with discussions of the concrete problems that the volunteers encountered. High-quality papers and group projects were the products of this experience. Some students also managed to complete independent studies with on-campus faculty, but most found the Indio project too demanding to permit any additional study. Gilbertson often stayed late into the night counseling individual students and conferring with County officials. He also garnered other Johnston faculty into making cameo appearances to speak on special topics. Class sessions were typically very lively, despite the frequently exhausting work days that preceded them.

The direct parallels to the founding of Johnston are intriguing. The Indio project offered students a new, exciting program which began as little more than a set of ideas. More experienced officials of the established institution — the Probation Department — were at first suspicious. There were no titles, there was no phone. Hours were spent determining what the volunteers should be called. "Intake counselor" was finally decided upon. It sounded professional without sounding *too* professional, and no offense was given to the regular staff. Negotiations had produced a workable set of relationships and had given everyone a sense of ownership in the program. It was like starting the college all over again.

Indio's great advantage was that it had a sharply focused context in a setting far removed from ordinary academic life. It embodied the Johnston entrepreneurial style at its best. Each night volunteers faced very difficult decisions: should this boy be released to his parents, or should he be sent to Juvenile Hall? Should this girl be freed on her own recognizance or can she be persuaded to call her parents in Iowa? Students not only had to master arrest procedure and detention laws, they had to learn to work with skeptical officials and hard-boiled police, the very authority figures many of them at least rhetorically despised. They had to confront distressed or fearful kids, and deal with angry, distraught parents. They had to face the consequences of their judgments — and of their sympathies.

Two case histories offer contrasting results while dramatizing the tremendous impact the program had on students. Stephanie Rosenberg worked in three internships during her Johnston career, but the crucial one was Indio. The experience confirmed her commitment to juvenile justice. She became a highly-placed official in the juvenile division of the Illinois Department of Corrections. She got that job as a direct result of a long *Christian Science Monitor* article about Johnston which featured the Indio project. And she affirmed that the contracting process and the team cooperation she found at Johnston and Indio shaped her managerial style.

On the other hand, Kathy Adorney was both exhilarated and frustrated by the Indio experience. "It seemed romantic to me when I began," she said, "but I soon learned that all we could do was clean up the filth, not stop the flow. I also became much more sympathetic with the police, whom I had thought of largely as cynical pigs. And I made some terrible mistakes in my arrogance. I remember especially a 13 year old girl I wanted to 'save,' and to protect from her family. Larry Bloom introduced me to what he called 'Mama's Law': 'Unless you want to take responsibility for this kid long after your internship is over,' he said, 'don't alienate her any further from her family. Mama is always right because Mama is going to be there long after you're gone. Don't undermine that law unless you're sure this kid has the maturity to deal with the freedom.' Experiences like that," Kathy continued, "enabled me to see the sense of the law, if not its truth. Finally I realized that social work was just too hard for me. I still wanted to help people, but I couldn't save anyone." Kathy went to Columbia for graduate work in clinical psychology and earned her Ph.D.; she is now a practicing therapist.

The Indio project taught her something important — what she did not want to do — and it somehow did so without undermining her commitment to a career in the helping professions. Kathy still sees the experience as the highlight of her undergraduate education: "It confirmed my conviction that you can't separate your academic and personal lives."

The combination of a full-time job, academic demands and careful on-site supervision made the Indio project both demanding and effective. This program alone among the Johnston UYA projects fulfilled the Federal guidelines. Students worked full time, lived in the target community and took classes on-site. The County was so impressed that it decided to underwrite the project after UYA funding dried up. In 1975-76 the County paid Johnston $55,000 to furnish volunteers and academic support services.

Indio's success was in large measure due to the work of Larry Bloom and Dan Gilbertson. Gilbertson set up the project and nurtured it for years; Bloom kept it vital on a day-to-day basis. Both men also kept the project somewhat outside the orbit of the Johnston Action program.

Contact between Indio and other Action volunteers, and between Indio and the "home office," was minimal, and Indio remained largely free from the political infighting that adversely affected so many education and community service volunteers. Indio was the result of entrepreneurial initiative rather than the creature of a bureaucracy.

The second section of the UYA program, the education projects, was largely supervised by American historian Bob Treacy. They enjoyed some success even though their original goal of providing tutorial assistance to Spanish-speaking and black students was not met because few Johnston volunteers were bilingual and few worked in schools with large black student populations. The few students who did speak Spanish had more impact, but this was more because of individual initiative and ability than because of support from the college.

The education projects took two forms: programs at San Bernardino and Redlands high schools to counsel minority students and develop college prospects; tutorial programs in local elementary schools.

The tutorial projects consisted of assigning "backward" or emotionally handicapped children to volunteers to work on specific academic and social skills. From documentary evidence it appears that these programs worked reasonably well. But there were difficulties: the integrative seminar in support of these projects met on campus and was not very well run; the job was never full-time; and no provision was made for replacement projects for volunteers during summer vacations. As a result, many education volunteers took several regular classes on campus, and some even lived in the dorms.

The high school counseling programs achieved more limited success; volunteers did indeed help set up and run Chicano and Black centers on high school campuses. But they did not succeed in lowering the dropout rate or in persuading people to go on to college. Further, a significant percentage of these volunteers were not Johnston students. Many came from San Bernardino Valley College, a local junior college from which the Johnston UYA recruited when it could not fill its ranks at Redlands. These volunteers received very little supervision and were not well prepared for their counseling roles. They also had virtually no contact with Treacy, and so no idea how their work was fitting into their academic program. Their work, then, took place largely in a supervisory and academic vacuum.

The third segment of the Action program, community development projects, was hydra-headed. At one time or another it included a legal aid clinic, a drug counseling center, job rehabilitation and training, care for the elderly, community health care, and probation. All these were under the direction of a full-time community action project director, not a faculty member. Full-time staff persons were needed because this set of projects was both more time-consuming and potentially more problematic than the others. In the Indio and the education projects volunteers were working with long-established local government or educational agencies. In the community service projects volunteers worked with small local groups or even individual sponsors; the field director had to make sure that these agencies provided proper supervision and quality control. When the agencies were too small to do so, the field director had to provide these services. And since working directly in the community posed more risks, because mistakes were public and had political ramifications, the field director had to run interference between volunteers and local citizens.

The legal aid and drug clinics best exemplify the community service projects. A group of volunteers decided to create a legal assistance clinic under the titular sponsorship of a local Protestant church which was dedicated to social action in the north Redlands barrio. The church was poor and could not afford to pay professional supervisors. Thus the volunteers had to find their own supervisors — lawyers who would be willing to devote time to overseeing volunteers and giving free legal counsel to clients. The legal aid volunteers spent a great deal of time trying to find legal support and ran the continual risk of being accused of legal malpractice.

But despite this muddling the clinic did survive and even prosper. It provided valuable assistance to local people, especially in divorce and credit cases. But the clinic was outside the structure of Redlands' "normal" social service agencies and received no funding once the Action grant was withdrawn. The church could not support it, and it died.

The most controversial program was the North Redlands Drug Crisis Center which, like the legal aid clinic, was sponsored by the Impact Presbyterian Church. At first the center was staffed by a mix of Anglo and Chicano volunteers. The Anglos were all young, middle class college-age students. The Chicanos were mostly older males with a great deal of street experience and long tenure as Chicano political activists. The project leader, Chano Gonzales, was a powerful, even charismatic figure for the Chicano volunteers.

Conflict developed quickly. The Anglos were intimidated by what they considered the bullying tactics of the Chicanos. They quit the clinic and transferred to the legal aid project, with the permission and support of the overall UYA director, Dr. Carol Cespedes. Cespedes did discuss the matter with Leo Hernandez, the field director of the clinic, but not with the Chicano volunteers. This offended the Chicanos, who wanted their side of the story heard. It also offended Hernandez, but for a different reason. He felt that the students had bypassed his authority and appealed to his Anglo female boss.[1] Cespedes' response, that she was afraid to visit the drug clinic because she would be subject to verbal and even physical abuse, did little to quell the protest.

This controversy led to two "crisis" meetings on campus during the summer of 1973. They offer comic, though telling, illustrations of the way in which political confrontation at Johnston unearthed strong personal feelings which then became the subject of the confrontation. McCoy's ideology prevailed; feelings at Johnston were always "beneath" everything else, and therefore a necessary starting − and ending − point for any serious discussion. Precisely because the principals were so open about their hostilities, the political and frankly racial conflicts between white leadership and Latino staff and students dissolved in a welter of emotion and general confusion. Once again Johnston subverted politics into psychology.

The meetings tried to deal with the issues, particularly whether or not Cespedes and Treacy were doing their jobs. The conduct of the first meeting on June 20 did not augur well for the next. The meeting − if it can be called that − took place in a room under the library which had been turned over to MECHA, the campus Chicano organization. The room was on the northeast corner of the building. It had two entrances from the outside but it was not connected internally to the rest of the building. Disputes had already occurred over the room itself. Originally agreements had been drawn up which permitted the room to be used for seminars during weekdays because it had originally been a classroom and space was scarce. But the Chicanos who currently ran MECHA saw this as an intrusion on their turf. Relations between MECHA and Johnston administrators were already strained.

The meeting's convener, Ed Williams, published an elaborate set of ground rules prior to the event, warning people rather severely to refrain from verbal attacks. Tensions were clearly running high to make this sort of preliminary statement seem appropriate. No other meeting in Johnston's history had elicited such elaborate preparation.

Gene Ouellette, Carol Cespedes and other faculty and administrators, the transferred Anglo volunteers, and some people who agreed with the Gonzales faction entered through one door. But no Chicano Drug Clinic representatives appeared. The group sat and waited. Then a representative of the Chicano volunteers appeared in a second doorway and asked a question about procedure. He disappeared, then popped in a few minutes later with a second question. He left again without responding to the answer, and college officials grew more and more irritated.

It was obvious that the Chicano complainants were in some nearby room issuing instructions to their spokesman, but declining, for unknown reasons, to appear. Finally the spokesman reappeared, only to announce that this meeting was not a "proper forum" for hearing grievances and that his group would "use other means to make their complaints known." Just what might constitute a proper forum was not made clear. All of the careful preparations led to nothing. Sheer nervous excitement led the assembled group to talk about their version of the issues for a little while, but the meeting broke up shortly. This pattern of dramatic beginnings, of issues fading into confusion, typified the next, decisive gathering of June 29.

On June 27 eighteen Action volunteers published and distributed a self-consciously formal "Petition for Redress of Grievances," which was signed by thirteen volunteers who had been at the June 20 meeting, plus five of the Chicano drug clinic workers who had instructed their peripatetic spokesman from offstage. A letter supporting Leo Hernandez was sent to Ouellette at the same time. This was signed by eight Indio volunteers, and argued that Hernandez was more suited to direct the overall program than was Cespedes. Since the entire UYA program only included about forty students at the time, and fewer than that from Johnston and the University (the only signers), the defection of twenty-six volunteers was indeed a very serious business and reflected real dissatisfaction with the Cespedes regime.

The petition listed a number of grievances. First it charged that "The administrative staff has not fostered honest and open communication with the volunteers." Next Cespedes and Treacy were explicitly accused of giving inadequate field support.[2] The proposed solution was radical: both Cespedes and Treacy should be removed from their jobs forthwith.

The third complaint was that "Johnston College and its Graduation Contract Committee refuses to recognize the UYA program as an educational experience. Evaluations of volunteers do not reflect the empirical educational value of project development and operation." The solution for this? "We propose that UYA volunteers be granted a full years (sic) credit for all work in their projects, and that subsequent evaluations be accepted in full measure in student graduation contracts." But this was exactly what the Action program was designed to do. The hidden issue came to the surface quickly: field director Leo Hernandez did not have full faculty status and his evaluations therefore had to be countersigned by a "real" faculty member, a sore point for a proud man. Hernandez felt that he, and the Chicano volunteers, were treated as second-class citizens even though he was an effective teacher and the Chicano volunteers were competent workers. Countersigning meant that Johnston trusted neither Leo nor the volunteers.

The closely related fourth grievance was the charge that the UYA program had too many administrators who tried to exercise too much control over the projects. They wanted a decentralized structure with control in the hands of on-site directors.

The final grievance was fiscal. The petitioners felt that too much of the Action grant went to administration and too little to the volunteers.

The June 29 meeting to address these grievances was attended by Ouellette and new Vice-Chancellor George Rupp.[3] Ed Williams and Doug Bowman attended for the faculty, as representatives of the Appeals Committee. Psychologist Don Miller was on hand to monitor group process; the college's full arsenal was mustered for the confrontation. Carol Cespedes and five students completed the roster. Of the five, three were present to represent the "Action 18."

The petitioners' representatives were Camilo Perez, a 36 year old Chicano activist; Mike Nixon, a black student who had spent a year in Indio and was in the middle of his second year as a UYA volunteer attached to the legal aid clinic, and Eddie Flores, who worked at the drug clinic. An Anglo volunteer still with the drug clinic, John Davey, was also present.

Gene Ouellette was at first angered that the whole petitioning group was not present but he agreed to work with the representatives. He began interrogating the complainants about each charge. To the first charge about honest communication the volunteers responded that the real problem was the ongoing feud between Carol and Leo. This led to confusion about who was responsible for what in administering the program.

As discussion continued it became clear that the volunteers themselves, even those supporting Leo, did not understand the reasons for the feud and wanted to know more about it. The confusion was sliding into farce; if there had not been racial tension in the air, things might have ended right there. In the event, the same old answers were given — Carol ran the program and Leo supervised volunteers — but no one was satisfied with that. It was becoming obvious that the charges were masks for feelings and fears.

The meeting dragged on in this vein, with faculty supporting Carol in spite of her obfuscations. They argued that problems with academics and with earning credit for internships were Hernandez' business. Charges that the Graduation Contract Committee was hostile to Action volunteers were easily refuted. When a volunteer responded that he had done poorly in his Indio evaluations because he did not know how to write well enough to pass his courses, political tension drained away. Once again, an allegedly general issue dissolved into a personal problem.

Doug Bowman stated that none of this seemed sufficient

grounds for dismissal and faculty began to make noises to the effect that the petition was thin. Under this pressure the real issues finally came clear: Carol, Leo and his cohorts charged, "was doing things the standard Anglo way," and not in "the standard Chicano way." Racism was at the heart of the matter.

To the petitioners, this meant that Carol had acted unilaterally in approving the transfer — even though everyone acknowledged that she had consulted on the issue with Hernandez. Her racism turned out to consist of the fact that she did not communicate the decision to Chano and his colleagues in precisely the right way at just the right time. Leo said: "Chano had to be in the right listening mood.... Chano had to be involved in this type of action, and it had to be the right way at the right moment. Differences can be resolved by talking to Chano at the right moment."

This seems extraordinarily indulgent to Chano, who was after all a volunteer and had no right to make decisions about other volunteers. Carol was perhaps insensitive in not talking to Chano before she approved the transfers, but she did have the power to make such decisions and the Anglo students did allege that Chano and the others had verbally abused them, a charge which was never denied. Leo felt that it was up to Carol and the Anglo volunteers to accommodate Chano; the problem was not his responsibility. Faculty and administrators did not agree.

A final point, easily the most legitimate, came up near the end of the meeting. Volunteers complained that they had to pay summer tuition, yet the faculty who were supposed to be their on-campus contacts were on vacation and unavailable to work with them. Here the administrators waffled; it was obvious that the volunteers were right. It was one of the more unsavory consequences of having faculty members double as UYA administrators.

By now feelings had taken charge of the meeting. Leo saved his bombshell for last: "It is because of all this sort of thing that I am resigning. The institution is racist." People shouted countercharges; discussion broke down entirely. At this point the student representatives, perhaps frightened at these unexpected results, backed off. They claimed that they did not really want to quit or have people fired; all they wanted to do was discuss some of their grievances. But that proved all but impossible in the Johnston milieu. They promised to go back to the "Action 18" and suggest that the group re-do their petition.

This was never formally done. The protest collapsed with Hernandez' resignation, which indeed followed close on the June 29 meeting. Shortly thereafter he filed a suit against the college, charging job discrimination. The suit failed. The drug clinic closed when Chano finished his year with Action, and with this, tensions between Johnston and its volunteers were sharply reduced. Although nervous memos about the relation between academics and Action projects continued to appear, this problem did not again become a matter for public discussion or protest. It is hard not to conclude that the crisis arose in good measure because Hernandez did not like taking orders from Cespedes.

Ironically, Cespedes herself was fired by Ouellette in December of 1973 for some of the very reasons advanced by the "Action 18": she simply did not work well with the volunteers, and did not administrate the program effectively. She stayed on until June of 1974 to finish her contract.

As this muddled protest indicates, the program suffered from mismanagement and inept political infighting. There were five Directors in five years and the turnover in field directors was nearly as heavy. A leading reason for this instability was the fact that most UYA directors were not well integrated into the Johnston academic system. Action also highlighted a further weakness inherent in Johnston's flexibility; programs could be set up without much careful planning. Once they were in place the programs were appreciated for the revenues they generated, and for the experiences they offered. But they were also left to prosper or perish without much support or long-range planning. The faculty who gravitated to the programs were not usually appointed to them because of special qualifications. Frequently they joined the programs because they were interested (Gilbertson) or because they had free time. Sometimes the faculty and the program fit beautifully; more often they did not. Johnston's love of academic amateurism was least successful here. In any case the college as a whole was not that interested in whether the programs were well-served. They remained "orphans" and only drew general interest when they caused problems.

This neglect was not cynical. Faculty were so caught up in the extraordinary demands that Johnston imposed on their time that they could not devote regular attention to all the programs which the college spawned. Programs could be in place before anyone — including the people involved in them — really understood their implications for the entire college. In such circumstances they had to make their own way in the world.

In the case of Action, faculty inattention had an adverse effect. Students were chronically puzzled about whether their job experience would be granted the academic credit they felt it deserved. Anxious, they often enrolled in several other courses, diluting the internship portion of their program. Too many advisors silently agreed with them, and approved the additions.

Overall, though, despite neglect and maladministration, the Action program survived and in a few areas even prospered for three and a half years. Individual volunteers accomplished remarkable things for themselves and for the community. But in late 1975 Federal evaluator Carl Manning found that the Johnston program had strayed too far from Action guidelines. A number of jobs were less than full time, administrative costs were too high, students too often lived on campus, and the ties between academics and jobs were unclear (though this last was not a major flaw in the eyes of the government). On these grounds Manning recommended the termination of the program. Johnston agreed, because by this time student interest in social action had so diminished that it was impossible to recruit more than a small minority of UYA volunteers from the college itself. In January 1976 the Action program died a quiet, even welcome death.

Action was only one of the programs at Johnston College. There were two other kinds of programs as well. The first, which included Cooperative Education, student-run internships and the Wilderness Program, shared Action's basic assumption that experiential learning was an indispensable part of undergraduate education. In these programs students went out into the world to learn. The second group of programs had precisely the opposite goal: projects such as the University Without Walls wanted to draw working adults back onto the college campus to add theoretical learning to life experiences. Both, of course, valued education based on a mix of theory and practice.

A typical instance of the first group of programs was Cooperative Education, a three-year, federally supported project run by physicist and computer expert Don Blachley. Cooperative Education students earned college credit for working at paid internships in government and industry. It was felt that such hands-on experience prepared students for life in the "real world." To quote the 1971 HEW "Report on Higher Education,"

> The longer students remain in the academic atmosphere, the more they become dependent on it because it is the only life they know. Most young people in college have no firsthand knowledge of any occupation save that of being a student. A great deal of student concern about the relevance of their

education can be attributed to their isolation. Many...students lack the experience and the sense of adult roles that would help them see how courses can be relevant.

College education is meant to prepare students for jobs, and exposure to jobs should begin as soon as possible so that students will enroll in the right courses. The Cooperative Education director contacted government agencies and businesses to arrange internships, preferably with salary. The internship would last for one year. Ideally, internships and student academic and career interests would mesh as closely as possible.

The program placed a dozen students per year in such diverse settings as the State Department, the United Nations, TRW, the Bronx Zoo and the *Los Angeles Times*. Nearly all the internships were successful. Students had a chance to find out how to operate in the worlds of government and business, and the companies and agencies had a chance to use student talent at minimal cost. Unfortunately, Cooperative Education was limited to a three-year funding grant and Johnston's chronic poverty prevented continuing the program.

There was also a student-run internship program which offered non-paying off-campus opportunities to students. Ironically, this was the longest-lived outreach program at Johnston; it survived from year to year without funding and with minimal faculty or administrative supervision.

Sherry Austin benefitted from this program. The student in charge that year, Patti Karlin, arranged an internship for Sherry with a San Bernardino law firm that took some public defender cases. The internship was primarily clerical and took up fifteen hours each week.

At first Sherry was restive with the routine jobs she was given. But Johnston forthrightness paid off. When Sherry told her bosses that she had to learn something about the law in order to have a serious internship, they gave her more research and allowed her in on several court cases. One visit to court involved jury selection:

> I watched the lawyer pay attention to every detail of the prospective juror's behavior. But he was acting as if he was just having a little conversation, as if jury selection were the last thing on his mind. I loved it! Subtle drama — I was hooked.

Sherry still thinks of the internship as one of the best parts of her education. But she really did it on her own, with almost no faculty guidance. Karlin and her successors did an admirable, if *ad hoc* job, but never did manage to institutionalize such experiences. That may well have been the key to their success.

Another long-lived outreach effort was anthropologist Roger Baty's "Community Insight" Program, which was designed to provide cross-cultural experiences. The program was funded in part by the Lilly Foundation (Baty was very adept in securing grants for the college). Though Community Insight underwent many changes in form, the basic model — preparing students for the experience with a class beforehand; the experience itself during the January Interim; a reflection course in spring — remained the same and helped many students to successful completion of the college's cross-cultural "requirement."

The primary form of Community Insight was foreign or domestic cross-cultural homestays on Indian reservations or in Mexico. Sherry also participated in this program, but with less happy results than her experience in the law office. "I guess I was just too young," she said in her interview.

> The family I stayed with in Mexico was really nice and things went pretty well for most of the month. It was hard getting used to sleeping in a room with three other people, and to speaking nothing but Spanish, but I coped with that. There was only one

shower in town, in the store, and it felt weird not taking one every day — but again, that was no big hassle. We all got along pretty well, and my Spanish sure got better!

But then right near the end there was a big party for the whole town. It was the saint's day, and everybody was out in the plaza dancing and drinking beer and *pulque* and eating. I made the mistake of dancing a few times with one guy — Jose Luis — who acted like he kind of liked me. I'd had a little beer and felt good — I hadn't partied in a month! Anyway, next day the women in the house I lived in acted really odd. The two sisters I slept with moved their beds out into another room, and people hardly talked to me. It was weird. Finally I got one of the sisters to tell me what was happening. I had danced with the other sister's *novio*, or fiance. And you just don't do that. They thought I was some kind of slut, like I was trying to steal this guy, and being really brazen. I felt awful and tried to explain but I don't think they really understood. The last few days were pretty uncomfortable and I couldn't wait to get out of there....

Sherry learned something but the learning was painful. "The reflection part of the course helped me pick up the pieces and not feel like such a jerk, but I still feel funny, and a little angry that nobody told me more about the customs...."

For Baty, of course, this experience was just as valuable — perhaps even more so — than one without any difficulties. Sherry's understanding of Mexican culture, and her self-understanding, increased enormously. Baty's model was so successful that it has remained part of the Johnston experience throughout the 1980's.

The University Without Walls (UWW) was an attempt to institutionalize the "free university" concept of the early

60's. The UWW student, usually a working adult, would build an education by assembling courses, independent studies and past life experiences. This assemblage would be worked out in contract form with a faculty advisor and approved by a faculty committee.

The key to the national UWW program was its use of local resources. The student would sign up with UWW, which would provide minimal academic opportunities on its own. The student would contract for work with artists, therapists, faculty members and the like who would be willing to donate time to working with the student. He might volunteer to do internships with local agencies. And he might take some regular courses at community or state colleges.

The role of the advisor in this system was to help the student find educational opportunities in the community, and to offer academic guidance and emotional support. Beyond this, the student was free to construct his/her own education by exploiting already existing resources.

The Johnston version of UWW was more campus-centered than this. Though students could receive credit for previous life experience, and though many of them did supplement this with courses taken at local colleges or as independent studies, many also began to join undergraduate seminars on campus. And they were encouraged to do this by advisors and by the Graduation Contract Committee, who felt that Johnston classes were well suited to adult learners.

The "infiltration" of adult students into campus seminars gave classes a salutory variety of members. And as the adults became involved in the seminars their surface practicality began to erode. They, as much as any undergraduate, were deeply interested in questions about values. They were thirsty for exposure to art and literature and philosophy.

A good instance of the effects of UWW infiltration was a Saturday morning seminar, "The Literature of Middle Age." The group was as yeasty a combination as Johnston could offer: five residential undergraduates (all male, it turned out) and twelve UWW students, nine of them women ranging in age from twenty-five to sixty. There was one married couple, and two of the women had just gone through ugly divorces. Attitudes ranged from radical feminism to midwestern conservatism. The residential students were all but overwhelmed by the vitality of the adults. Discussions moved rapidly from the readings to personal/societal issues and back again. For the adults it was an instance in which personal and academic experience meshed perfectly.

UWW added more than interesting students to the campus. It added new revenue and helped stem the precipitous enrollment decline. UWW meant a ten percent increase in "full-time tuition equivalents," and it took relatively less faculty time than on-campus work. So UWW was welcome, and it took four variant forms during the early 1970's. One succeeded, one lasted for a year, and two never passed the planning stage. One of the successes and one of the failures merit comment.

The "failure" was a plan to provide a coordinated UWW experience for groups of people in the same industry. The specific proposal was to provide on-site classes and advising to a group of middle management staff at Kaiser Steel in nearby Fontana. Johnston would provide some direct faculty support and administrative services, and would hire part-time faculty to teach some of the courses. This program foundered because the project was simply too large for Johnston to handle and because it demanded highly specialized coursework which was unavailable from a small liberal arts college. Such business-oriented programs were better handled by institutions specifically created to manage them.

The most successful offshoot of UWW was the Master's Degree program in Humanistic and Transpersonal Psychology. The psychology contingent at Johnston had always included more members than any other, and its emphasis had always been experiential and clinical. But as the institution gradually de-emphasized T-grouping, the psychologists found themselves without a clear-cut role. So, during the Era of Programs, they turned outward as well. This UWW program was approved in principle in 1973 as a program in clinical psychology. By the time it began to operate in 1975 it had been transformed, under UWW influence, into an external degree program. And the key word "transpersonal" had been added. One of the most successful operations in Johnston's history, the program deserves a more careful look.

Johnston in the mid-seventies still attracted some students whose interest in community service and social change was undiminished by the national turn from such matters toward what Christopher Lasch terms the "culture of narcissism." But it also included many people whose interest in personal growth was paramount, and who saw psychology as a way to inner peace and tranquility in an unacceptable world. And even those more interested in therapeutic work still believed with Pres McCoy that the road to social change was through the individual, not through immediate political or community work.

From the first Johnston had been a home for humanistic or "Third Force" psychology. Even when sensitivity training lost its hold over the entire community, there remained a significant portion of students who valued such groups and the therapeutic psychology which empowered them. Throughout its ten year history, more students concentrated in psychology at Johnston than in any other field, and by a wide margin. By 1974-75 the phrase "interpersonal dimension" still appeared in the catalog, but not in the campus patois; the standard term "psychology" was more than adequate for this new group of Johnstonians. But the term did not connote a strictly disciplinary approach to the field. Course offerings remained heavily experiential. A student could choose among encounter and Gestalt groups, psychodrama and biofeedback, psychosynthesis and meditation, Rolfing or structural patterning, and spiritual healing. More career-minded students had several counseling internships available to them in the Redlands area. Or they could work as an apprentice psychodramatist on campus, or on a crisis hotline, or conduct supervised counseling at the Women's Center.

There were, of course, a number of more theoretical classes which bolstered the experiential work. But little experimental or behavioral psychology was taught; it appeared largely as an alternative, or more frequently a straw man, in discussions of humanistic theories. Humanistic psychology was defined in several different Johnston publications as "a kind of therapy and theory which evolved out of a concern for a more positive and growth-oriented, person-centered and integrative approach," in contrast to classical Freudian analysis. Its special interests and topics were listed as "identity, authenticity, self-actualization, transcendence, the search for meaning, personal growth..." and its methods were Gestalt, psychodrama, client-centered therapy, T-grouping, biofeedback, movement and dance. Its goal was "to develop the whole person — physical, emotional, intellectual and spiritual." It traced its intellectual roots to continental phenomenology and its existential descendants as interpreted by psychotherapists such as Rollo May, Carl Rogers, and Abraham Maslow.

The transpersonal (or "Fourth Force") emphasis developed gradually at Johnston during the early 1970's. Hugh Redmond was hired in 1971 as an urban planning specialist. But he soon turned from that subject — Johnston's radically entrepreneurial system even allowed faculty to redefine their positions — to a loosely defined set of practices which explored psychic territory beyond the range of the conscious ego (hence "transpersonal"). Johnston publications defined this field as "that branch of an overall integral and humanistic approach to psychology, which makes a scientific study of the farther reaches of human nature." "Farther reaches" turned out to be: "the peak experience; mystical, transcendental and religious experience; pathways to self-realization; spiritual growth and practices; esoteric sources of wisdom; meditation, Akido, Yoga and T'ai Chi."

The nub of the transpersonal movement was a rediscovery of the spiritual dimension in the individual. True to its sources in the counter-culture, transpersonal psychology did not usually look to the Western religious tradition for spiritual renewal. Rather it adopted the Romantic fascination with Buddhism, the Tao, and other Eastern spiritual practices. Its leading Western lights were Jung, Reich, Assagioli (for psychosynthesis) and East-West eclectic thinkers such as Allan Watts. Self-evidently an interdisciplinary field, it was also rooted in American, specifically Californian, sensibilities; natural healing, for example, involved nutrition as well as psychopharmacology. Massage and altered states of consciousness were worthy subjects, as were intuition and creativity, and the psychic roots of gender difference.

Transpersonal students had quite different interests than the existential and humanistic psychologists. Most notably, they were not interested in group therapy but individual renewal; the development of the inner spirit took precedence over solving specific psychosocial problems. But their interests, finally, were not incompatible with humanistic approaches; all they argued was that there was a level of human awareness deeper than consciousness. Any psychology which embraced the value of the person led naturally to studying all dimensions of that person.

The "scientific" portion of transpersonal psychology might seem hard to locate amidst this welter of practices and methods. And, frankly, it did not strike the fancy of wide numbers of transpersonal students. But the faculty did keep careful investigation − of psychic phenomena, for example − an important part of the program.

So the humanists and the transpersonalists were able to work together. They were joined by other faculty whose interests overlapped: religionist Doug Bowman had always been interested in Eastern spiritual practices, and 1974-75 visiting faculty member Barbara Gibson wanted to explore the feminine as a spiritual principle. New developmental psychologist Barbara Coulibaly felt that she could teach alternative theories of learning based on both humanistic and transpersonal theories, and older student David Zeller contributed his extensive personal experience in meditation techniques. The old hands in psychology — Whitlock, Miller, Tubbs, Blume, Smith — participated in transpersonal inquiries with varying degrees of enthusiasm.

The psychology faculty developed a remarkable class list, one which any traditional liberal arts professor would find positively exotic. Familiar classes in Developmental Psychology and Theories of Personality operated in happy co-existence with such arcana as psychic healing, out-of-body experiences — the transcendence of the body in certain meditative states — and "the path of the heart" — a self-tranquilizing practice based on meditation on ancient Hindu body centers.

This made the psychology program at Johnston extraordinarily lively; there was something to intrigue everyone interested in the avant-garde California psychotherapy-cum-spirituality. And the program did attract talented students who found in it a spiritual reaffirmation missing in the other aspects of their lives. In 1974 Johnston offered the only undergraduate degree in transpersonal psychology in the country.

The program also fit in well with Johnston's implicitly religious character: if education could save, why not specific forms of it? No matter how skeptical other faculty might be, the psychology program did carry forward the saving mission of the college, and thus sustained its idealism during a period when idealism was becoming more and more difficult to sustain. The path from Pres McCoy's philosophy of education to the concentration in transpersonal psychology is a direct one.[4]

In her first semester, Sherry Austin avoided what she

termed the "far-out California" transpersonal courses. But the enthusiasm of friends and a secret desire not to be a parochial Easterner eventually persuaded her to try a course with High Redmond. The one she chose was an introductory seminar entitled "Right Brain Education: Psychosynthesis and Other Approaches." Sherry went to the first meeting with the promise to herself to be open-minded, but she was ill-prepared for what happened. The class met in a specially designed "Meditation Room" in the attic of East Hall; the room had been carpeted and wired for sound. Sherry had never been in the Meditation Room. The first thing she noticed was that there were no chairs. Large pillows were produced from a closet, and everyone took up comfortable positions on the floor.

There was no syllabus and Hugh made no opening statement about the course. Instead, he said: "Just settle back and close your eyes. Take a deep breath. Another one. Feel your feet and ankles relaxing. Let the tension leave your knees. Feel your hands dangling free. Roll your head until it seems to flop on your neck. Now you're fully relaxed. Okay?" There was a full minute of silence, and then an almost imperceptible sound entered the room. It seemed to come from everywhere. Sherry didn't know what instrument it was, but after a few moments she stopped wondering. The sound swelled and faded, surrounded her − she felt herself drifting across an open, blue-grey space, carried by the music, borne almost out of herself. Even that nagging little voice that so often made her feel self-conscious fell silent. Gradually the music fell away to a whisper, then silence. Dazed, even grateful, Sherry opened her eyes. A few others did the same, but no one spoke. As the silence lengthened, Sherry started to fidget; "This is a college class, after all," she thought. Hugh sat perfectly still, his eyes shut. Another student, as impatient as Sherry, finally spoke: "What do we do now?" he said.

Hugh smiled a little, but without a trace of condescension. "Where have you just been?" he asked. "Can you tell us?"

"Not very well," the boy answered. "I don't feel as though I 'was' anywhere."

"That's the subject matter of this course," said Hugh.

Most of the semester was devoted to exploring these altered states of consciousness via music, meditation, guided fantasy, even physical exercise. The initial stage was always to achieve a state where the critical, verbal faculties of the mind were not in control of consciousness. And Sherry did experience what she still calls "other states of mind." "I haven't done much of that sort of thing since I left Johnston," she reported, "I don't know why. I still have the journal I kept during that semester — we had to keep one for the course. I was never sure if I was making up all the things I experienced, or whether they were actually happening to me. But things sure happened. And it was very good for me to be in a class where I wasn't trying to show off, or impress the teacher, or do a better job than the other students. There was a little reading, but it was mainly an experiential course. It was some contrast to go from the scurry of a law office to losing yourself in the aftertones of a Tibetan gong!"

The "MA in Humanistic and Transpersonal Psychology" began operation in the second semester of the 1974-75 academic year. It had no founding grant, but it did have ample faculty support. Crucial to its success was Hugh Redmond. His energetic interest in the field, backed by his excellent organizing skills, gave the new degree the impetus it needed. The program defined itself as follows: there would be seven contracts written for the degree: one in an "experiential colloquium," one in research methodology and five in other areas, including an in-service internship if that was appropriate. Several "concentrations" were possible: humanistic psychology, humanistic education, and transpersonal psychology. Each candidate would also complete a final thesis or project. The program was designed to be completed in no more than two years. Contracts could be written with residential faculty or with a list of approved "adjunct and support" faculty. Only the colloquium need be taken on campus, though in practice many contracts were written with residential faculty. But contracts typically included a great deal of experiential as well as theoretical work.

The program was perfect for Southern California, and the staff was able to attract a number of capable students despite the stiff tuition. Their presence on campus, as with the UWW students, diversified the student body and enriched a number of seminars. It also attracted a host of practitioners to campus to offer workshops and demonstrations. In a typical year fourteen people offered workshops on subjects ranging from Amerindian medicine to psychic healing, movement and music, and Zen meditation. This list, as well as the list of available off-campus study centers, indicates how strongly transpersonal interests and Redmond's organizational talents had shaped the program. Perhaps more than any other Johnston program this one succeeded in creating a relatively self-contained world which was a safe haven for students and faculty, and which developed a highly specific identity on a national level.

Further, this program offered a clear alternative to the liberal arts tradition of learning for its own sake and for intellectual development. Some more traditional faculty were as skeptical as Sherry Austin had been. The transpersonal program was openly based on intuition, feeling and practice — and to these it attached a saving power. The quasi-religious and frankly "trans-intellectual" character of the program was a yeasty irritant which made traditional faculty address the relations between reason and feeling in a more serious and practical way. Transpersonal psychology was, in the last analysis, the only serious challenger for educational hegemony; the entrenched humanist "gurus" resisted and sometimes ridiculed it, but in the long run learned to respect it as a serious counterweight to their control of education at the college.

Why was it such a serious threat? Because it did successfully combine experience and theory, and offered both as a way to effect radical change in the individual. This was something that Johnston had always promised but which it had never developed a consistent program to deliver. Encounter groups were too disorganized and too monochromatic to offer the change; off-campus internships never did succeed in bridging the gap between academe and action for large numbers of students. As valuable as they were, they tended to remain separate from academic development. The transpersonal and humanistic program alone offered a simple marriage of theory and experience, primarily because the marriage was an internal one between oneself and oneself, and because the techniques used were ancient and well tested. Further, its goals were more modest; it did not purport to change the world but only the individual practitioner by opening up spiritual possibilities which had been denied, through neglect, to a great majority of modern college students. So this very lively and successful program formed a unique focus: a largely on-campus experiential program which effectively wedded theory and practice at both the undergraduate and graduate levels. It was an ideal Johnston program.

One final corner of the Johnston academic arena deserves mention. The physical education "program" at Johnston was one of those wonderfully *ad hoc* developments which appeared unpredictably, flourished without outside support, full-time faculty, or any discernible organization, and managed to import the Johnston ethos into the realm of sports.

Some students, following the original plan, took activity courses at the University, and a small number even went out for varsity sports. But Johnston's own zany version of "PE" classes appeared early in the college's history. The Kazoo band, which so maddened University officials when it ran around the football field at Homecoming, was perhaps the first example of organized physical activity a la Johnston. There was a widespread interest in aerobics, a concept which had just burst on the national scene. Faculty and students who had watched in amazement as Doug Bowman ran around the Pilgrim Pines parking lot in 1969 were themselves jogging in 1970, years before it became fashionable.

There was even a series of Johnston intramural flag football and softball teams. Johnston attracted good high school athletes who had tired of the Devil's Island disciplinary manias of their high school coaches. Consequently, the intramural football team regularly challenged the "jock" fraternity teams from Redlands for the University title. It was always a shock to see a Johnston receiver streaking under a perfectly thrown deep pass with his pony tail streaming behind him. Some frat teams, to their cost, couldn't take the "hippies" seriously.

A quintessential Johnston product was a coed touch football team which flourished for a few years in the early 70's. That team was so talented that it played coed teams from other California schools and developed a local reputation as one of the best such teams on the West Coast. It also routed an all-male faculty team foolish enough to challenge it.

But competitive sports were something of an anomaly at Johnston. Most physical activities tended to be therapeutic rather than aggressive. Eastern self-defense techniques were always popular as aesthetically pleasing and individualistic forms of exercise. There was even a class on "Zen athletics" in which students learned track and field events through using Zen mind-cleansing techniques.

A related project was the Wilderness Program, proposed during 1974-75 and approved the next year. This was a more modest version of the Outward Bound program used at Prescott College to test students' mettle. In the Johnston program students would hike, camp out, rock-climb, and master survival techniques. But they would also learn the ecology of the local forests and how to operate in the wilderness without harming it. In addition the courses would focus on cultivating attitudes toward physical fitness based on self-development rather than competition. So there was a spiritual/philosophical reason even for the PE program. And yes, Sherry Austin did manage to scramble up a rock face which two months earlier had terrified her.

Thus the off-campus, internship and experiential aspects of education at Johnston College. In community service, homestays, in-service clinical training, transpersonal/spiritual experiences, and working internships Johnston College offered a rich set of possibilities to the student who wanted "hands-on" education. Whatever the administrative problems raised by some programs, and whatever the academic resistance to others, the family of experiential programs at Johnston is strong testimony to the power of McCoy's vision. Johnston at its zenith did in fact make real McCoy's idea that education must reach out into the world and also deep inside the individual learner, to turn experience into a form of enlightenment.

NOTES:

1. Hernandez had been a candidate for Cespedes' job. Her academic background (Ph. D. in anthropology) made her a more desirable candidate on a purely academic basis. But Hernandez was more popular with the volunteers because he spent a good deal of time with them in the field, and had more field experience than Cespedes. A power struggle was unavoidable.

2. This second charge is interesting because it follows closely a complaint that Leo Hernandez had made in writing to Gene Ouellette on June 15. He accused Ouellette and Johnston of racism and detailed what he called Cespedes' "dereliction of duty." He claimed that Carol had missed inordinate amounts of time on the job because of family problems (a sick child) and a broken hand, and that she never appeared in her office at all on Thursdays. The tone is petty and carping. But its substance is repeated in the later volunteer petition, which strongly suggests that Hernandez gave this information to the petitioners, who would not otherwise have been in a position to know it.

3. Williams, Rupp and McDonald had, for eighteen months, met daily

as an informal administrative team to discuss issues facing the Vice Chancellor. Mischievously named the "Trimurti," the Hindu trinity of creation, preservation and destruction, the group decided to rotate the official title from Williams to Rupp (McDonald's term came later). George Rupp "rotated" out of Johnston to several more distinguished positions in American higher education; he is currently President of Rice University. Williams reassumed the post in 1976.

4. It has even turned out, by 1985, to be a personal line as well. McCoy has developed major interests in meditation, self-realization, and out-of-body experiences, which, if economic realities allowed, he would deeply love to pursue full-time.

CHAPTER 7

The Politics

The academic complexity of the college was mirrored in its social and political organizations. As the academic dimensions splintered into smaller communities of learning, so the monolithic community which once ruled political and social life underwent centrifugal transformation.

The community meeting system of governance was still in existence in 1974-75 but had undergone fundamental changes. Consensus proved too cumbersome a decision-making process as soon as the community began to change from an undifferentiated unit to a complex political body with self-conscious interest groups. Standardization produced standard politics; consensus was replaced in 1972 by majority rule. And the committees of 1970, whose power had been carefully circumscribed, now assumed a more central place in campus politics. The committees would handle all minor issues and only bring "major decisions" (vaguely defined) to the Community Meeting, and then only in a form appropriate for "yea" or "nay" voting. Further, certain committee decisions — on approving graduation contracts and faculty retention/firing — were only brought to Community Meetings as information; the committees had the power to make such decisions and to refer them directly to the Chancellor.

The growth in power of the committees produced a balkanization of political power analogous to the balkanization of academic programs. It also reduced dramatically the importance of the Community Meeting. Things had become so difficult in 1973 that a system of governance by dorm lobbies rather than the central meeting was attempted. But this proved too fragmentary, and the 1974-75 academic year saw a return of the Community Meeting to a position of at least nominal significance. The meeting was again held each week, and could occasionally reassert its one-time vigor. But for the most part the Community Meeting was a relic of the past — ill-attended, ridiculed for time-consuming, boring discussions, and beset by backwater issues; student budget allocations were easily the leading items on the 1974-75 agendas. The forum that had been the political lifeblood of the college became a place to decide how much to pay the band for the Halloween dance.

The withering of the Community Meeting did not, however, mean that political life at Johnston suffered a like fate. That was alive and well in the labyrinthine world of the committees which emerged as the seat of effective political power.

In the academic year 1974-75 there were eleven full-fledged committees at the college, as well as the Community Meeting. These groups, nearly all of which were staffed by equal numbers of students and faculty, dealt with such areas as personnel, academic policy, long-range planning, and student life, as well as with the various programs. A special Chancellor's search committee was convened in the spring of 1975, shortly after Gene Ouellette announced his resignation. There was even by this time a steering committee — bureaucracy indeed! — to coordinate the activities of all the other committees. In addition there was a regular faculty meeting, meetings of faculty subgroups, a Chancellor's advisory group, and community memberships on the Board of Overseers and the Board of Trustees. Beyond all this were the various

University-wide committees on which Johnstonians — nearly always faculty — had to serve.

This plethora of committees offered students ample chances to participate in the political life of the institution. There were some sixty committee slots open to students, so that approximately one-fourth of the student body was directly involved in governance. Students were also organized by dormitory lobbies, and served as dormitory hall managers. They also worked in the Women's Center, and as interns — not just campus guides — for the Admissions office. And since students on off-campus internships couldn't serve on committees or act as dormitory managers, the percentage of students involved in politics was actually about one-third.

At Johnston as elsewhere, committee work was less an opportunity than an imposition for faculty. With eleven committees (including the two graduation committees) and other assignments at the University and on the Boards, professors normally served on two committees in addition to attending faculty and community meetings. Thus faculty tended to be preoccupied with political obligations, sometimes to the detriment of their time commitments to classes and almost always to the detriment of their research. But such commitment was necessary because Johnston *was* so complex and so labor-intensive. In order to produce Johnston education faculty had to help run the school day-to-day; they also advised students, negotiated class and graduation contracts, taught seminars and wrote evaluations. In a student-centered educational institution they chose, most of them, to surrender a great deal of their development in areas other than teaching, advising and administration. Those who didn't so choose either left, or lost the respect of their colleagues. There was indeed a right way to behave for Johnston faculty which partially tempered the entrepreneurial tone of the campus. Faculty might manage to change their academic fields in mid-stream, but if they didn't "do their fair share" of teaching and governance, they were ostracized.

The committees dealt with every aspect of college business. The Personnel Committee evaluated, hired and fired faculty. The Academic Policy Committee grappled with general issues of quality control, record-keeping and operational definitions of contracting. Other committees treated of life in the dorms, long-range plans and a variety of other issues. We will focus here on the Personnel and Academic Policy Committees because they were the most powerful.

Of these, the Personnel Committee offers the richest insight into the Johnston political process. That committee at Johnston was, from the first, caught between conventional expectations for faculty review and retention and the radically egalitarian ethos of the community. As we have seen, "professional behavior" for Johnston College faculty included personal openness, direct confrontation, and commitment to all facets of college life. The membrane between living and learning was as permeable for faculty as it was for students. At the same time, mistakes inevitably were made in faculty hiring, and responsibility for redressing these fell upon the Committee, with its delegated power from the Chancellor to "formulate personnel recommendations for my office and the Board of Overseers."

Given the intensity of personal relationships at Johnston, however, this charge was extremely difficult to fulfill. It is one thing for a large department or tenure committee to dismiss an assistant professor because the requisite articles and books have not been produced; it is quite another to vote to fire a person with whom one has shared T-grouping, solidarity against outsiders, indeed the founding of a college. Yet faculty were not all equally gifted, and discriminations, whatever the ideology, were in fact made by community members all the time. But "officially": could such a community police its own ranks, weed out weaker members?

Perhaps the most common opinion concerning

Johnston College on the main campus, held especially by those who were generally friendly to the enterprise, was that Johnston simply couldn't cull its own. "You guys kept too much deadwood — that's what hurt you more than anything else" — the quote is from President Douglas Moore in 1981, and he was the last of a long line to say much the same thing. And many Johnstonians agreed.

We strongly suspect that in 1974-75 most Johnston faculty would have ranked themselves and their peers in much the same order; the same half dozen faculty would have appeared near the top and bottom of nearly everyone's list. But those at the bottom were never seriously threatened, even though the institution proclaimed outstanding teaching as its greatest strength. From 1969 to 1979 only one professor was actually fired, and that involved such a painful, complex and ultimately legal confrontation that any repetition of it was virtually unthinkable.

Personal relationships aside, there were two enabling reasons for this. First, Johnston was adept in persuading some faculty that they really did not belong at the college. Whatever the reasons — academic ambition, impatience with hazy structures, fear of openness or simple exhaustion — several persons left on their own, or after informal talks with colleagues; the "bottom six list" wasn't static. So in this important sense the Johnston personnel style worked admirably; a combination of direct confrontation and discrete counseling led a number of faculty — we calculate eight in the first five years — to resign. Second, the almost continuous conflicts with the University over the proper number of faculty positions for Johnston made dismissal seem more suicidal than strengthening; to fire a person could well mean the loss of the position as well. As Frank Blume observed, "It was certainly better to have 'X', even if he was mediocre, than to have no one at all." This was doubly true because most disciplines at Johnston had just one or two representatives; the loss of a position meant in effect that an entire field could no longer be offered.

However, both these reasons, while compelling at times, also became convenient rationalizations. In fact, Johnston faculty and students alike, when the moment to vote actually came, simply could not fire one of their family. There were only two Personnel Committee votes to fire a faculty member in the history of the college. One was an impulsive vote in 1970 after very brief discussion to fire physicist Allen Killpatrick. Cooler heads at the meeting pointed out that the reasons given for the firing — unpopularity of physics and personal dislike — were entirely unrelated to the Committee's criteria. The vote was immediately reversed (and kept secret). The second occurred in January of 1974, when the Committee recommended unanimously that philosophy professor George Derfer be given a terminal one year contract.

A full history of the Derfer "case" would run to several hundred pages, and we have no desire to retry it. But that there could have been such a bitter confrontation at Johnston is the direct result of the clash between the college's theology of unlimited human growth and the *Realpolitik* of legal contracts and detailed regulations. A little background on the tenure and evaluation policies at Johnston will make the reasons for that clash clear.

The development of personnel regulations at Johnston is a study in well-meaning carelessness. The leading issues were tenure (yes or no?), faculty protection against Trustee or administrative interference from the main University (the legacy of the Jeanne Friedman case), and criteria for evaluation. The issue that would have aroused most American faculties — students as voting members of the Committee — was taken for granted from the beginning; only one faculty member opposed it, and he left shortly afterwards.[1]

The assumption in all personnel policies was that face-to-face evaluation would replace closed door committees and arbitrary administrative decisions. No one felt the need to (or even thought much about) the possible legal dilemmas of such a policy. Representative of this ameliorist view is a "Personal Position Paper" written for the Committee in April of 1970 by Bill McDonald and endorsed by McCoy. One paragraph contains the following two passages:

1. "I would hope that the trust level at Johnston College would be sufficient to keep the structures (for retention) fairly simple: a review committee of administrators, faculty and students could be established to investigate and make fairly authoritative recommendations to the Chancellor." ("Fairly authoritative"?!)

2. "All AAUP (American Association of University Professors) regulations should be followed, of course. To structure the procedure any further... seems to me unnecessary at this point."

That these two points are at odds, if not contradictory, seemed to have escaped the attention of virtually everyone for the next three years. The reasons are in part understandable. The AAUP was invoked here only to protect faculty against the sort of high-handed interference exemplified by George Armacost in the Jeanne Friedman affair. The fact that AAUP has very specific and very detailed regulations governing faculty dismissal was calmly ignored.

The working conceptions of "tenure" at Johnston divided along exactly the same grounds. It may surprise Johnstonians to learn that during the Pres McCoy era it was widely assumed that Johnston faculty would be tenured, even though the idea itself generated little enthusiasm. There were practical reasons: conflict with University policy wasn't considered worth the trouble (McCoy, 10/22/70), and no one wanted to bring AAUP wrath down on the fledgling experiment. McCoy contacted the General Secretary of the AAUP to ask whether long term contracts rather than tenure were acceptable to the organization. He received a rather condescending reply, together with a Prof. Machlep's rigorous defense of strict tenure (seven years full-time teaching equals tenure no matter where the individual is currently employed). The Secretary apparently read McCoy as an administrator trying to pull a fast one on his faculty, and never actually answered the question. Only two schools — Goddard and Prescott — out of 141 surveyed had long term contract systems rather than tenure. (Don Miller even wrote a psychological analysis of the need for tenure among faculty: a classic Johnston essay). But Johnstonians were clear about one thing: "tenure" here did not mean the *de facto* lifetime contract it meant at most universities. Evaluations had to be real and serious; everyone agreed to that. It was even specified in faculty contracts. So an ingenious — or ingenuous — split was made in the traditional concept of tenure. Johnston faculty would accept the "external protections" of tenure (free speech, freedom to choose textbooks, and so forth), but not the internal protections (dismissal only for moral turpitude or gross incompetence), which in practice rendered evaluations impotent. A proposal along these lines went to the Board of Overseers in February of 1971. But they were too embroiled in McCoy's firing to consider the matter. Johnston faculty came that close to having, officially, at least some sort of tenure.

In April of 1971 a group of students proposed to the Community that no Johnston faculty member be tenured. They recommended instead five year contracts. The proposal was not officially endorsed, but its intention was widely applauded. Discussions with AAUP officials indicated that if the faculty itself endorsed a "no tenure" policy, then the organization would not in principle have any objections.[2] By October of 1971, therefore, the word "tenure" was banned from enlightened conversation. But the split between external and internal protections remained a cornerstone of Johnston belief even if it did not translate itself directly into policy. It was virtually a common law understanding among the faculty.

A set of personnel policies finally passed the Board of Overseers in February, 1972. It stressed the "educative" rather than the "punitive" purposes of faculty evaluation, and urged that the criteria for hiring and retention be the same. The criteria themselves are predictable: professional background (Ph. D. or appropriate terminal degree expected but not required); teaching (excellence in the classroom, but also a "commitment to experimental education, to the basic academic design of Johnston College, and to continual peer and student evaluation"); "institutional responsibility" (teaching a full load, doing "one's fair share" of administrative work, and committing oneself to Johnston's community life); and "implementation," which claims that categories 1-3 require "that the Fellow commit himself to openness in his interactions with others in the Johnston College Community." Contracts were to be renewed every three years.

Everyone recognized the difficulty of being both "educative" and "evaluative" at the same time, and various elaborate schemes were devised by different Personnel Committees to reconcile the split. None of their solutions proved permanent. The pressure of making contract renewals on a third of the faculty every year made the tension between the two especially sharp. The tension was great enough, in fact, to drive nearly every committee toward one pole: the educative.

As a result, the business of faculty evaluation looked much more ominous than it really was. The general mode of operation was as follows: each faculty member would write a detailed self-evaluation. Next, his evaluations from students and colleagues would be collected, read and summarized by a Personnel subcommittee composed of one student and one faculty member. Then an open meeting would be held at which students could voice both complaints and praise. Students were also invited to communicate their views to the student member of the subcommittee if they felt intimidated or feared reprisal (in fact, this privilege was almost never used). The faculty member under review would then meet with his subcommittee faculty member and another colleague of his own choosing to review his self-evaluation and his work generally. All this information would find its way into the subcommittee report, which would be discussed by the Committee as a whole. Independent (in theory) of this discussion, the Committee would also make a contract recommendation to the Chancellor. The grounds for the recommendation were not specified, on advice of University counsel. (The irony of this in an "open community" was especially galling.)

Evaluations, especially from students, were generally positive. Even faculty regarded as mediocre by a majority of community members received respectable reports; the educative principle, supported by institutional loyalty, almost always took precedence. And, as a result, the Committee usually did not perform either its educative or its evaluative function especially well. The evaluation system, incredibly time-consuming, usually produced positive enough results that faculty were not seriously threatened. But precisely because they were so positive they tended not to be educative. And faculty widely perceived as weak were, far from being "educated," all but told to continue as they had been. Even the faculty who grumbled most about load inequities refused to terminate underemployed colleagues' contracts when it actually came to a vote.

The one negative vote, on George Derfer, was reached by a process we consider just and fair. Yet it must be said that the previous year's Committee, unable to make a decision on his contract, had deferred that decision for a year in order to "work with" Derfer to improve his performance. They in fact did very little, if anything. The Committee's relatively vague procedures maddened Derfer, who saw them as an implicit *carte blanche* for whatever the current committee wished to do (to him). This view was heartily supported by the AAUP, who sent a blistering letter to President Dawson about alleged violations, and about the *de facto* tenure which Derfer, a Redlands faculty member since 1967, allegedly possessed. On the other hand, to provide the kind of fully explicit criteria and guarantees that Derfer wanted would have rendered Johnston just the sort of institution that it was created to supersede. Ultimately, the college was forced into technical maneuvers and self-serving reinterpretations of its own documents in order to justify what twelve of its members, after a participatory and equitable process, voted should be done. The Johnston process, finally, was humane, perhaps too humane.

On the hiring side of its responsibilities, the Committee fared a little better. Pres McCoy had set a high standard, and successive Committees worked very hard to find a number of excellent faculty to augment the original group. Recall that this was the early 70's; there was still some mobility in higher education, and still hundreds of faculty openly disaffected with traditional academia. The Committee received hundreds of "Help me, I'm stuck in ... and want to get out" letters each year.

Hiring procedures were less academic than personal. There was no required paper presentation, for example. Candidates met with most of the faculty and at least twenty students during a typical two-day interview. Academic style and personality were considered more valuable than a major intellectual pedigree. But by 1975 enrollments were dropping, and the opportunity to hire significant numbers of people had largely vanished.

The only dramatic hiring opportunity of 1974-75 arose when Gene Ouellette resigned to take a high administrative post with the Union for Experimenting Colleges in Yellow Springs, Ohio. A "Chancellor Search Committee" composed of four faculty, six students and a secretary who practically became a voting member of the group, illustrates the Johnston Committee "system" at its best. The Committee solicited nearly 200 applications, conducted phone interviews with over twenty of the strongest candidates, and arranged complex two to three day interviews for no less than twelve finalists. There was a convener, but no real chairman; everyone assumed as much responsibility as they could. Students were, if anything, more dedicated than the faculty members. Meetings and candidate evaluations were direct and detailed; the legacy of T-grouping was much in evidence. The Committee painfully chose its four finalists (two men and two women) as instructed by the Board of Overseers, and ranked them (though the Overseers had instructed them not to do so). When their first choice was not elected — members were not allowed to attend the Overseer interviews — Committee members were bitter for a few hours, but the solidarity produced by months of hard work proved to have more value for them than the outcome of their labor. Cathleen Crider — now a Ph. D. in psychology — said that it was the most important learning experience for her at the college.

The Academic Policy Committee seemed to be dealing with important issues in 1974-5, but appearances deceive. By this time the basic structure of education at Johnston was in place. Major issues concerned the design of transcripts, the approval of new programs, the advisability of granting WIPs and the question of equal work loads for faculty. The first issue had to do with weighing Johnston courses with respect to each other. Should all courses count the same toward graduation? It was clear that some classes took much less time to complete than others, yet on student transcripts all courses appeared as if they were equal. This meant that a student *could* graduate with a slate of very "light" classes, while another student with the same number of classes might have done twice as much work for the same degree.

This problem was solved, not by the Committee but, once more, by the ingenious Ed Williams, author of the contract system. He had proposed as early as 1971 that Johnston courses be assigned units but not credits in order to avoid basing graduation on earning a fixed number of credits. Units would be assessed using the Carnegie method: each hour in class would entail two hours' work outside class, or more. A four-unit class would mean 160 hours of work per semester; a three-unit class would mean 120 hours, and so forth. Contracts should specify just how much actual time a student would devote to the class. In this way outsiders reading transcripts and Johnston people reading graduation contracts could use the hours as a guideline.

By 1974 it was an idea ready for official adoption. It was already used by a number of faculty and students. The Committee discussed and gave its tacit consent to this policy without ever taking a formal vote. But that was of secondary importance at Johnston. The hours system did become a common feature of contracts, though it was not in universal use.

The second issue — the granting of WIPs — has already been discussed. There was one interesting intersection of the WIP policy and the hours policy that does deserve mention. It became standard practice to eliminate incompletes by renegotiating the hours stipulated in the contract. So, rather than completing a piece of work to finish the contract, the student would close the contract by stating that he wanted to be evaluated for the number of hours he had actually spent to that point. He would thus complete the contract by reducing its unit value to fit whatever work he had actually put into it. The Committee approved this procedure, but several more conservative faculty were strongly opposed to it on the grounds that it undermined the validity of the original contract. Students in effect could fulfill whatever portion of the contract they wanted, and receive credit for it. This conflict, like virtually all other similar disagreements, was never formally resolved. There was no institution-wide authority to force conformity on an issue. In theory the Chancellor and Vice-Chancellor had the legal power to do so, but in practice that rarely happened. Those faculty who strongly dis-

liked this policy simply ignored it, or made their understanding of contractual obligation clear to their students.

The issue of equal faculty loads took up a good deal of
the Committee's time during 1974-75. Certain faculty were
unhappy because they felt that they were doing more than
their share of work, while other faculty seemed to be
underemployed. This reflected the unequal popularity and
energy of faculty members, and points to the fact that it
was possible to survive as a faculty at Johnston with a
very light teaching and advising load. There was no uni-
versally accepted number of classes that faculty were
required to teach. From 1969 on there was a policy of
"doing your fair share," a phrase that was deliberately left
unclear. The "guideline" was two seminars and three
tutorials per term, but that was never made a rule. The
hope was that moral persuasion and individual responsibility would make unnecessary all the Byzantine calcula-
tions of workload that beset most American universities
(how "much" for an independent study? a science lab?
committee work? music lessons?). And with most faculty
this deliberately naive policy worked brilliantly. Many of
those who found themselves underenrolled in a given
semester volunteered for more administrative work;
physicist Allen Killpatrick's work with the budget is a
leading example. Those who did not do their "fair share"
were the object of grumbling and scorn, and their reputa-
tions suffered. But there were no official sanctions, only
peer pressure. Even when the Academic Policy stipulated
the number of classes the policy was not honored by
everyone and, like the WIP policy, proved unenforceable.

When one looks at comparative student and class loads,
the inequities are indeed glaring. In the fall of 1974 some
faculty taught as few as ten to sixteen students and worked
almost exclusively in team-taught courses in which their
responsibilities were less onerous than in classes taught
alone. Others taught primarily independent studies which
required less preparation, and still others pleaded special
administrative duties which reduced their teaching time.

On the other hand, several faculty worked with as many as fifty students. In a system which demanded detailed written evaluations and a good deal of work with individuals outside of class, the difference between teaching ten students and fifty was enormous. It was especially burdensome because the imbalance in numbers persisted over the years.

The final major issue was the question of approving programs. The pattern for program development at Johnston had been that programs were developed independently and then presented to the Academic Policy Committee as *faits accomplis* seeking official sanction. The Committee did not create programs or really oversee them: it accorded them legitimacy. During 1974-75 this pattern continued. The Committee approved the M. A. in psychology with little discussion, and began deliberations on the relatively smaller wilderness program, which they also approved once it had produced a coherent statement of purpose.

But the real day-to-day business of the Committee, the task to which it devoted the majority of its time, was assessing small budget requests for various projects. The Committee had a few thousand dollars to dispense, and it was besieged for funding by the new Women's Center, by the wilderness program, by a group which wanted to produce an original play, by another group planning a symposium to discuss the relation between the individual and society, and by a variety of people who wanted money for art supplies and a movie series and poetry readings and the like. The parallel with the 1974-5 Community Meetings is exact; the minutiae of small budget allocations had supplanted the consideration of fundamental issues. Yet for all the triviality of these requests, they do throw valuable light on the activities which provoked them. Not only was Johnston academically and politically complex, it was also bursting with social and cultural energy.

It is finally our conclusion that the political structures

of Johnston provided several vital functions: they gave students (more than faculty) a place to practice political skills; they provided for a discussion of crucial campus issues; they occasionally made painful decisions — the Derfer contract, or denying a weak graduation contract — which needed corporate endorsement. But, for all their authority, they were finally a secondary loci of power because power at Johnston did not reside in formal political structures. For one thing, institutional memory was comically poor; some difficult decisions, hammered out over long weeks of meetings, were forgotten two years later and the process begun again. But more important, individual persons, whether administrators, faculty or students, were the fundamental centers of authority — in the classroom, in the inauguration of programs, with outside groups, even in community meetings. It was not a place where committees laid down policy and community members docilely complied. Johnston politics finally proved a useful training ground, but not the vital center of the community. McCoy's conviction that persons, not society, came first, was borne out in his college's style long after he had departed.

NOTES:

1. Voting splits along faculty-student lines were virtually non-existent in the Committee; indeed, splits along student-faculty lines were a rarity in all facets of the college's political life. The most dramatic example of this occurred in 1978-9, when faculty welcomed a Personnel Committee composed of the two academic administrators and six students, with no faculty members at all.

2. There is nothing in writing to this effect, only notes from a phone conversation between Gene Ouellette and the national AAUP office. But by September of 1971 the Personnel Committee had been "assured that abandonment of the word 'tenure' from our statement would involve us in no difficulties with AAUP." President Dawson also pointed out that the protections desired by Johnston faculty were already available even to nontenured faculty in AAUP regulations, and that the use

of the word "tenure" was therefore redundant. To our knowledge, no one (for once) questioned Dawson's motives.

Section Three

1976-79:
Endings —
and New Beginnings

CHAPTER 8

Reorganization and Integration

1976-1978

The University's 1976 reorganization was not, for a change, concerned solely with Johnston. Financial troubles could not all be consigned to such a small part of the whole. The University had suffered growing deficits for several years, deficits which its officers seemed less and less able to control. At the time of the reorganization in 1976 the annual deficit was hovering around $300,000 and the University owed the Bank of America $1.5 million. Paying this off both restricted cash flow and made other borrowing difficult. The Trustees had demanded a balanced budget for 1976-77, yet preliminary budget figures showed a whopping deficit of nearly one million dollars.

Johnston, of course, was blamed for a considerable share of the deficit. The Trustees had reluctantly approved a $100,000 deficit for the college for 1975-76, and declining enrollments promised even larger shortfalls in the near future. Even though the University as a whole was running in the red, historical resentments caused Johnston to be a leading focus of plans for change. The current Vice President for Academic Affairs, Bill Moore, proposed a plan which would make Johnston an external degree institution. Most faculty and administrators would be fired, and the rest would run the off-campus program or work in other departments of the University. President Dawson endorsed the plan and forwarded it to a Select Committee of the Trustees assembled to study reorganization recommendations. When that body endorsed a much less radical version of the Moore plan the President supported that as well.

The reorganization plan approved by the Trustees created a third college, soon to be named Alfred North Whitehead College. This institution was to take over the off-campus programs currently administered by the University's office of Special Programs. It would have a larger staff and would expand these programs as quickly (and profitably) as possible. Its target population was working adults who needed a bachelor's or a master's degree to advance their careers. Though the new college did have an educational mission, it was also quite openly a money-making scheme.

The creation of a third college saved Johnston — for the time being. But there were significant changes. Any faculty members who resigned or whose contracts were not renewed would not be replaced, except in special circumstances. The Chancellor was renamed "Provost" and reported directly to the President and the Trustees rather than to the Overseers. Future faculty appointments, if any, were to be approved by the Trustees. Jim and Anita Allerdice, arguably the best Student Life staff members ever to work at the college, were fired. Lee Jones, the talented grant-writer and publicity officer, was transferred to the University's Development office and Johnston lost its best seeker of outside funds. Even more damaging, the Johnston Admissions office was closed and the two admissions counselors, Ben Tate and Oscar Porter, fired. Doris Stockman, now administrative head of UWW, was fired. The new post of Chancellor's Assistant was abolished and its first-year occupant, Ed Angus, fired.

Three secretaries were fired. And most galling to the undergraduates, the Johnston Commons was closed and Johnstonians were again required to take their meals at the University Commons as they had in the early fall of 1969.

There were small victories. The Overseers remained, though their role was radically reduced. The faculty was saved, and with it, Johnston's hard-earned separate accreditation. But these offered little consolation.

The losses in people were terribly painful on both a personal and an institutional level. Johnston lost some of its best talent, especially in the areas of public relations and recruiting — the areas where it most needed people in the face of declining enrollments. Bill Moore's prediction that the University's staff could do just as good a job proved disastrously wrong.

The reorganization also produced the most famous anecdote in the college's history. The Trustee meeting which confirmed these reorganization plans was held in the Redlands Room of the Armacost Library. The large room has a false ceiling to allow for lighting and air conditioning equipment; the ceiling is formed by light plexiglas panels resting on flimsy aluminum framing. During the meeting one Trustee thought that he heard noises from this ceiling. "Who's up there," he suddenly shouted, bringing the sedate meeting to a halt. There was silence for a moment, and then a small voice said, distinctly, "No one." Immediately thereafter a foot suddenly appeared between dislodged and falling panels. Enraged, the Trustee grabbed the foot and pulled; Johnston student Art Henning tumbled onto the meeting table. Small and lithe, he had managed to inch across the delicate tissue of the ceiling, and had overheard a good portion of the meeting. The story made the wire services and several eastern papers the next day.

Johnston survived the reorganization with its academic integrity intact and many of its programs still functioning. It maintained a remarkable vitality despite being virtually "occupied" by the University. But the decisions demoralized everyone. Students left in large numbers, and faculty adopted a doomsday approach. The end of the college was no longer in question — the only issue was when it would finally occur.

The old problem of compatibility had returned to haunt the community. Under pressure the University turned on Johnston and made decisions which effectively made it impossible for Johnston to survive. The decisions did not save the University from ongoing — and increasingly larger — deficits, nor from yet another reorganization in 1983 which led to the termination of some fourteen University faculty positions. Johnston was not the central problem. But that came clear only in retrospect. The final act of the drama, the "integration" of Johnston with the University, had still to be acted out.

The years 1976-79 were a valiant but predictably unsuccessful series of attempts to overcome the destructive effects of the 1976 reorganization and the national trend away from alternative education. Gene Ouellette, when he had accepted an administrative post with the Union for Experimenting Colleges, presciently took a two-year leave of absence from his tenured position on the University faculty. Bill Thomas, Ouellette's replacement as Chancellor in the Fall of 1975, lasted just one year. In a few months Thomas had spent whatever good will had existed between himself and President Dawson. They were openly at war by the second semester.

Thomas resigned in the Spring of 1976 and Ed Williams, long-time Vice Chancellor and principal architect of Johnston's accreditation, became the interim provost.[1] It was not a job that Ed sought but he accepted it with the same devotion that typified all his services to the college. He encountered difficulties from the first. University administrators soon grew impatient with his oblique, understated style, and some Johnston faculty felt the institution needed a more dynamic leader. When Ouellette, disenchanted with the Union, decided to resume his Redlands professorship, the search committee for the permanent provost's position approached him with the idea of returning instead to Johnston. After negotiations which assured him greater control over personnel and student life decisions, he accepted.[2] It was a painful moment for Ed Williams.

In retrospect the choice of Ouellette seems the right one. He did have a history of stormy relations with Dawson, but the two year cooling-off period had healed many of the irritations, and a core of mutual respect remained. His strengths were numerous. He could marshall support for the remaining external degree programs, which were now necessary to offset falling residential enrollments. And he had the loyalty and support of nearly everyone on the faculty, and knew how to provoke them to develop new programs. His efforts, together with those of Hugh Redmond and Dan Gilbertson, were bearing fruit by 1979.

The two years between Ouellette's two administrations were years with strong but large graduating classes whose members were not replaced by equal numbers of new students. Johnston continued to shrink. As student numbers dropped, so did those of the faculty. Old hands — European historian Michel Landa and biologist Isobel Contento — left, and faculty numbers were reduced to twenty. The social outreach programs continued in severe decline, but fascination with the self was as strong as ever; as we have seen, the programs in humanistic and transpersonal psychology were very popular. Old patterns were now set in cement. By 1979 residential Johnston was split firmly between two camps: psychology and the humanistic disciplines. Relations between the groups were friendly but there was very little intellectual exchange between them, except in the person of students or the occasional faculty member who moved from one sector to the other.

There was also a widening split between Johnston on-campus and off-campus programs. Some faculty worked comfortably with both external degree and residential students, and some external degree students blended well into campus classes. But there was limited interchange between these two groups of students, and considerable suspicion among the residential population that the external degree program was "easier" than their own.

Yet these internal bifurcations were not debilitating. They were the legacy of the emphasis on program development, and so seemed tolerable, even typical, to faculty and students. Johnston was still united, especially when it faced external threats. And it was slightly more conservative. Both faculty and students, taken as a whole, were more traditionally academic than in the earliest years. A review of course offerings for the period in question reveals a significantly greater proportion of traditional academic titles and a drop in both "flaky" and brand-new courses. The reasons for this are not hard to locate: growing student caution and conservatism; the heavy drain of continual experimentation, especially for traditionally trained faculty; the excellent reputation of certain repeated courses; and the success of certain programs, notably psychology.

Of the innovations, the most spectacular was Kevin O'Neill's semester-long travel course to classical Greek sites in 1977-78. This trip was unique in that it followed a very rigorous schedule of site and museum visitations and class meetings but otherwise left the students to fend for themselves. They had to find their own meals and hotels, make their own travel arrangements and otherwise adjust to the demands of living in a foreign country. Thus there was no break between living and learning. The experience of travel itself became one of the trip's contracted classes, equal in value to the study of classical texts and the site visitations.

As the students moved through Greece, Aegean and Mediterranean Turkey, and Sicily, they had ample opportunities to travel on their own or in small groups. Challenging cross-cultural encounters were thus unavoidable. When the group reassembled for class, students gave papers based on research they completed, using books they carried in their packs. They studied classical civilization through primary texts; they studied the history of the Mediterranean basin; they studied Greek art and architecture and city-planning.

The results of the trip were dramatic. Lives were changed, vocations discovered. Those who went acquired a certain cult status among succeeding classes. The old "international dimension" had at last been revived and attained its *arete*.

1978-1979

Gene Dawson was president of the University of Redlands for eight of Johnston's ten years. Increasingly isolated during the last years of his term by financial problems and the imposition of Alfred North Whitehead College upon an unwilling residential faculty, Dawson ended his term at Redlands with Johnston College as an improbable ally. Dawson did several favors for the beleaguered community in 1977-78, notably in connection with thirteen members of the faculty who were up for contract renewal in the spring of 1978. There was powerful Trustee pressure not to renew these contracts for their full three-year term, or even not to renew them at all.

But Dawson, now a lame-duck president, made an impassioned plea at the May, 1978, Trustees' meeting for the contracts and for the college in general. At one point he nearly broke into tears. Members of the Board's inner circle, its Executive Committee, were less than moved. But many other members, less familiar with the tension between Dawson and their leaders, were obviously stirred. We conjecture that perhaps the Board leadership, used to a docile acceptance of their views, was caught off guard. In any case, the contracts were renewed, albeit with a financial rider: the college was given a $23,000 ceiling on its deficit for the coming fiscal year. Should costs exceed that figure, the Board reserved the right to abrogate the contracts. But it was a vital and unexpected victory. The Johnston observers at the meeting frankly expected that only one-year contracts would be approved. They returned to a spontaneous celebration in the Orton Center. A few weeks later, at the end-of-the-year faculty party, Dawson took much good cheer with his former enemies, and was voted an impromptu "Comeback of the Year" award.

When Dawson first arrived in Redlands — humanistic psychologist, friend of Pres McCoy, supporter of innovative education — he had been welcomed eagerly by the Johnston community. In the Fall of 1978 the University's new president, Douglas Moore, appeared to be just as desirable a leader. He had not made much of an impression on the Johnston community during his on-campus interviews; almost no one turned in an evaluation sheet on him, and another candidate, Samuel Babbitt, was a clear favorite. But once in office Moore began to gain support. He held degrees in theology and psychology, subjects dear to the hearts of Johnstonians. He had also spent some years as a Methodist minister, which gave him a homey charisma when he delivered his "sermons" to the assembled University community. And his Texas accent, still discernible, coupled with a low-key manner, made him seem approachable and well-meaning. As a professor in Kansas, Moore had used the idea of class contracts, and he had served as provost of Callison College, the experimental wing of the University of the Pacific. Finally, he had put in several years of work with external degree programs as president of Metropolitan State University in St. Paul. With his tall frame, close-cropped grey hair, florid complexion and academic pipe, Moore was a master of one-on-one dialogue and a polished raconteur. He seemed safe and sympathetic.

In the Fall of 1978 Moore also seemed to be saying all the right things. In an interview he granted to the Johnston student magazine, *The Forum*, students Mark Phillips and Jonathan Diskin found him to be a thoughtful and candid subject. Taking one of Johnston's favorite phrases, he declared "learning how to learn" to be the central task of liberal arts education. He praised the college's distinctiveness and tendered a shrewd analysis of its political and financial difficulties. Moore even offered accurate criticism, noting that small, intense communities such as Johnston are conformist, even rigid, making political flexibility difficult and placing special stresses on new faculty members, who "really have to earn their stripes."

The same interview, however, contained more ominous statements which Moore repeated to his many constituencies during his first months in Redlands:

> ...I don't think this institution, over the last ten years, has projected a coherent image of what it is.... You come in here and you pick up the literature and you have to sort of hunt for all the bits and pieces and then put them all together, rather than the University having said, "here it is all together".... I think that Whitehead and Johnston and the old parent institution have to be more integrated, integrated again not in the sense that everybody at the University and at Johnston are doing everything alike — but there is an integration in terms of mutual respect and understanding and tolerance.

And there were other themes: "duplication must be avoided"; "resources must be used more wisely"; "...the institution can destroy itself by responding to every opportunity to make a buck, and therefore find itself more in an entrepreneur posture than in keeping to some very important principle in education...." "One of the first questions I asked Gene Ouellette was 'What are the principles or tenets of Johnston College that are the most worth preserving?'"

Johnston supporters had to face some disquieting facts in the fall of 1978. The student-faculty ratio, which had hovered near 14:1 for the years 1971-75, had fallen to 10:1 by 1977. It fell even further in the fall of 1978, when 32 students withdrew after the spring semester, citing loss of faculty as a major reason. The 1975 faculty of 24, with 11 administrators, had become a faculty of 19, with 4 administrators. The number of residential students had dropped from 280 in the fall of 1974 to 212 in 1975 and finally to 92 in 1978. While growth in the External Degree and Masters programs offset these losses to a degree, the number of full-time tuition equivalents was only 136 in the fall of 1979, compared to nearly 300 in 1974. There was hardly a residential college left.

The shrinkage was physical as well. West (or Fokat) Hall had been abandoned to the University, and East (or Kofap) now housed 30 non-Johnston students and still had empty beds. In addition, the University as a whole was suffering losses in enrollment, though not to the extent of those suffered by Johnston. Despite the 1976 reorganization deficits were a still regular occurrence, and Johnston bore some responsibility for the shortfall. In all, the prospects for the future looked grim as the University entered a decade in which the numbers of the traditional college-age students would decline significantly. President Moore was more than aware of these imposing problems and immediately instituted a self-study to reorganize the University once more and halt its downward spiral.

There were positive aspects to the Johnston picture and Ouellette was quick to point these out to the president. The external degree and M. A. in psychology programs were thriving. Ouellette encouraged the establishment of satellite campuses for both programs to increase their draw. Johnston's psychology program had established a liaison with Sonoma Institute near San Francisco; this afforded Institute students the opportunity to earn an accredited degree and it provided valuable new faculty for Johnston's Master's candidates. The undergraduate external degree program established relations with a similar program at the University of San Diego.

Ouellette believed that further development of these and other off-campus or adult-oriented programs would be Johnston's salvation. He encouraged Roger Baty's plans to establish an M. A. program in International and Intercultural Studies; this program passed successfully through the University committee structure but implementation was held up by Moore until the planning committee made its report at year's end. Ouellette could also point to an excellent core of humanities faculty who could teach the smaller numbers of residential students while social science faculty launched new non-residential programs.

At first it was not clear what Moore thought of Johnston's chances. He met with Ouellette weekly and relations seemed friendly; he kept re-emphasizing, to faculty, his sympathy with experimental education in general and with Johnston in particular. But at the same time he continued to talk about "lack of focus" and a "confusing image."

By late fall, 1978, the clouds grew darker. The weekly meetings between Moore and Ouellette became bi-weekly. The San Diego connection began to grow stale and the International Studies M. A. remained on hold. During Interim, as the President's March deadline for reorganization of the University drew near, the Johnston faculty met off-campus with Moore, hoping to provoke fresh ideas in a fresh setting.

For some reason lost in history the meeting took place in a gloomy, rather sleazy upstairs banquet room of a restaurant in San Bernardino. It was late afternoon; the sun dappled a tacky, multicolored carpet which had not seen a vacuum cleaner for at least a month. The faculty sat on plastic chairs around sterile Formica-topped conference tables.

Moore finally made his plans clear, though he continued to insist on their provisional nature. "Reorganization" was the watchword. Graduate programs belonged under the aegis of the dean of graduate studies; all external degree programs belonged at Whitehead. The first point was not too troubling; the Johnston graduate program already had close relations with the graduate dean and inclusion of it under this person would not mean serious structural changes to the college. But the inclusion of the growing external degree program would take students away from Johnston at a time when it needed them desperately. Under the new arrangement, M. A. students would still be Johnston students and take Johnston classes. But if external degree students went to Whitehead they would take Whitehead classes. Moore ended by uttering heresy: "There should be one faculty" for the University and Johnston, though he quickly added that this could be accomplished in many different ways. It was clearly the moment for a counterattack. The situation sharply echoed other perilous times in the history of the college. McCoy had fended off Armacost's plans for an international business school. Ouellette had neutralized the worst features of the 1976 reorganization. Now he must try again.

The community, always most unified when threatened, swung into action. Petitions were drawn up, telegrams and letters were sent to the Trustees and Overseers. New designs were proposed, and the Johnston case was argued at Board meetings in the first months of 1979. Ouellette offered three possible models for reorganization: the "fold-in" plan, which would mean the end of Johnston as a separate entity; then a plan in which there would be two residential colleges, one for liberal arts and another for "nontraditional liberal arts and career preparation for students of all ages" with emphasis on graduate and external degree programs. This was really a plan for uniting Johnston and Whitehead; it had no serious support. The third plan was the real Johnston proposal and it essentially called for maintaining the *status quo*. In this plan the "restructuring" would not affect Johnston's academic autonomy, and it would leave the Board of Overseers intact. The only changes would be that graduate faculty would report to the graduate dean (which they already did), and Johnston faculty would "work more closely (with University faculty)...to avoid expensive duplication." Faculty contracts would be rewritten so that the University would have no responsibility for paying Johnston faculty salaries should the plan fail. Ouellette ended his argument by suggesting that if the "fold-in" model was used the University would lose more than $400,000 in tuition, and room and board. It would also lose revenue to pay off the mortgage on the Johnston buildings and it would be stuck with paying several Johnston faculty salaries.

Ouellette's analysis was clear. It was an article of faith at Johnston that the experiment could only succeed if it were separate from, and protected from, the bureaucratic processes of the University. Thus the achievement of separate accreditation had been the cornerstone of Johnston's success. To take that away meant taking away Johnston's control over its own destiny; it meant, in effect, the death of the experiment or, at best, its trivialization. And separate accreditation could not be maintained without a separate governing Board.

As the college moved into the spring semester, Ouellette continued to believe that Moore shared his dedication to preserving Johnston's autonomy. On January 18 he wrote a letter based on the assumption of a "University of Redlands commitment to preservation of the Johnston College philosophy, educational design, programs and personnel." Moore had never explicitly rejected any of this, and he did ultimately preserve the philosophy and the educational design. In Ouellette's view Moore had no intention of closing the college. He trusted Moore and, canny political veteran that he was, this trust must have been based on some foundation. But Moore's public statements were consistent, if somewhat general. As the day of reorganization loomed, these statements grew more specific; his intention was to reorder the campus so that it would survive the travails of the 80's. At no time did he explicitly state that in so doing he would preserve Johnston in its current form. Nor did he explicitly state that he was going to close it. Nor is there written evidence in the archive to suggest that he was hired to close Johnston. It appears that he kept an open mind on this question during much of the 1978-79 school year.

The showdown came on February 16, 1979, at the Pauma Country Club north of Escondido. While Overseers' meetings were typically held on campus, the Board nominated one meeting a year as a "retreat" and held that meeting in quieter and more elegant surroundings. This was especially appropriate since the meeting would deal with reorganization plans, whose airing needed a certain degree of privacy.

Ouellette recalls that he shared lunch with Moore and Milo Bekins, chair of the Trustees. This was the first time he got an inkling of what was about to happen. Several times during the meal, as reorganization plans were discussed, Bekins, never a model of diplomacy, pushed Moore — "But you are going to close Johnston, right?" Moore remained noncommittal. "That was the first time," continued Ouellette, "that I even suspected that a decision had already been made — and therefore that everything must have been decided beforehand. But I refused to believe it." The fateful meeting itself was conducted in the cool, expensively decorated conference room, a sharp contrast to the shabby haven in which Moore had met the Johnston faculty a month earlier. The familiar long rectangle of tables covered with spotless white cloths and name cards was in place. Standard business was dispensed with quickly.

Moore led off in his low-key fashion, painting with a large brush the facts about national student demographics, inflation and the University's lack of a clear image: old stuff. But now came sharper phrases, and with them Moore's sermonic intensity increased:

In order to meet the challenges of the future we must redefine our goals. We are at work on models of Johnston College as an integral part of the University rather than an appendage.... The whole must see the value of the parts, and the parts must see the value of the whole. And the models that Dr. Ouellette is about to present to you are not necessarily anyone's position, but working models from which a plan may be derived.

Ouellette then went through the three models, devoting most of his time to the third. He emphasized the importance of rewriting faculty contracts to protect the University from potential financial loss, and he presented the entire plan with energetic conviction. Long discussion followed, with money the central issue for most Overseers. Student Overseers Judith Braber and Jonathan Diskin, with the confidence typical of Johnston's best, welcomed the opportunity to educate the Overseers and spoke eloquently about the academic strengths of the college — strengths which no one questioned.

The most telling moment of the three-hour meeting came at its end. Overseer Alexander "Sandy" Power, a long-time generous supporter of the college, asked whether definite reaction to the three models from the Board of Overseers was required at this time. Gene Ellis, the chair, turned to President Moore and said, "It's up to you, Mr. President. Do you want such a reaction?" Moore shook his head; nothing more was required of the Board of Overseers. To any objective observers, the final outcome was now clear.

Johnstonians, still misreading the signs, returned to

232 A HISTORY OF JOHNSTON COLLEGE

campus with unrealistic if pardonable euphoria about the college's future. The meeting seemed to have gone well; the Overseers were generally supportive. But their mood was also shaped by what they were returning to — the tenth anniversary reunion, Johnston's first official gathering of alumni.

Unlike most Johnston efforts the reunion was meticulously planned. Gene Ouellette made it a leading priority and student intern Larry Singer turned the project into a full-time job. The notion of "alumni" was liberalized to include everyone who had ever registered as a Johnston student.

The event was a stunning success. Eighty-three former students signed up before the weekend, and over one hundred more were registered for the major reunion events on Saturday and Sunday. Time had not dulled the Johnston tendency to trifle with deadlines. Nearly all the faculty, staff and ex-faculty were there to greet them.

The real reunion began with lunch in the Johnston commons. Impromptu performances by current students punctuated the meal. The weekend was officially titled "Johnston Celebrates!" and that spirit swept through the Orton Center as the community meeting began. Nearly all community meetings in Johnston's history were held in the Orton Center's spacious foyer adjacent to the dining hall. As the alumni came out from lunch the familiar scene greeted them, and the mood was set. For the first time in years the room was full. Old students and new, faculty, spouses, friends — there were nearly 300 people pressed around the open space in the center of the room where, as per tradition, a faculty member (Bill McDonald) and a student (Patty Polinger, class of 1975) co-chaired the meeting.

The meeting opened with a report on the present state of the college, delivered by several undergraduates. They were unaccustomedly tongue-tied. The highly energetic alums had taken over their school, and they felt temporarily dispossessed. Then people spoke movingly of their experiences at the college and especially of the ways in which Johnston had shaped their lives. Alumnus Davis Masten impulsively started a pass-the-hat money-raising scheme to "save Johnston." Excitement ran high; speakers interrupted one another. Johnston's present plight and future prospects were discussed, and shortly both old and new students joined the meeting as equals.

Doug Moore showed courage. He attended this volatile meeting and took the brunt of Johnston's bitterness at the turn things had taken in the past few years. As he left, one community member shouted at him to take a good look at what Johnston really was. Moore did not turn around.

Then Pres McCoy spoke. He had arrived earlier in the day, smiling broadly and still greeting old colleagues with the slightly distracted charisma of a man running for office. People clustered around him, honoring him for what he had become for them − a legendary figure, now suddenly come to life. When he was introduced to the meeting applause and shouts continued for five minutes. Obviously moved, Pres spoke, using the old jargon − "growth of the individual," "living-learning community," "affective and cognitive" and all the rest. He ended by a reaffirmation of the Johnston project:

> I feel so fortunate to have been here at Johnston, to have had the chance to put some of these ideas to work. And even in the most miserable times I have never regretted it for one minute. You don't get that many opportunities for building something with a group of people...and look at this community now. I'd do it again!

That evening, fresh from various Redlands watering holes and a catered dinner in the Orton Center (which featured for "entertainment" a set of dreadful skits produced in typical fashion by O'Neill and McDonald), the alumni were treated to the climax of "Johnston Celebrates!" Paul Cornell, a talented photographer as well as scientist, had put together a Johnston multi-media show primarily for recruitment purposes. Two slide projectors flanked a film projector. There was a narration and musical sound track. The seven-minute show gave a quick overview of the Redlands area, the Johnston program and the feel of Johnston-style learning. But for old Johnstonians it did more than that. The fast-paced show was a brilliant condensation of the college's history: from the drive into Redlands in Ed Williams' familiar orange Fiat convertible, through Doug Bowman's cartoon panels of graduation contract building, to the scores of beautifully photographed candid shots taken from 1969 to 1978, the essence of the Johnston experience unfolded before the audience. What began as entertainment became a religious celebration.

Just before the end, pictures of the 1976 reorganization meetings bled across the screen, with a piercing atonal lament on the sound tract: Gene Ellis' set jaw, Gene Dawson's angry eyes, the floors and walls of the empty Orton Center littered with telegram drafts and tattered worksheets. But then, in Paul's history, the college rises from its ashes. The music quickens with a compelling beat, slides of delighted faces at graduation flash by, the campus in California sunset fills the side screens. The center panel then shows trainer Phil Smith leading a dozen students down a high-grass slope as the finale of a long T-group session. They skip and jump, serpentining, long hair flying as they follow their bounding, laughing leader.

Everything was there: the joy in learning, the sheer celebration of feeling, the freedom and trust of shared community, the promise of the 60's, the dawning of Aquarius. The Dream.

As the lights came on, the room exploded. It was the single most intense public moment since the firing of McCoy. Many people were weeping. Others embraced, shouted themselves hoarse, saw the same wild-eyed joy in the faces of strangers. It was cultic — the best and the worst of Johnston. Everyone celebrated the epiphany they had made together.

It remains now only to see how the sock finally unraveled in the late spring of 1979. Moore, though welcoming opposition in the speech with which our book began, in fact withdrew, Buddha-like, from the process. Questions had to be directed to his chief academic officer, Don Shockley. Shockley was new to the office and was suddenly faced with a host of unfamiliar issues and histories — and with a very angry group of Johnstonians.

Shockley saw himself as a friend of Johnston but that commitment was simply incompatible with his current responsibilities. With everything now up in the air — faculty contracts, control of programs, the political future of the community — people pushed Shockley for guarantees that he was unable to give. Unification and retrenchment were his two constant replies to any attempts by Ouellette and Williams to find some breathing room in the President's mandate.

Long negotiations over the Johnston external degree program went nowhere, and the program was closed down by the following fall. Five faculty whose contracts were up for renewal were given notice during the summer. Frank Blume negotiated for his job and eventually won it back. After a stint as Redlands' Institutional Research officer, he is now Director of the Johnston Center and a tenured member of the psychology department. Dan Gilbertson was hired as a Director of Summer Programs for the University, a job that he held for a few years before resigning. The rest were let go. Despite Shockley's best efforts at conciliation, the situation deteriorated. In June Ouellette wrote to Moore expressing "shock" over the non-renewal of faculty contracts, and referring bitterly to broken promises. Words from the March reorganization speech were thrown back in the President's face to prove his hypocrisy and his desire to "eradicate all things Johnston."

Ouellette, to no one's surprise, resigned his post and returned to his tenured position in the communicative disorders program at the University. He was finished with Redlands politics in any form. Biologist Kathy Shumaker, a relative newcomer to the Johnston faculty, took over as the first Dean of the "Johnston Center for Individualized Learning." Shockley left that summer to become the chaplain at Emory University, exhausted by an impossible job. His replacement, biologist Gerry Gates, became the leading architect of the new relationship between Johnston and the University.

In the midst of this there were several signs of the healing that the president hoped for. Johnston student Judith Braber was elected president of the University-wide Associated Students. Bill McDonald was voted in as president of the University Faculty Senate for the coming year. In fact, the 1979-80 Faculty Senate had no fewer than five Johnstonians in its twelve member constituency. The remaining Johnston faculty were assigned to University departments and given a paltry three years' credit toward tenure. Yasuyuki Owada was appointed chair of the sociology department and Kevin O'Neill became chair of philosophy and, shortly thereafter, of history as well. Roger Baty became the director of the library and Doug Bowman became the University chaplain. Ed Williams took over direction of graduate research at Whitehead, and Dave Bragg became chair of the math department, joined there by physicist Allan Killpatrick. Andy Shumaker continued part-time in photography. Only the Shumakers and McDonald were officially assigned to work at Johnston Center.

The programs that were entirely destroyed by this reorganization were both the graduate and undergraduate psychology programs and the external degree program. The University psychology department with its traditional outlook wanted nothing to do with psychodrama,

Gestalt or the transpersonal. Only Frank Blume was kept on; Coulibaly, Miller, Redmond, Tubbs, Smith — all were gone. Glenn Whitlock was permitted to teach clinical psychology for two years until his retirement. Essentially, the core of the humanities faculty were kept. From a high of twenty-eight full-time faculty in 1972-74, eight Johnstonians remained as full-time faculty on the residential campus in 1987. All were tenured and occupied leading positions in both the academic and political life of the institution. Ed Williams remained at Whitehead, again in a position of leadership.

On May 26, 1979, at 2 p.m., in the 97 degree heat and smog of the Southern California summer, Johnston College graduated its last full class on the lawn before Orton Center. The ceremony had been conducted eight times before and its spontaneity was now a familiar pleasure. It once again proved itself to be one of Johnston's most resonant inventions.

Traditional commencements stress the impersonally ceremonial. Every student wears the same inappropriately heavy black garb and marches in vaguely military fashion across a stage to the reading of their full name before returning to the anonymity of his or her seat in the crowd. The ceremony is more stuffy than celebrative.

At Johnston each senior's graduation was his or her own. The diploma was presented by people of his or her choice — parents or lovers, friends or children, professors or grandmothers or dogs. Most presenters spoke, at greater or lesser length, of their feelings for the graduate. Some faculty gave books to their seniors, others quoted from freshman applications as graduates squirmed. Most people simply expressed admiration and love. A few snickered at the sentimentality before or after the ceremony. During it everyone seemed caught up; hugs and tears were the order of the day.

The families of external degree graduates were especially touching. They had often sacrificed more than the money and patience demanded of the parents of residential students. And parents were frequently as moved by the ceremony as the graduates; in the reception following, at which champagne always flowed freely, their praise for the school and for the faculty was often effusive. Small liberal arts colleges regularly promise individual attention and respect for the person to justify their high tuition. At Johnston, graduates and their families took part in a ceremony which enshrined that promise and gave it full life.

At that final ceremony eleven M. A. degrees in psychology were awarded along with fifty-four baccalaureate degrees and the only B. F. A. ever earned at the college. Bill McDonald, following tradition, gave a short faculty address. He described the day as one of commencement not only for seniors but for the college itself as it sought to begin a new life at the University. President Moore sat in the front row and endured several not-so-subtle barbs from the graduates before leaving during one of the intermissions. Mark Fleckenstein was the last student called to the podium (Johnstonians refused to graduate in alphabetical order!). Long after the ceremony, long after the last of the reception champagne had disappeared and the maintenance crew had carted away the folding chairs, people lingered, talking quitely in the darkening air. No one wanted to leave.

NOTES:

1. The history of the college may be traced in miniature in the titles of its chief officer: 1968-75, Chancellor; 1975-79, Provost; 1979-80, Dean of Johnston Center; 1981-present, Director.

2. Ouellette, in his interview of June, 1984, made clear that he had definite plans in both areas. Most dramatically, he intended to get rid of five faculty whom he considered weak. But the growing threat of yet another reorganization made him fight for every faculty position.

Conclusion

Killing a college is like trying to kill a barrel of snakes. As soon as you think it's dead, it rears its head again.

— Douglas Moore, 1/9/85

After a lost war, one should only write comedies.

— Novalis

We began this history with a dramatic scene — President Moore's announcement that Johnston College would no longer exist as a separately accredited institution. As we complete our work some eight years after that event, the Johnston Center for Individualized Learning has just graduated eighteen students in a ceremony identical to Johnston College graduations of the past. Only the location is different — the lawn of Bekins Hall, a smallish dormitory on the main campus quadrangle. But this was unmistakably a Johnston graduation for students who had gone through the time-honored graduation contract and review process, and who had chosen a favorite person to present their diploma. There was once again a faculty

239

speaker, grateful parents and tearful graduates.

The continued existence of a Johnston program on the campus of the University of Redlands raises questions which this conclusion will try, in a combination of summary and analysis, to answer. There are four such questions: first, why is Johnston no longer a college?; second, why does it survive as a "Center"?; third, what is it like today?; and finally, what does the Johnston experience offer to other American institutions of higher learning?

In the foregoing narrative, we have shown how Johnston's demise as a college came about, and we have discussed President Moore's public reasons — money, and the "incoherence of the Redlands image" — for such a move. The financial and image arguments were indeed crucial, and we have no wish to minimize their importance in what follows. But we also believe that there are several structural reasons why the college was closed and why it continues today in a new form. These reasons lead us to the fourth and most difficult question: what does the Johnston experiment offer to higher education generally?

Why is Johnston no longer a college? It is important to say first that Johnston did not close because it suffered an internal collapse. Up to and beyond Moore's 1979 announcement the educational life of the college remained vigorous. Classes offered in 1979, though more traditional, were nearly as varied as those offered in 1975-7, and students were just as engaged and enthusiastic as they had ever been. It could even be argued that the Johnston of 1979 was academically superior because the faculty was more experienced, and because the students of the post-Watergate era were generally more serious (though less imaginative) about their studies.

Moreover, the faculty did not appear to be suffering the burnout so often encountered at experimental colleges. At least they were not suffering any more than they had four years previously and, if such burnout manifestations as late evaluations, the "cult of bitching" and reduced office hours are any indicator,[1] the 1979 faculty in fact was less harassed than it had been in '75. Over a decade of trial and error people had learned to cope, and by 1979 most faculty were working well within their limits. The smaller number of students obviously helped as well.

The centrifugal patterns established after the departure of McCoy were still dominant factors in the structure of the college. To review quickly, the gradual withering away of the social action programs left the psychologists on one hand and the liberal arts faculty on the other as the two prevailing "cliques." Both groups were solidly established; each had its cadre of loyal students and there was relatively easy movement of students between the two informal circles. The sometime acrimony which had once existed between the groups had markedly diminished. Members of both groups remained deeply loyal to the Johnston system, and this shared loyalty overcame any points of disagreement. Longtime coexistence had established a degree of mutual trust and respect.

And of course there were many fewer students, despite the health of the academic program. By 1979 Johnston had shrunk to only a third of its former size; from representing more than 20 percent of the residential student population at Redlands, it had diminished to less than ten percent of that total. And nothing seemed able to arrest the trend. Faculty joined the beleaguered University admissions office in spending a good deal of time on admissions work, but there no longer seemed to be much interest in alternative education.

This brings us to the most important internal fact affecting the closing of the college. As student numbers diminished, faculty numbers did not — or at least not proportionally. Faculty ranks were somewhat thinned by resignations but in 1979 there were still eighteen faculty, a reduction of about 35 percent from 1975. But during the same period Johnston had lost nearly 70 percent of its students. Since the faculty had never taken pay cuts (though raises were few and modest) and nearly all revenue was derived from tuition, budget deficits became severe.

It was clear to the University that something had to be done. Pressure to reduce faculty numbers by non-renewal of contracts, postponed by a hair's-breadth in 1976, again became intense. But Johnston was intransigent. The college believed, rightly, that if the number of faculty was reduced past a certain point it could no longer pretend to offer a real college curriculum, and it was not willing to accept the obvious alternative — to reduce faculty and to cease being a college. Johnston people also resented University pressure because it threatened the fiercely-defended academic autonomy on which so much of Johnston's identity was based, and for which it had fought so hard. Finally, it was difficult for Johnston people to believe that their experiment was really in trouble because its day-to-day life remained so vital. Empty dorm rooms aside, poverty was a disease with few surface symptoms; it was easier, and more in keeping with Johnston tradition, to assume that the University had made a false, or at least a hasty, diagnosis.

It is also important to recall another factor which was not directly linked to hostility and mistrust of the University. The strong feelings of community, and a personnel system that emphasized the educative rather than the punitive aspects of evaluation, made it all but impossible for Johnstonians to fire incompetent or underworked faculty. The combination of this inability to clean their own house, and an equal inability to take seriously the University's plaints about financial crisis, made the Johnston people firmly resistant to any fundamental changes.

We need to add a final note. The years of opposition between Johnston and the University had eroded compassion. Johnston people just could not see that the University was experiencing serious, perhaps fatal problems; if

Johnstonians saw it, they did not care because they had lost the ability — if they ever had it — to identify the problems of the University as their own. If the lack of empathy was relatively unimportant when Johnston was paying its own way, it became a decisive factor when the University asked the college to see itself as part of a larger enterprise and to make sacrifices accordingly.[2]

Johnston's continuing survival as a Center is best understood in terms of the complex circumstances facing the University in 1979. The parent institution was in a difficult bargaining position. Its years of obstruction and snipping at the ideology of Johnston — if not at its educational program — made its more rational concerns about finances suspect. Johnston people cannot be blamed entirely for imagining that University fiscal concerns or President Moore's dissatisfaction with an "incoherent" campus were simply blinds for imposing its mores on Johnston. And the University can be charged, with considerable justice, with grossly neglecting Johnston admissions, public relations and the excellent outside grant support record of the college after the reorganization of 1976.

Further, the University was not only in a financial bind, but, just as important, a structural one as well. Like so many small liberal arts colleges it had expanded eagerly during the prosperous days of the late 60's, and it had committed itself heavily, in its residential undergraduate program, to an Arts and Sciences curriculum. But in post-Vietnam America, under the pressure of a faltering economy, students joined their parents in looking for immediate, tangible results from a college degree. The typical college student of the late 70's was more interested in training for a career in business than in personal development. And fewer eighteen to twenty year olds were going to college at all.

The University now found itself poorly equipped to deal with the shift in student interest and with reduced enrollments. It had not invested heavily in business, economics, engineering or computer science faculty, and it was dominated by a large number of liberal arts faculty whose advanced courses were drawing fewer and fewer students. This faculty had been trained to be **academic professionals** — people who measured success in terms of scholarly accomplishment within strictly defined disciplines. As teachers, they were acculturated to offer sequences of courses leading to disciplinary majors. Such sequences were ideally suited to prepare students for graduate study in the field. But by the late 1970's the academic life had not only lost its charm to allegedly more hard-headed interests, it was heavily overpopulated. Jobs in such disciplines as philosophy or the classics were literally non-existent. So students quickly lost interest in training for graduate school, and the disciplinary structure of all but a few majors became, from a market point of view, outmoded. Faculty trained to produce others like themselves were compelled more and more to offer "service" courses — mostly lower-division — to students whose primary interests lay elsewhere.

The Arts and Sciences faculty had a difficult time adjusting because the shift in student interest threatened their hegemony over the curriculum, put their livelihood in jeopardy, and sharply qualified the value of their professional training. Morale was low and the future looked threatening as Business Administration became the largest major in the residential program. Even in that bastion of liberal arts professionalism, the English department, more and more students wanted to be trained as writers, and fewer and fewer showed interest in traditional courses in literary history and criticism.

Faculty fears were only exacerbated by the foundation of the Alfred North Whitehead Center for Life-Long Learning. Whitehead, to repeat, was founded in an attempt to exploit a new population of learners — working adults who for one reason or another needed a college degree but who did not have the time or the means to become full-time students on campus. Whitehead was only one of many such programs developed during the period and, despite the political blunders which attended its founding, has turned out to be one of the University's saner decisions. Adult learning has proved to be the one expanding market for higher education in the 1980's. Whitehead grew like Topsy and did indeed produce desperately needed revenue for the residential program. But it also threatened the residential faculty, many of whom saw in Whitehead a crass abandonment of the University's dedication to liberal learning and a pandering to students whose only interest in college was in acquiring the technical certification necessary for career advancement.

Whitehead itself in the early 1980's was under very serious attack because it had hired a highly suspect "headhunter" organization to garner students for its far-flung programs. The University was doing all it could to extricate itself from its contract with that organization because its accreditation was suddenly at risk.

The University was thus in trouble on several fronts. Johnston remained recalcitrant in the face of shrinking revenues; the University faculty were understandably agitated by a redefinition of their role as professionals and pressed for clarity about their future; the University needed to find the means and the structural genius to add faculty in technical areas without giving up its longtime commitment as liberal arts education; finally, it needed to exert stringent quality controls in the Whitehead program so that it would not further damage its already shaky reputation by in effect selling degrees to all comers. This raft of problems had to be solved, moreover, in the face of a shrinking residential population and sharply increasing costs.

All this argued strongly for a centralization of power in the administration and for much more coherent planning at the top. If the University were to survive the 80's it needed to establish firmer control over its many parts. One of the parts was of course Johnston, and here the problem was relatively simple: the University had to establish hegemony over Johnston faculty contracts, which were beyond its power to control under current arrangements. There were two ways to do this: the University could close Johnston once and for all and cut its losses, or it could restructure the program to give it the control it felt it needed. Gene Ouellette had offered a third way — linking faculty contracts directly to income — but this was mere temporizing for anxious University officials. Melodramatic metaphors were common in meetings and in memos; the ship had to be righted before it was too late.

But closing the college outright would have had negative effects without addressing these structural issues. In the first place the Johnston program did have a national reputation among educators, even if that reputation did not currently produce many matriculants. Sacrificing such an advantage made little sense when the University was struggling to establish itself in a more competitive market. And there were obvious advantages in retaining the small but real Johnston student body: ninety tuitions at $5000 each were not to be sneezed at.

A second series of reasons for retention, not directly part of the original calculus, began to emerge in 1979-80 as negotiations between Gerry Gates, Johnston Dean Kathy Shumaker, and the McDonald-led Senate proceeded. Johnston did have an excellent faculty — at least some excellent faculty — which the University had good reason to retain. Even though long-term interests might be served by reducing the relative proportion of liberal arts faculty on campus, some of the Johnston people could be assimilated at small cost by assigning them to faculty slots recently vacated by retirement or resignation. And the Johnston faculty members were especially attractive because they had expressly given up their strict disciplinary and professional loyalties when they signed on at

Johnston. If the University did plan to restructure, it could not hurt itself by hiring people without such loyalties. Finally, the Johnston program could be retained, without Johnston College, at relatively little cost. If faculty were either let go or reassigned, all the new program, Johnston Center, would need would be a Director and a secretary. Faculty could teach courses at Johnston as needed, and also fill any emerging gaps in the University's curriculum, particularly in the low-status "service courses" category.

So the University decided to close the college but keep the program. And Johnston was no longer in a position to resist. The small number of students sharply reduced the college's bargaining power, and its persistent deficits since 1975 made its case even weaker. Part of the price paid for autonomy was that Johnston had virtually no political allies in the administration, and it certainly had few adamant supporters among the Trustees. Equally important, it could not at this juncture make common cause with any of the University's other constituencies. It had little in common with the University faculty, which was fighting to retain the very departments and strong disciplinary majors which Johnston had specifically abjured. Indeed, the University already had more than half the number of programs and sub-programs as it had faculty! And Whitehead was no ally, since Johnston was not a pre-professional school (except in the field of humanistic and transpersonal psychology, a program which had virtually no relationship to Whitehead's aims). And of course the Trustees and administration were bent on gaining control over Johnston faculty contracts and could hardly be expected to embrace their opponents. The ideal community which had gathered at Pilgrim Pines to revolutionize American higher education was, or seemed to be, irretrievably shattered.

But then something happened that surprised the Johnston diehards. Once Johnston faculty contracts were securely under University control and the faculty "massacre" carried out, the University did an about-face and made real efforts to preserve all the other trappings of the Johnston system: narrative evaluations, graduation contracts, even a good measure of living autonomy. The reason quickly became clear: what the University administration wanted was complete administrative and fiscal as opposed to academic control. The old fears that the Trustees or the University Academic Policy Committee would make short work of the experiment itself proved groundless. In fact, the opposite turned out to be the case. The University genuinely wanted to retain the Johnston program, and not only for the pragmatic reasons cited above. The University was still, despite its various crises, an academic as well as a political and economic institution, and it acted at least partly as such with respect to Johnston. Doug Moore's own experience at Callison College, now closed, no doubt helped shape this fresh attitude. Administrators recognized Johnston's inherent educational value and were loath to give that up because it represented a standard of excellence which they considered valuable to the future of the institution as a whole.

In the lengthy negotiations during the fall of 1979 over the details of Johnston's amalgamation, only one serious point was forced on the community without its consent. First semester freshmen were not allowed to enroll in Johnston; new students had to become Redlands students before they could become Johnston students. After two years, as enrollment pressures continued, even this qualification was quietly dropped.

So the Johnston process remained in place. The new Center was relocated in Bekins Hall, the smallest and oldest of the University dormitories. There, about forty students could live and four or five faculty offices could be established. There was sufficient space for classrooms, a communal kitchen and rec room, the meditation and dark rooms, and a central lobby in which community and graduation contract meetings could be held. In fact, Bekins has proved much more amiable than the sterile

East and West Halls, and there the Johnston communal spirit has continued, unfettered by University interference or fueled by University opposition.

Under the new dispensation the Center was more closely integrated with the life of the University. Since relatively few Johnston courses could be offered by the remaining faculty, who had assumed new departmental responsibilities, students took the majority of their work at the University. And, happily, a number of University faculty began to list their classes in the Johnston section of the catalog. Among certain segments of the faculty there even developed a friendly competition to woo Johnston students into classes because they proved to be more vocal and generally more committed than the normal run of Redlands students. In addition, Johnston students could ask any University faculty member to write a narrative evaluation for a standard University class; indeed, the evaluation option now appeared on official registration cards, marking both the domestication of Johnston and the seduction of the University. Roger Baty's old vision of Johnston as the "Trojan Horse" that would infiltrate the citadel of Redlands suddenly seemed credible.

The natural increase in contacts between University and Johnston students which the new order created also produced some unexpected results. Many University students began to enroll in the few "pure" Johnston courses offered through the Center. Some — between fifteen and twenty a year — transferred into the Johnston program and others became Johnston fellow travellers, spending a good deal of their leisure time at Bekins without officially joining the Center. Conversely, about half of the Johnston student population now lived in other University dormitories either because of sheer numbers, or because they did not feel comfortable with the vaguely countercultural life at Bekins. Thus the violent antagonism between the two student groups began slowly to diminish, and Johnston and its processes have become, in 1987, a familiar alternative to standard patterns of study. Naturally, Johnston continues to proclaim its differences, but these are now more of degree than of kind. Johnston is still seen as "weird" by some University students, but Bekins is hardly the forbidding ghetto that East and West halls once were to the main campus undergraduates.

The "old" Johnston faculty ended up in perhaps the most ironic position of all. At the time of this writing all eight who were kept on are tenured full professors in positions of academic and political authority. Several have won Outstanding Teaching awards. Nearly all of them still spend time advising Johnston students and serving on graduation committees, and a few regularly offer old-style Johnston seminars and keep full-time offices in Bekins. But these faculty have also adapted to life at the University and their enthusiasm, along with the quality of Johnston students, has lured many University faculty into association with the Center. This has allowed those who so desired to devote more time to their research activities. A college such as Johnston can create an almost feudal dependence of faculty members on the specialized institution; it demands so much that transfer to a mainstream professorial life is very difficult. The reincorporation of Johnston into the main University has made a more balanced professional life possible for those Johnstonians who needed it.

Students can still move through the old Johnston process as they did in the past and the few faculty (Blume as Director, Childs, O'Neill, McDonald, and Andy Shumaker) who still have Johnston offices provide the appropriate instruction in Johnston contracting traditions and offer those essential "in" classes that help create and consolidate communal ties. True, Johnston is no longer a place to study "new wave" psychology and its ambitions are considerably moderated, but for students primarily interested in the classic liberal arts it provides as rich an academic and social environment as it ever did. And the heritage of humanistic psychology has not disappeared entirely; Frank Blume regularly leads a T-group, and graduate Kate Kelley offered a psychodrama workshop in the spring of 1987 which was exotic — and popular — with current undergraduates.

The numbers, when compared to 1971, are still small. But the trend is very encouraging. From a nadir of 35 students in the days immediately following reorganization, the Center this year, thanks to an increasing number of internal transfers, passed 100 enrollees toward the end of the spring semester. There are now more students enrolled at Johnston than when the college closed. Ironically, growth has become something of a problem; a move to a larger dormitory has been negotiated for the summer of 1988. And applications are burgeoning: three years ago fewer than ten high school seniors applied directly to the Center; this year the number of applications exceeded seventy. The University's investment in new admissions materials, and the dedication of a new, very supportive admissions staff, have paid off. And the quality of those students is, if anything, stronger than the entering classes of the 1970's. Of the twenty-two new students who enrolled in the Center in the fall of 1986, five were National Merit Finalists. (One University administrator noted, waggishly, that the Johnston freshmen had higher SAT scores than the entering freshmen at Stanford) Among the 23 graduates of the Johnston class of 1986, there were six Phi Beta Kappas, more than a quarter of those elected from the entire University.

At the same time the Center has strongly resisted several informal overtures from University officials that it become the "honors program" for the institution. The offer is tempting because it appeals to the elitism that schools such as Johnston have consistently maintained toward more traditional institutions. But the egalitarian impulse remains equally strong. Johnston continues to do its best work, we believe, with the student who, whatever the reasons, has compiled a very mixed academic record in high school, or even in the first two years of college.

Johnston has enabled many of these students to discover and then work right to their potential, producing persons who can accomplish goals, academic and otherwise, which they once thought entirely beyond them. The tight-knit community encourages such students to learn in concert with more talented or more industrious peers, and in turn to influence those entering students who have similarly ambivalent educational histories. This commitment not just to self and institution, but to fellow students as students, is one of the distinctive features of schools such as Johnston, and one whose implications for the greater society we are especially proud.

We attended the American Association of Higher Education national convention in 1985. The principal focus of this convention was the presentation and discussion of two major national studies of American higher education, studies conducted by the Carnegie Commission and the National Institute for Education. The findings of these studies, and their energetic presentation by such authorities as Charles Muscataine and Alexander Astin, left us with feelings of exhilaration and bitterness. The reason was simple: the list of their recommendations read like an outline of a Johnston College catalogue. These reports elaborately confirmed that Johnston-style education is in fact what best produces learning in undergraduate students. Thus what Johnston and a number of schools like it have been doing over at least the last fifty years is still lauded by experts in higher education, and is still unavailable to the great majority of American college students. It is true that the reports focused more on the sins of large research institutions, who have practically abandoned undergraduates in pursuit of more lofty goals. And it is equally true that it is easier for a school such as Redlands to develop student-oriented learning communities than it is for a campus with 30,000 matriculants. But the fact remains that undergraduate education in America, taken whole, blatantly ignores the established results of its own researchers and philosophers. Such a tremendous gap between widely acknowledged theory and actual practice would not be tolerated in any other profession; imagine a law firm or a medical group that would permit institutional inertia to override so completely an established form of legal defense or medical treatment. A colleague at another alternative college has succinctly confirmed what the two national reports made clear:

> Educational institutions are by their nature ultra-conservative. Their mission is not to lead but to follow the dictates of the community.... Even the most casual look at the history of academic institutions will show that few meaningful social changes have their start inside the ivy-covered walls. Scientific and technological discoveries, yes. But changes in the way people act toward each other, how they structure their government or spend their money, or treat the environment — these don't begin in academic institutions — at least not as a planned part of the mission of the institutions.[3]

The painful truth is that alternative programs, taken whole, have done little, except on a local level, to change the repressive conditions that gave them birth.

It is also true that Johnston is no longer an experimenting school. There are no new conceptions or procedures which the Center is systematically testing. The burden of experimentation at Redlands has, appropriately, shifted to Whitehead Center, where new ways to deliver quality education to adult learners are being developed and evaluated. The Johnston experiment succeeded, a fact confirmed not only by the national studies we have just discussed but by its graduates.

Johnston does remain an alternative school, however. While it has liberalized academic attitudes at Redlands to some extent, it remains different enough, and therefore separate enough, to maintain a distinct identity on the

campus. One must be suspicious here, since it is characteristic of intentional communities to lose their critical edge;
experiments regularly become orthodoxies, and self-
obsession replaces any challenging political life. The
genius of the Johnston design is that it remains flexible
enough (i.e., individualized enough) to resist calcification.
Johnston began largely as a critique of education, and
over time developed a set of positive achievements in
undergraduate learning. The *form* of a Johnston
education has indeed become an orthodoxy, and no one
within the community has suggested that the contract
design be abandoned. But it is an orthodoxy which allows
for wide variety in content, and in the development of
both course and graduation contracts. And ongoing points
of difference with the parent institution make complete
self-absorption difficult. Johnston faculty and students
are regularly required by their political situation to deal
in realistic terms with more powerful (if well-intending)
outsiders. It was much easier in the days of separatism to
ignore all but the chief officers of the University. Happily,
that sort of isolation is no longer possible.

There are a number of other Johnston successes that
deserve to be shared with those interested in American
education. First is the results of a Johnston education. We
can of course point to a large number of lawyers and a few
doctors and professors, to persons now engaged in social
work, in counselling, and other helping professions. But
this hardly distinguishes Johnston, and in any case
valorizes criteria used by research institutions to justify
their programs. Consider instead the following. In our
interviews with nearly one hundred Johnston graduates,
one finding far exceeded all others. Whether they had
become white collar professionals or, like one woman,
drove heavy equipment for the city of San Diego, the great
majority of them (73 percent) stated that Johnston's
major impact came with how they conducted their working professional lives. Egalitarian politics in operating an
office or a business was mentioned most frequently,

followed by the interdisciplinary, problem-solving style of education and related internships. As one remarked, "Job interviews are a snap, even if I'm not terribly well qualified, after all the things I had to do on my own at Johnston. It was more entrepreneurial than American business." Graduates experienced direct carry-over from their undergraduate experience to their "real world" living. Also mentioned frequently by early (before 1976) graduates of the college was the cognitive-affective mix in their education; this too had carried over into both their personal and their economic lives. Those who had entered academia, or the law or medicine, tended to praise the joy they discovered in learning, the sheer satisfaction of it, rather than any isolated intellectual attainments. The virtues of an academic community, and of close intellectual and emotional ties with faculty, were held to be of greatest value.

Second, the Johnston experience makes clear that separatism within a small institution finally fails. However necessary in the beginning it was for Johnston's integrity, the separatist model finally made it impossible for the college to gain support in the mother institution, and made the mother institution largely indifferent to, and therefore ignorant of, the many worthy experiments taking place a hundred yards from their offices. Current Johnston faculty have exhausted the patience of their University colleagues by pointing out that Redlands innovations of 1987 are reruns of programs tested at Johnston fifteen years earlier. Johnston indeed was the best kept secret in Redlands, and both sides of the street conspired to keep it that way. Granted, there were *sub rosa* influences; Johnston was a catalyst, especially in the area of student life, in urging the University away from its Baptist parochialisms into the modern educational world. But in the main the two campuses were invisible to one another. Separatism diminished one institution and was fatal to the other.

Third, the Johnston experience is one among many

that confirms the importance of learning communities for humanistic education. Much of Johnston, admittedly, was shaped by negative affirmations; we were against impersonal education, hierarchical politics, the perceived tyranny of the University. But this had little to do with the academic commitment which, after the first year, took hold in the beleaguered community. That commitment arose directly from shared enthusiasm among faculty and students for the intellectual enterprises they designed together. Both were committed, without snobbery or defensiveness, to developing the best in one another. As we have noted in several places, it was peer pressure as much as faculty urging that gave so many seminars their intensity. The same sort of commitment obtained in fieldwork and in experimental learning; psychodrama groups, or a class of interns at Indio, developed a commitment out of shared experience that had demonstrable effects on their later careers and self-perceptions, as well as their immediate learning. The Center in 1987 continues to thrive on just this sort of commitment; it is a legacy shared by alums, faculty, and current undergraduates.

Finally, Johnston has contributed, like the individual member of a species, to the persistent life of intentional communities in America. This contribution is nebulous, even romantic, but nonetheless significant. The line from the Oneida community, from Brook farm, indeed, from the Shakers and the *isolato* Pilgrims themselves, through Micklejohn and Black Mountain, to Hampshire and Santa Cruz, to the Paracollege at St. Olaf's or Fairhaven at Western Washington, is a line, now underground, now dramatically visible, that has sustained humanistic — and humane — education in our country.

And Johnston, for all its self-importance, did so without forgetting the injunction of its founding benefactor. We did offer personal joy and personal commitment to students who refused to see themselves as raw material for the great educational factories. Some of Johnston was comically inefficient, and some of it was frankly silly, but it was never impersonal or indifferent.

In his whimsical way, Jimmy Johnston may not have cared about the details of what we were doing, but we cared passionately, and at the same time managed to "have a good time" — the only request he ever made of us.

NOTES:

1. Holmquist, Nisonoff, and Rokoff, "The Labor Process at Hampshire College" in *Against the Current, Reform and Experimentation in Higher Education* (Cambridge: Schenkman Publishing Co.), pp. 203-9.

2. And Johnston did pay its own way from 1969 to 1975. A historical summary prepared by the University's own Business Office showed that the college had a cumulative deficit of less than $20,000 by the end of that fiscal year. The college's final four years, however, were another story.

3. Comments by former Callison College faculty member Roger C. Mueller as quoted by Larry Jackson in an unpublished paper entitled "Concluding Unscientific Postscript: Impressions, Reflections and Reminiscences about Callison College of the University of the Pacific, 1967-77."

Postscript (2003)

Years later, historian and C. S. Lewis scholar Stan Mattson told us this final episode in the history of the College's demise. In 1979 Stan served as a development officer for the University, and attended a President's Cabinet meeting at which Doug Moore had pretty much decided to dismiss the remaining faculty and close the College. In the midst of the discussion someone - Stan doesn't recall who -brought in the latest issue of U.S. News and World Report. It featured the magazine's national rating of colleges, an annual feature that has now become something of an institution. The brief review of Redlands spoke almost exclusively about Johnston, naming it as the best reason for coming to the University. So much for closing. The Johnston Center came into being at that moment. Our rescue at the eleventh hour by a conservative news magazine remains the most delectable irony in our history.

APPENDIX

Communion:
Notes from a Journal

This excerpt from the journal of Vice Chancellor Ed Williams conveys more clearly than any description the emotional power and integrity of Pilgrim Pines.

We have been in session four days and it is Sunday morning. Yesterday afternoon it rained heavily in some places, but the sky was bright as we sat around listening to Cynthia and Angie, sisters whose voices harmonized well together. Angie is a skillful guitarist. Gradually we were drawn into group singing, and then the kitchen staff brought out doughnuts, coffee, and Kool-Aid into the camp area where we all sat. The doughnuts were left over from breakfast, and they had been cut into halves to be sure there would be enough to go around.

I was wishing the group might sing "Mine Eyes Have Seen the Glory," which is a favorite of mine, but the time never seemed right to ask, and the other songs that came out were better for the occasion. They sang "Coom by 'Eah," which is a touching thing, and then they sang the words, "Somebody's dying, Lawd," which moved me deeply because my father is old and very delicate, and I stopped singing.

Revalee came over near me and the coffee, and we had a little whispered conversation. We had coffee and took doughnut pieces when they were passed to us. I wasn't really hungry but took something anyway because, as I said half jokingly, it would be almost irreligious not to. Pres had already given us the idea; a moment earlier he had said, "Now for a communion service of some kind we will pass the doughnuts."

I suddenly wanted to write down some fragments of German verse, though I didn't know German well, and I couldn't be sure of anything. I took out my notebook and began printing in crude form the words as best I could remember them:

Wer nie die kummerfollen Nächte
Wer nie das Brot mit Tränen aß
Auf seine Bette saß —
Der kennt euch nicht, ihr himmlichen Machte...

Revalee saw what I was doing and said she too kept a notebook. I whispered to her that I was all wound up suddenly — or unwound. There were things that went back thirty years, and I found myself astounded to be seeing them again so clearly. I promised to tell her about them sometime. Then, partly because I was blowing my nose a lot and feeling like a fool, I left the circle and went to my cabin. Then I began to write it all down, and this is where I am now. What I am writing is for Revalee, and me, and all the people in that communion service, if they want to share it, and for John I. Church especially, who may be dead, and others.

John I. Church was in the room next to mine in college, more than thirty years ago. He was taking German and I guess really liked it, because he used to recite it a lot, in a nasal and somewhat arrogant tone, sometimes accompanying himself on the cymbals. He was redheaded, skinny, and authoritative. He played in the band, I sang in the choir, and maybe this could speak for bonds and differences between us. (I was taking French, and barely surviving with consistent D's). John had acne and various minor health problems, and I was completely healthy, though not particularly athletic, having just spent the summer in construction work.

One of my proudest possessions was a used typewriter my mother (now three years dead) had got for me at some sacrifice. Someone had told me that I should save the platen by putting a piece of paper around it to absorb the punishment of continual use, and John liked to use that paper as a locus for his brainstorms, graffiti and personal messages. I was going with Elaine then, and one of the things that bothered me was John's habit of typing off conjectures about my love life. "Elaine is pregnant!" was an incremental refrain in one of the messages he left, and I found the remark maddening. I suppose I secretly thought it flattering but at the time I only knew my reaction as "heated" — angry, dismayed.

John was one of a group of us who were rather happy together: my roommate, another John, Frank Macek, a giant man from Montana, and another fellow, old Bennett, I especially liked, who aspired to become a doctor. He never made it, so far as I know.

John and I never really had it out about my typewriter, but he knew I was upset pretty badly. At the end of the school year, because I was in the choir, I had to stay around a little longer to sing at commencement exercises. I never did know just when John I. Church left, but I came back to my room once and found he had been at my typewriter again.

What was there were the words of Goethe's poem, but at the time I hadn't the slightest idea what they were or said. I puzzled over them and even kept the fragment for many years. Eventually I asked someone how to pronounce the German and what it meant, and got a rough idea of the meaning. But it didn't quite make sense to anyone I showed it to, and I finally lost the bit of paper or threw it away. I didn't know the lines came from a poem of Goethe's, or where I could find the original.

Many years later I found myself back in school, studying to be a teacher, reading and learning almost frantically, trying to be ready to pass my doctors orals. I ran across the remark of William Lyon Phelps that everyone should read Carlyle's translation of *Wilhelm Meister* because the novel is really the combined triumph of two great geniuses, in its English version. Desperate to read that which "everyone must read," I started *Wilhelm Meister* and in fact got hooked on it. Finally I got to the place about the old mad arsonist, the maniac who finally recovered his sanity (and in the process continually carried a bottle of poison on a string around his neck). He recited, at some point in the story, the lines that I remember about as follows:

> He who never has eaten bread with tears
> He who has never, the livelong night,
> On his bed, weeping, stayed,
> He knows you not, you heavenly powers.

Suddenly and with great astonishment, reading that, I remembered John I. Church, and I went to the original of *Wilhelm Meister*. The link was made at last, and I could understand, fifteen years later, what John I. Church had said to me. But I have never been able to find him and tell him so. On the twenty-fifth anniversary of the class (from which I was a dropout) his name was missing from all the lists, and the alum director, when I wrote him, told me that John was the only member of the class he hadn't been able to locate, and he thought maybe John had been lost in World War II combat.

Now, sitting here thinking about this morning's communion service, I remember believing that the doughnuts were a kind of holy bread for me, and I regretted that we did not have real wine, as we Episcopalians would have had. We had coffee and Kool-Aid to share, and now I find myself sharing the wine of my own tears — for John I. Church, for Elaine, for Revalee, for Carlyle, for Geothe, for my mother and father, for my brother and brothers, dead and living, and Phyllis, and all my loves.

ISBN 141200946-4

9 781412 009461

71951037R00157

Made in the USA
San Bernardino, CA
20 March 2018